A Crisis of Global Institutions?

The legitimacy of global institutions which address security challenges is in question. The manner in which they make decisions and the interests they reflect often fall short of twenty-first century expectations and norms of good governance. In addition, their performance has raised doubts about their ability to address contemporary challenges such as civil wars, weapons of mass destruction, terrorism, and the use of military force in international politics.

This book explores the sources of this challenge to multilateralism – including US preeminence, the changing nature of international security, and normative concerns about the way decisions are taken in international organizations. It argues that whilst some such challenges are a sign of "crisis," many others are representative of "normality" and continuity in international relations. Nevertheless, it is essential to consider how multilateralism might be more viably constituted to cope with contemporary and future demands.

Addressing topical issues, such as the war against Iraq in 2003 and terrorism, and presenting provocative arguments, this dynamic book will have broad appeal amongst specialist readers interested in international relations, security and international organizations, as well as students generally.

Edward Newman is Director of Studies on Conflict and Security in the Peace and Governance Programme of the United Nations University.

Routledge Global Institutions
Edited by Thomas G. Weiss
The CUNY Graduate Center, New York, USA
and Rorden Wilkinson
University of Manchester, UK

About the Series

The Global Institutions Series is designed to provide readers with comprehensive, accessible, and informative guides to the history, structure, and activities of key international organizations. Every volume stands on its own as a thorough and insightful treatment of a particular topic, but the series as a whole contributes to a coherent and complementary portrait of the phenomenon of global institutions at the dawn of the millennium.

Books are written by recognized experts, conform to a similar structure, and cover a range of themes and debates common to the series. These areas of shared concern include the general purpose and rationale for organizations, developments over time, membership, structure, decision-making procedures, and key functions. Moreover, current debates are placed in historical perspective alongside informed analysis and critique. Each book also contains an annotated bibliography and guide to electronic information as well as any annexes appropriate to the subject matter at hand.

The volumes currently published or under contract include:

The United Nations and Human Rights (2005)
A guide for a new era
by Julie Mertus (American University)

The UN Secretary General and Secretariat (2005)
by Leon Gordenker (Princeton University)

United Nations Global Conferences (2005)
by Michael G. Schechter (Michigan State University)

The UN General Assembly (2005)
by M.J. Peterson (University of Massachusetts, Amherst)

Internal Displacement (2006)
Conceptualization and its consequences
by Thomas G. Weiss (The CUNY Graduate Center) and David A. Korn

Global Environmental Institutions (2006)
by Elizabeth R. DeSombre (Wellesley College)

The UN Security Council (2006)
Practice and promise
by Edward C. Luck (Columbia University)

The World Intellectual Property Organization (2006)
Resurgence and the development agenda
by Chris May (University of Lancaster)

The North Atlantic Treaty Organization (2007)
The enduring alliance
by Julian Lindley-French (European Union Centre for Security Studies)

The International Monetary Fund (2007)
Politics of conditional lending
by James Raymond Vreeland (Yale University)

The Group of 7/8 (2007)
by Hugo Dobson (University of Sheffield)

The World Economic Forum (2007)
A multi-stakeholder approach to global governance
by Geoffrey Allen Pigman (Bennington College)

The International Committee of the Red Cross (2007)
A neutral humanitarian actor
by David Forsythe (University of Nebraska) and Barbara Ann Rieffer-Flanagan (Central Washington University)

The Organization for Security and Co-operation in Europe (2007)
by David J. Galbreath (University of Aberdeen)

United Nations Conference on Trade and Development (UNCTAD) (2007)
by Ian Taylor (University of St. Andrews) and Karen Smith (University of Stellenbosch)

A Crisis of Global Institutions? (2007)
Multilateralism and international security
by Edward Newman (United Nations University)

The World Trade Organization (2007)
Law, economics, and politics
by Bernard Hoekman (World Bank) and Petros Mavroidis (Columbia University)

The African Union
Challenges of globalization, security and governance
by Samuel M. Makinda (Murdoch University) and Wafula Okumu (McMaster University)

The World Bank
From reconstruction to development to equity
by Katherine Marshall (Georgetown University)

Organisation for Economic Co-operation and Development
by Richard Woodward (University of Hull)

Non-Governmental Organizations in Global Politics
by Peter Willetts (City University, London)

Multilateralism in the South
An analysis
by Jacqueline Anne Braveboy-Wagner (City College of New York)

The International Labour Organization
by Steve Hughes (University of Newcastle)

The Commonwealth(s) and Global Governance
by Timothy Shaw (Royal Roads University)

UNHCR
The politics and practice of refugee protection into the twenty-first century
by Gil Loescher (University of Oxford), James Milner (University of Oxford), and Alexander Betts (University of Oxford)

The International Organization for Standardization and the Global Economy
Setting standards
by Craig Murphy (Wellesley College) and JoAnne Yates (Massachusetts Institute of Technology)

The International Olympic Committee
by Jean-Loup Chappelet (IDHEAP Swiss Graduate School of Public Administration) and Brenda Kübler-Mabbott

The European Union
by Clive Archer (Manchester Metropolitan University)

The World Health Organization
by Kelley Lee (London School of Hygiene and Tropical Medicine)

Internet Governance
The new frontier of global institutions
by John Mathiason (Syracuse University)

Shaping the Humanitarian World
by Peter Walker (Tufts University)

Contemporary Human Rights Ideas
by Bertrand G. Ramcharan (Geneva Graduate Institute of International Studies)

For further information regarding the series, please contact:

Craig Fowlie, Publisher, Politics & International Studies
Taylor & Francis
2 Park Square, Milton Park, Abingdon
Oxford OX14 4RN, UK

+44 (0)207 842 2057 Tel
+44 (0)207 842 2302 Fax

Craig.Fowlie@tandf.co.uk
www.routledge.com

A Crisis of Global Institutions?

Multilateralism and international security

Edward Newman

LONDON AND NEW YORK

First published 2007
by Routledge
2 Park Square, Milton Park, Abingdon, Oxon, OX14 4RN

Simultaneously published in the USA and Canada
by Routledge
270 Madison Ave, New York NY 10016

Routledge is an imprint of the Taylor & Francis Group, an informa business

Transferred to Digital Printing 2009

© 2007 Edward Newman

Typeset in Times New Roman by
Taylor & Francis Books

All rights reserved. No part of this book may be reprinted or reproduced or utilized in any form or by any electronic, mechanical, or other means, now known or hereafter invented, including photocopying and recording, or in any information storage or retrieval system, without permission in writing from the publishers.

British Library Cataloguing in Publication Data
A catalogue record for this book is available from the British Library

Library of Congress Cataloging in Publication Data
Newman, Edward, 1970–
   A crisis in global institutions? : multilateralism and
international security / Edward Newman.
      p. cm.–(Routledge global institutions ; 17)
   Includes bibliographical references and index.
    1. Security, International. 2. International organization. I. Title.
JZ5603.N49 2007
355'.033–dc22
                                                   2006039780

ISBN 978-0-415-41164-6 (hbk)
ISBN 978-0-415-41165-3 (pbk)
ISBN 978-0-203-94709-8 (ebk)

Contents

Foreword viii
Acknowledgments xii
Abbreviations xiii

Introduction 1

1 Multilateral malaise – sources and manifestations 10

2 The United States, power, and multilateralism 30

3 Collective security and the use of force 43

4 Humanitarian intervention 56

5 Weapons of mass destruction 78

6 Civil war, state failure and peacebuilding 95

7 Terrorism 117

Conclusion: revisiting institutionalism in a
post-Westphalian world 140

Notes 156
Select bibliography 176
Index 181

Foreword

The current volume is the seventeenth in a dynamic series on "global institutions." The series strives (and, based on the volumes published to date, succeeds) to provide readers with definitive guides to the most visible aspects of what we know as "global governance." Remarkable as it may seem, there exist relatively few books that offer in-depth treatments of prominent global bodies and processes, much less an entire series of concise and complementary volumes. Those that do exist are either out of date, inaccessible to the non-specialist reader, or seek to develop a specialized understanding of particular aspects of an institution or process rather than offer an overall account of its functioning. Similarly, existing books have often been written in highly technical language or have been crafted "in-house" and are notoriously self-serving and narrow.

The advent of electronic media has helped by making information, documents, and resolutions of international organizations more widely available, but it has also complicated matters. The growing reliance on the Internet and other electronic methods of finding information about key international organizations and processes has served, ironically, to limit the educational materials to which most readers have ready access – namely, books. Public relations documents, raw data, and loosely refereed web sites do not make for intelligent analysis. Official publications compete with a vast amount of electronically available information, much of which is suspect because of its ideological or self-promoting slant. Paradoxically, a growing range of purportedly independent web sites offering analyses of the activities of particular organizations has emerged, but one inadvertent consequence has been to frustrate access to basic, authoritative, critical, and well-researched texts. The market for such has actually been reduced by the ready availability of varying quality electronic materials.

For those of us who teach, research, and practice in the area, this access to information has been particularly frustrating. We were delighted, then, when Routledge saw the value of a series that bucks this trend and provides key reference points to the most significant global institutions. They are betting that serious students and professionals will want serious analyses. We have assembled a first-rate lineup of authors to address that market. Our intention, then, is to provide one-stop shopping for all readers – students (both undergraduate and postgraduate), interested negotiators, diplomats, practitioners from nongovernmental and intergovernmental organizations, and interested parties alike – seeking information about the most prominent institutional aspects of global governance.

A crisis of global institutions?

When we began thinking about this series, the preeminent role of the United States in the post-Cold War world was very much on our minds, especially in the wake of the attacks of 11 September 2001 and the decision to go to war in Iraq without Security Council approval as part of the so-called Global War on Terror. The record of the United Nations (UN) in this period reveals and accentuates the implications of the post-Cold War trend toward an international system based on a sole superpower. The preponderance of the United States – militarily, economically, and culturally – is ever more striking. This reality represents a serious threat to the health of the UN, captured well by the European Union commissioner of external relations Chris Patten's characterization of Washington's current gear as "unilateralist overdrive."[1]

Former French foreign minister Hubert Védrine described American preeminence as *hyper-puissance*. On the one hand, major power politics have always dominated the UN. On the other hand, there is no modern precedent for the current dimensions of the US Goliath. In many ways, UN Secretary-General Kofi Annan created his High-level Panel on Threats, Challenges and Change and convened the September 2005 World Summit, according to a host of diplomats, "to keep Washington in the tent."[2]

What exactly is the meaning of a collective security organization in a world so dominated by US power? Washington is, at best, indifferent to the UN and, at worst, has a penchant to weaken or destroy it. Much of the contemporary UN debate could be compared with the Roman Senate's effort to control the emperor. Scholars speculate about the nuances of economic and cultural leverage resulting from US soft power, but the hard currency in the international system remains military might. Before the war on Iraq, the "hyper-power" was already spending more on its military than the next 15 to 25 countries (depending on who was counting). With additional appropriations for Afghanistan and Iraq, Washington was spending more than the rest of the world's militaries combined.[3] And even in the domain of soft power, the United States remains without challenge on the world stage for the foreseeable future although some analysts see hegemony as more Western than American.[4]

Washington's multilateral record in the twentieth century conveys "mixed messages," as Edward Luck reminds us.[5] The United States sometimes has been the prime mover for new international institutions and norms but just as often has kept a distance or stood in the way. This historical pattern is not about to change. The reality of US power means that if the UN and multilateral cooperation are to have a chance of working, let alone flourish, the globe's remaining superpower must be on board. This undoubtedly will have to await the 2008 presidential election.

Understanding the current dimensions of international peace and security are essential for readers of books about global institutions. The sub-title of this book, "Multilateralism and international security," suggests why Edward "Ted" Newman was at the top of our list of desirable authors when we decided to have a book on the crisis of global institutions. He is Director of Studies on Conflict and Security in the Peace and Governance Programme of the United Nations University (UNU). Prior to that, he was lecturing at Shumei University in Japan, a position he took up after he finished his doctorate at the University of Kent and published his dissertation on the changing role of the UN Secretary-General in the post-Cold War period.[6] While at UNU his research and writing have revolved around most of the topics in this very readable volume. He has co-edited a number of volumes dealing with the post-Cold War peace and security agenda[7] and he has published widely in such journals as *Conflict, Security and Development; International Peacekeeping; The International Journal of Human Rights; International Studies Perspectives; Security Dialogue*; and *Studies in Conflict and Terrorism*.

Ted Newman's insights and knowledge are visible on every page. This book deserves to be read by all interested in the role of the UN and of the remaining superpower in the world organization's successes and failures. As Newman notes in the first page of the book, "The values and institutions of global multilateralism have always been challenged – or even sometimes seemingly undermined – by the realities of power politics in international relations, even though they are a creation of these same realities."

We may or may not be in a post-Westphalian world, but Newman challenges us to think about the consequences. As always, comments and suggestions from readers are welcome.

Thomas G. Weiss, The CUNY Graduate Center, New York, USA
Rorden Wilkinson, University of Manchester, UK
March 2007

Acknowledgments

I would like to thank Tom Weiss and Rorden Wilkinson for creating this series and for their suggestions on earlier drafts of this volume. Tom is an inspiration to so many of us and it has been a pleasure to work with him. I have also enjoyed the experience of working with Routledge and I wish to thank the people there for their support.

This book was written while I was an academic officer at the UNU, and it draws upon eight years of research and program management in the UNU Peace and Governance Programme. I am grateful that I had the opportunity to bring my thoughts together and I appreciate, in particular, the conversations I had with Ramesh Thakur, the Senior Vice Rector throughout almost my whole time at the UNU. I also thank Paul Bacon from Waseda University, and I regret that I could not act on all of his excellent suggestions. Needless to say, the contents of this book are the responsibility of the author. Moreover, as a UN staff member, I would like to point out that the contents are the personal opinion of the author.

Abbreviations

ABM	Anti-Ballistic Missile Treaty
ANC	African National Congress
BWC	Biological Weapons Convention
CD	Conference on Disarmament
CTBT	Comprehensive Nuclear Test Ban Treaty
CTC	Counter Terrorism Committee
CWC	Chemical Weapons Convention
FMCT	Fissile Material Cut-off Treaty
FRELIMO	Front for the Liberation of Mozambique
GDP	Gross Domestic Product
HLP	High Level Panel on Threats, Challenges and Change
IAEA	International Atomic Energy Agency
ICAO	International Civil Aviation Organization
ILO	International Labour Organization
LTBT	Limited Test Ban Treaty
MTCR	Missile Technology Control Regime
NATO	North Atlantic Treaty Organization
NGO	Non-Governmental Organization
NPT	Non-Proliferation Treaty
ONUC	UN Operation in the Congo
OPCW	Organisation for the Prohibition of Chemical Weapons
PLO	Palestine Liberation Organization
PNET	Peaceful Nuclear Explosions Treaty
PSI	Proliferation Security Initiative
SCO	Shanghai Cooperation Organization
SIPRI	Stockholm International Peace Research Institute
SWAPO	South West African People's Organization
TTBT	Threshold Test Ban Treaty
UNDC	UN Disarmament Commission
UNEF	United Nations Emergency Force

xiv   *Abbreviations*

UNESCO	United Nations Educational, Scientific, and Cultural Organization
UNHCR	United Nations High Commissioner for Refugees
UNIDIR	United Nations Institute for Disarmament Research
UNPROFOR	United Nations Protection Force
UNSC	United Nations Security Council
UNTAC	United Nations Transitional Authority in Cambodia
UPU	Universal Postal Union
UTA	Union des Transports Aériens
WMD	Weapons of Mass Destruction

Introduction

The values and institutions of global multilateralism have always been challenged – or even sometimes seemingly undermined – by the realities of power politics in international relations, even though they are a creation of these same realities. Despite this apparent paradox, inherent in the nature of the international system, multilateral organizations have made a valuable contribution to the regulation of international affairs. The circumstances at the beginning of the twenty-first century, however, have led many commentators to seriously consider if multilateralism is in crisis. This volume considers if it is correct to think in terms of a "crisis." It explores the sources and manifestations of the challenges to multilateralism in the area of international peace and security, and envisages how multilateralism might be more viably constituted to cope with contemporary and future demands.

US unilateralism and hegemony, weakening and failed states, the growing salience of non-state actors, the evolving nature of the security agenda, the social impact of globalization, normative changes regarding human rights, governance and sovereignty – these and many other factors provide an environment quite different to that which existed when many international organizations were established after the Second World War. In addition, the future of multilateralism has become embroiled in a transatlantic split and vying visions of world order.

The signs of crisis are also multifold. The rules governing the use of force, embodied in the UN Charter, are arguably under threat. The principal arms control conventions are increasingly challenged. Leading UN members have questioned the efficacy and legitimacy of the organization and promote alternative *ad hoc* coalitions. The "liberal peace" ethos of the United Nations in its peacebuilding work is problematic in countries such as East Timor, Afghanistan and Bosnia.

2 Introduction

The UN fails to develop a workable doctrine for preventing and responding to civil war. Its members also fail to address egregious human rights abuses including genocide, one of the most glaring affronts to humankind. The extent to which a global united front against terrorism can be constituted multilaterally is also questionable. And as the agenda of multilateralism – no longer the preserve of "high politics" and diplomats – has penetrated deeper into societies, it has resulted in a clash of values which reminds us that there is no consensus on what global governance should actually mean. In the world of academia, realist scholars have become particularly skeptical of international organizations. Liberal internationalist scholars, in principle supportive of international organizations, bemoan an erosion of traditional multilateralism; some of them accept that the constitutive principles of international organizations are partly to blame for this.

And yet from a different perspective all of these difficulties simply indicate a perennial reality in international relations: there are, and have always been, limitations to international institutions, organizations and regimes, but these limitations do not undermine the rationale of multilateralism. Indeed, the limitations and weaknesses of multilateralism are more characteristic of "normality" than "crisis." Formal and informal multilateral arrangements arguably remain significant across a wide range of security issues, judging by the preference that most states have for working through multilateral means when possible. This has not definitively changed as a result of the war against Iraq, US preeminence and the other challenges to global security institutions. Multilateralism is "a highly demanding institutional form" – especially in the security realm – but it can also be resilient.[1]

A number of questions can be raised. Is the "institutional bargain" upon which the US created and maintained multilateral arrangements – accepting constraints upon its foreign policy and the material costs of supporting public goods, in return for regularity in international interactions and having its interests reflected in the international institutional architecture – breaking down? Can institutionalized multilateralism, as currently conceived, offer a viable basis for international order in a unipolar world? Do the challenges faced by the UN and other security regimes suggest a broader challenge to multilateralism? Is the UN really at a "fork in the road," or are these challenges – in one form or another – essentially perennial and an inherent feature of international relations? Is the value system which underlies global multilateral organizations becoming untenable? Is the prevailing institutionalist theory of multilateralism conceptually viable in the area of international security? Do alternative forms of cooperation – such as *ad hoc* alliances and arrangements amongst "democracies" – suggest a fraying of global multilateralism, or is this simply "business as usual" in international politics?

The legitimacy of the UN and other global regimes – in terms both of operational processes and performance – is under challenge. But it has always been under challenge, and support for the UN in terms of membership is almost universal; states continue to work with, and through, the UN. This volume attempts to bring clarity to these debates and seeks to put the multilateral "crisis" into perspective. It considers the sources and manifestations of challenges to multilateralism in the area of international peace and security broadly defined, and the possibility of alternatives to existing multilateral forms. On this basis it considers how the values and institutions of multilateralism may have to be re-envisioned according to the evolving realities of a "post-Westphalian" world.[2] That is, a world where notions of inviolable and equal state sovereignty – never actually a reality but often respected as a norm – are breaking down; where states are no longer the sole or even the most important actors in certain areas of international politics; where the "national interest" cannot be defined in one-dimensional terms; where power takes many different forms, both soft and hard; and where the distinction between "domestic" and "international" politics is irreversibly blurred. According to the conventional Westphalian model, threats to international security come primarily from recalcitrant or aggressive states; in the twenty-first century, threats are equally likely to come from failing or weak states, or even non-state actors.

Much of this book focuses upon the UN, and yet the title emphasizes the theme of multilateralism. The explanation for this is that the discussion which follows, while focusing mainly on the UN, seeks to present conclusions which are relevant to – and engage – the broader theoretical debates on multilateralism. The UN – as the preeminent global multilateral organization – receives the greatest attention, but a range of other organizations or regimes are considered so that general conclusions regarding "multilateralism" can be proposed. This means that this book is consciously at odds with the views of some scholars on one point. While Ruggie, for example, might suggest that the relatively recent emergence of formal international organizations should not be confused with the "generic institutional form of multilateralism," I argue that international organizations are in fact important multilateral forms.[3] Although they are historically recent they do cover a very wide array of foreign policy, and since they involve formally

4 Introduction

binding obligations, they are emblematic of the most demanding challenges of multilateralism and thus *can* point to broader conclusions about multilateralism. (In fact, Ruggie himself does occasionally succumb to such an approach.[4])

Above all, while supportive of multilateralism in general and the UN, the volume argues that we must be realistic about the role and prospects of multilateralism – and especially formal international organizations – in the field of conflict and security. Indeed, given the environment in which they operate – one of sovereign states and power politics, in which traditional conceptions of national interest still largely prevail – the record of and prospects for multilateralism are quite healthy. Ultimately, however, the judgment rests upon subjective and contestable perceptions of the nature of international political life, and also different state perceptions dependent upon contextual circumstances: not all states are the same. For some states, multilateralism, both formal and informal, is an organizing principle; for others, it is one tool amongst many for achieving foreign policy goals.

Overview

Chapter 1 examines the sources, manifestations and consequences of multilateral malaise. International organizations and other multilateral arrangements have always faced difficulties – and even crises. The chapter illustrates why, however, there is a widely held perception that the values and institutions of multilateralism are fundamentally challenged at the beginning of the twenty-first century. The chapter begins with a discussion of the theories of multilateralism – the practice and principle of states committing to collective action to address common problems and opportunities – with reference to theories of international relations. It provides an overview of the main signs of multilateral problems and the debates relating to this, and it suggests a framework for considering if multilateralism is truly in "crisis" or if political problems are merely "business as usual."

The chapter argues that challenges to multilateralism can be found in three areas: structural or systemic challenges which derive from the structure and nature of the international system, including the evolution of state sovereignty and the nature and impact of different types of actors; hegemonic challenges which relate to the exercise of power (especially American) in international politics; and normative challenges to multilateralism which concern the way that decisions are made and implemented in international organizations. This chapter also introduces a key argument of the book: the problems of multilateralism in the twenty-first century are inherent in the nature of the international system – and not a sign of crisis.

Chapter 2 explores the impact of American power and ideology upon multilateral arrangements. It suggests that American antipathy towards international organizations – and sometimes unilateralism – is a result of a number of factors: American power, the changing international security environment, and America's perception of its historic exceptionalism and its unique place in the world. The chapter argues that America's preeminent economic and military position allows it to pursue certain foreign policy objectives unilaterally "when necessary" and operate outside – or withdraw from – established multilateral arrangements. However, American preeminence does not automatically result in antipathy towards multilateralism or a general malaise in multilateralism. The pattern of US behavior suggests a declining respect for international rules and treaties, yet it does recognize the value of multilateral approaches in promoting its interests. It seeks, through persuasion and sometimes coercion, multilateral channels that are convergent with US interests, and it may create new or alternative forms of multilateralism to better fit its values and needs when necessary.

Chapter 3 addresses collective security and the use of force. It considers the role of formal multilateral organizations – especially the UN – in international security and particularly in regulating the use of armed force by states. Specifically, it considers whether a legal, or rule-based, framework exists for the use of military force. If such a framework existed, was it undermined by the war against Iraq of 2003 and the doctrine of the preventive use of military force? Is a rule-based system of collective security amongst states of widely different levels of power and interests, in an anarchic international environment, viable? The chapter argues that norms regulating the use of force were not destroyed by the war against Iraq in 2003 or strategic ideas of preventive or unilateral military force, because these norms never in reality constituted a perfectly viable system. Some of the claims of a crisis of international order seem to be based upon the presumption that the UN system of collective security worked effectively until the US-led coalition invaded Iraq in 2003. But this is not the case. In fact, historically, the international use of force has declined. International law regulating the use of force – as with other areas of policy – has always been violated but it essentially remains intact because most states, generally, support a norm which proscribes aggression. The role of the UN Security Council at the time of the war against Iraq – when it served as a diplomatic focal point – and in relation to other international

6 Introduction

security challenges since then suggests that states attach real significance to rules of conduct.

Chapter 4 addresses "humanitarian intervention," a more complex challenge to multilateralism. The use of force for human protection presents another area where rules governing the use of force, embodied in the UN Charter, have come under question as moral arguments to alleviate widespread suffering have challenged legal restrictions on the use of force. At the same time, global organizations – specifically the UN – have a responsibility to respond to the worst abuses of human rights, but they have mostly failed to develop a doctrine and the practical means to protect humans in dire circumstances. This represents a moral challenge to the legitimacy of international organizations. It also raises a paradox: the use of military force for human protection can be controversial when it does occur and when it does not occur. The chapter argues that the failure of the UN to assemble a robust response to egregious human suffering represents the most significant (moral) challenge to multilateralism. It thus concludes that there is no consistent norm of a "responsibility to protect."

Chapter 5 examines multilateral arrangements to regulate the development, stockpiling, transfer and use of weapons of mass destruction. It demonstrates how and why these arrangements are under challenge, as a result of changing strategic demands, arms control verification and enforcement loopholes, and the erosion of the norm of nuclear non-proliferation. It also gives attention to the military preeminence and ideology of the US and the effect this has upon WMD multilateralism. Nuclear proliferation is a particularly acute challenge and the actions of a number of states – such as India, Pakistan, Iran and North Korea – have demonstrated the limitations of multilateral arms control arrangements. The trade-off which lies at the heart of the Non-Proliferation Treaty (NPT) regime – the obligation of nuclear weapons states to disarm and the obligation of non-nuclear states to refrain from developing nuclear weapons – is under severe strain. At the same time, considering countries which are targeted for opprobrium for breaching non-proliferation norms – and those which are not – raises claims of double standards at the heart of the non-proliferation regime. All of this weakens the legitimacy of the regime and increases the risk of countries rejecting the norm of non-proliferation.

Chapter 6 focuses on civil war, state failure and peacebuilding, and also finds significant challenges to multilateralism. It considers whether the record of international organizations such as the UN in preventing and resolving civil war – as a humanitarian as well as a security challenge – undermines the legitimacy of multilateralism in this area. It focuses upon the functional effectiveness of the UN's approach to civil war; the normative stance of the UN, which has traditionally been based upon ideas of impartiality and neutrality; and the "liberal" value system which accompanies international peacebuilding efforts. The chapter suggests that there has been progress in the international community's approach to civil war and state failure. The Security Council now employs a broader definition of peace and security which allows a multifaceted involvement in conflicted societies and in 2006 the UN Peacebuilding Commission began work to improve effectiveness and coordination amongst all agencies involved in peacebuilding. The remit of the Commission is progressive, based upon the idea that development, peace and security and human rights are interlinked and mutually reinforcing. However, the chapter concludes that a radical change in thinking amongst states towards civil war is unlikely, indicated by the modest – and not proactive – ambitions for the new Peacebuilding Commission. A fundamental question thus remains unanswered: what responsibility does the international community – through the UN and regional organizations – have to intervene in societies which are afflicted by conflict and state failure?

Chapter 7 explores multilateral responses to terrorism. From an institutionalist theoretical perspective, terrorism presents acute challenges to collective action, for a number of reasons. Political and legal disagreements as to what constitutes terrorism have hindered agreement on a definition of terrorism, which has obstructed a common approach to the challenge. During the Cold War the organization was therefore characterized by ambivalence, stymied by the politicization of the issue. After the Cold War, in the 1990s, consensus emerged in the Security Council especially in addressing state-sponsored terrorism. And after 9/11, the UN took a particularly active leadership role in strengthening norms and coordinating state policy against terrorism. However, a number of challenges remain: do the structure, decision-making processes and legal bases of the UN allow it to take an effective role in addressing terrorism? Does the UN have the means to compel state and non-state actors to conform to counter-terrorism measures? Is the UN's approach limited by the politicization of the terrorism debate globally, and in particular the US dominance which is reflected in its "war on terror"? Has the UN neglected its commitment to human rights and the root causes of conflict in addressing terrorism? Despite these remaining questions, the chapter concludes that the UN has not been inhibited by the unconventional nature of terrorism as a security threat. The UN can tackle new and unconventional security challenges, but only if the political will exists.

The conclusion of this book has the theme of "Revisiting institutionalism in a post-Westphalian world." In light of the evidence of the preceding chapters, it suggests that multilateral values and institutions must be constituted according to contemporary principles of governance and legitimacy, and capable of addressing contemporary challenges effectively, if they are to be viable and legitimate. This involves moving beyond the Westphalian roots of multilateral institutions based upon sovereign equality, reassessing the values upon which multilateralism is based and is promoting, and recognizing that contemporary challenges demand greater flexibility and pro-activity. A number of – mainly liberal internationalist – proposals follow from this. However, the reality appears to be different from the liberal internationalist vision. The book illustrates that the incentives which exist for states to commit to formal multilateral arrangements, according to the dominant institutionalist theory of multilateralism, falter in important policy areas related to security. The principles of non-discrimination, indivisibility and reciprocity – which have functioned well in many areas of policy since 1945 – appear less viable in more sensitive and less predictable areas such as the use of military force and intervention, weapons of mass destruction, terrorism and civil war. There *are* incentives to commit to formal multilateral arrangements with regards to international security issues, and such arrangements do exist; however, there are inherent limitations and these are unlikely to be overcome at the global level.

These limitations, which have become particularly acute in some policy areas, have led to alternative forms of multilateralism. Many analysts have increasing faith in regional cooperation, or cooperation based not upon elusive global interests but upon exclusive shared values. The idea of cooperation amongst democracies has been promoted in a number of Western states. Other alternative forms of exclusive multilateralism exist amongst allies: for example the Proliferation Security Initiative and the Shanghai Cooperation Organization.

The volume concludes that the fundamental *principle* of multilateralism, with all its limitations, is not in crisis. Indeed, this principle is validated and vindicated by the demands of the contemporary interdependent world. However, the values and institutions of multilateralism as *currently constituted* – and with them, the conceptual tools with which multilateralism has been approached hitherto – are arguably under serious challenge. In some areas of security, the tenets of multilateralism (indivisibility, generalized principles of conduct, and reciprocity) are not functional. The notion – held dear in some regions of the world, notably Western Europe – that multilateral processes, by their very nature, have greater legitimacy than unilateral or *ad hoc* coalition approaches is also questionable. Multilateralism in the twenty-first century is likely to focus more on performance legitimacy rather than process legitimacy. In the past, according to the Westphalian model of multilateralism that emphasized consensus and sovereignty, ineffectiveness and status quo were often tolerated according to the lowest common denominator. This cannot remain the constitutive principle of multilateralism in the twenty-first century.

1 Multilateral malaise – sources and manifestations

Multilateralism is the practice and principle of three or more states committing to collective action, according to established rules, to address common problems and opportunities. Scholarship on multilateralism analyzes regularized interaction amongst states in many areas of policy, although studies on economic cooperation and trade have become the most theoretically mature. In particular, this explores the incentives that states perceive in creating and supporting multilateral institutions and regimes – which can be both informal arrangements or formal organizations. Much of this scholarship approaches the subject of multilateralism within an anarchical model of international politics where the state is the primary actor and power is the prevailing organizing principle. Anarchical, but "not lacking in rules and norms."[1]

Within the broad scholarship on international relations, the institutionalist (sometimes called liberal institutionalist or neoliberal institutionalist) approaches have invested the greatest effort in describing and explaining the potential and limitations of multilateralism. A major part of this scholarship has sought to explain how international rules are constituted, how regimes emerge and evolve, and how changes in the international environment are reflected in and absorbed by international regimes and institutions. The institutionalist approach clearly believes that multilateralism is important to international politics. Multilateralism brings stability, reciprocity in relationships, and regularity in behavior. It is necessary because all states face mutual vulnerabilities, all share interdependence, and all need to benefit from – and thus support – public goods. Even the most powerful states cannot achieve security, environmental safety and economic prosperity in isolation or unilaterally, and so the international system rests upon a network of regimes, treaties and international organizations.

Sources & manifestations of multilateral malaise

Regimes can be defined as "sets of implicit or explicit principles, norms, rules, and decision-making procedures around which actors' expectations converge in a given area of international relations."[2] Institutions can be thought of as "persistent sets of rules that constrain activity, shape expectations, and prescribe roles."[3] Multilateralism can be taken as "a generic institutional form in international relations ... that coordinates relations among three or more states on the basis of generalized principles of conduct: that is, principles which specify appropriate conduct for a class of actions, without regard to the particularistic interests of the parties or the strategic exigencies that may exist in any specific occurrence."[4]

There are a number of corollaries. The principles of multilateralism "logically entail an indivisibility among the members of a collectivity with respect to the range of behavior in question."[5] This means that members of a multilateral arrangement should follow the rules for all issues which are relevant to the arrangement – and not pick and choose – and not discriminate amongst the other members. In addition, multilateralism involves a credible expectation of what Keohane calls "diffuse reciprocity," whereby members can expect to receive roughly equivalent benefits over time, if not necessarily on every decision or occasion.[6] Keohane also demonstrated that multilateral institutions perform important roles for states by reducing the costs of making, monitoring and enforcing rules (transaction costs), providing information, and facilitating the making of credible commitments.[7]

Clearly, these well-established and widely accepted definitions of regimes, institutions and multilateralism are not confined to formal international organizations, and the concept of multilateralism should not be confused with or confined to formal international organizations. This distinction is fundamentally important in order to differentiate a discussion of a crisis in multilateralism as a general principle from a discussion about a crisis in a specific formal international organization. It is essential to reiterate that the general principle of multilateralism is different from specific forms of multilateralism, such as international organizations, which are a much more recent phenomenon (and, according to Ruggie, "still of only relatively modest importance" especially in the security field[8]). A crisis in a formal international organization most certainly does not mean a crisis in the general principle of multilateralism, despite the tendency of some commentators to conflate the two things.

As a conceptual construction, this institutional form – the state-centric model of multilateralism – can certainly be challenged. The role of non-state actors such as civil society organizations and multinational corporations, and norms and values that constitute international society and human rights, have serious implications for inter-state multilateralism. Nevertheless, the multilateral logic is clear.

While the logic of multilateralism is clear, this logic is still problematized by an inherent paradox in international politics. All countries depend upon multilateralism and the maintenance of regularity, reciprocity and public goods in the international system. But the international system is nevertheless basically anarchical. States vary in power, political outlook, and interests. They are formally sovereign, and generally driven by self-interests which are frequently in conflict. Leaders and hegemons – invariably the chief sponsors of international regimes – decline or increase in relative power and perceive negative changes in cost-benefit equations related to international regimes. Thus, multilateral arrangements are basically a reflection of the dynamics and processes of international power. This does not mean that formal or informal multilateral institutions are not effective or important, or cease to be effective in changing circumstances. It does, however, suggest that they are conditioned by the exigencies of changing international power configurations, and by conflicts which exist within the broader international system. Multilateral arrangements are *inherently* under strain. Institutionalist scholars, therefore, have sought to demonstrate that, in addition to the primary incentives for forming multilateral institutions, multilateral forms endure for a number of reasons, even when the environment which led to the emergence of the institution has changed. These include sunk costs, continued functional utility, and institutional inertia.[9] Ruggie adds that the durability of multilateral arrangements is also a function of domestic environments within which constituencies of support develop.[10]

Challenges to multilateralism: themes and debates

In November 2003 United Nations Secretary-General Kofi Annan observed that "The past year has shaken the foundations of collective security and undermined confidence in the possibility of collective responses to our common problems and challenges. It has also brought to the fore deep divergences of opinion on the range and nature of the challenges we face, and are likely to face in the future." His comments echoed the analyses of many others, in both the policy and academic worlds. The evidence of problems across a range of international norms and institutions is ample. The United States and its allies undertook a war against Iraq in 2003 without the clear authority of the UN Security Council. Many bemoaned what they claimed was a war pursued illegally outside the framework of the UN, while others decried the apparent inability of the UN to address the perceived threat of Iraq and its violation of Security Council resolutions: "the Security Council's failure to reach agreement on Iraq."[11] This came in the wake of similarly controversial NATO military action in Kosovo in 1999. Some observers have interpreted this, and other developments, as a shift amongst some major powers towards an *ad hoc* "coalition" model of military action. Some states openly question the established rules governing the use of military force (only in self-defense, collective self-defense, or with reference to Chapter 7 of the UN Charter) and suggest that preventive force outside the UN framework may be necessary in response to latent threats and a changing strategic environment.

Other policy areas also reflect a perceived multilateral malaise. The United States, China, Russia and many other countries do not support the International Criminal Court and thus render its jurisdiction limited. According to a 2004 high-level panel report endorsed by the UN Secretary-General, the main global multilateral regime responsible for promoting and protecting human rights "suffers from a legitimacy deficit that casts doubts on the overall reputation of the United Nations."[12] The Kyoto protocol to regulate climate change is jeopardized by key abstentions. The effectiveness and legitimacy of a number of multilateral arms control treaties and conventions are being eroded, including the Anti-Ballistic Missile Treaty and the Non-Proliferation Treaty. Others, such as the International Convention to Ban Anti-Personnel Landmines, are not supported by key states.

Notably, many of the challenges experienced by multilateral institutions have been associated with the idea of US military and economic preeminence in what has been called a unipolar world, and an attendant pattern of US unilateralism. While some analysts might argue that multilateral institutions are being sabotaged by the forces of power politics, others have concluded that organizations such as the UN have moved towards "self-marginalization" as a result of their idealism and ineffectiveness.[13]

Are the values and institutions of multilateralism under challenge, or even in crisis? There are a number of elements to this. First, there are structural or systemic challenges: challenges which derive from the structure and nature of the international system, including the evolution of state sovereignty and the nature and impact of different types of actors. Classic models of multilateralism are premised upon regular and stable relations amongst viable sovereign states akin to a

"Westphalian" model of international relations. This privileges states as the principal actors, along with the preservation of their independence and territorial integrity. However, this has conceptual and practical limitations; many observers would agree with Heinbecker's view that the UN Charter was "written in and for another age."[14] States are not necessarily all viable; state weakness and failure are characteristic of a number of regions in the developing world. Indeed, state incapacity is an underlying source of a wide range of pressing problems. One of the principal objectives of international organizations is the maintenance of international peace and security amongst states, yet most instances of armed conflict are clearly domestic rather than inter-state, albeit with transborder consequences. The traditional security problematique is still very much relevant, but most violent conflicts occur outside the classic inter-state paradigm. International organizations, while not legally precluded from being involved in civil war, have had difficulty in finding a consensus or doctrine about the international community's role and responsibility in civil war.

In a more general and less explicit sense, sovereignty is arguably itself under challenge, again with implications for multilateralism. Sovereign statehood remains a core characteristic of the international system. However, the legalist model of international politics – premised upon the primacy of sovereign autonomy and sovereign equality, where domestic forms of government are irrelevant as long as states conform to international norms – is demonstrably out of touch with reality in a number of respects. International norms regarding human rights have developed an importance that significantly conditions state sovereignty and goes beyond the voluntary nature of international human rights instruments. As Slaughter observes, "membership in the United Nations is no longer a validation of sovereign status and a shield against unwanted meddling in a state's domestic jurisdiction."[15] This has given rise to a solidarist norm of "individual sovereignty," whereby the legitimacy of state sovereignty rests not only on control of territory and international recognition, but also upon fulfilling certain standards of human rights and welfare for citizens.

As a corollary, the sovereignty of states which are unwilling or unable to meet certain basic standards of human rights may be in question. The use of military force for human protection purposes – "humanitarian intervention" – is the starkest example of this idea, although a wider range of transnational norms and processes regarding human rights and governance also underscore the normative challenge to the conventional narrow principles of sovereignty. Sovereignty, and respect for its legitimacy, rests in part upon the recognition of other states and territorial control, but it is arguably now also premised upon a broader set of criteria, including human rights. Yet existing international organizations essentially rest upon the basis of a narrow reading of state sovereignty, and prioritize sovereignty and non-interference above human rights. They may therefore be out of step with important normative changes.

Some analysts may not accept that human rights are becoming a more significant factor in international politics or that they are meaningfully conditioning sovereignty.[16] However, the evolution of sovereignty goes beyond this issue. State sovereignty traditionally implies control of territory, along with independence and reciprocal recognition. Historically, there are countless cases where this was a fiction, and yet the international community stressed the norm of sovereignty, avoiding any legal derogation of that institution. However, it is becoming increasingly difficult to uphold the idea of sovereignty in cases where states are unwilling or unable to uphold even the most basic foundations of the institution of sovereignty, especially when they can have serious negative repercussions across borders. This is represented in a number of forms. When viable public authority and control cease to exist, the rights and needs of citizens cannot be met, and relations with other international entities cannot be meaningfully pursued. Moreover, a lack of control over territory, cross-border movements of illegal activities and refugee flows affect other states. In addition, the association of certain countries with terrorism, weapons of mass destruction and other "errant" behavior has further challenged the Westphalian order. For conservative policy-makers in the US, what President Bush calls the "deadly combination of outlaw regimes and terror networks and weapons of mass murder" requires entirely new thinking about the idea of sovereign equality.[17]

Conceptually, the contemporary reality of international politics also raises a challenge to the way that scholarship on multilateralism has emerged. Traditional analysis of multilateralism has been premised upon rational, unitary and autonomous actors which follow the same rules of logical behavior, irrespective of sociological factors or the particular circumstances of a country. However, it is increasingly recognized that sociological perspectives are important to understanding how multilateralism works.[18] State behavior is not entirely dictated by the system (as neorealism would contend); domestic political and cultural factors, and civil society actors, are relevant.

In many ways and for different reasons, the challenge to the conventional model of state sovereignty, as the foundation of multilateralism, represents a challenge to formal institutionalized multilateralism. At the beginning of the twenty-first century, it is necessary to acknowledge a controversial and perhaps uncomfortable reality: the concept of equality of state legitimacy – that all states are endowed with equal rights to legal respect, sovereign prerogatives and inviolable territorial integrity – is not universally accepted.

A further problem with the state-centric nature of international organizations is that many challenges and problems are transnational and involve non-state actors. In the most extreme illustration of this, the idea of multilateralism – or even international order – as constituted by states is being challenged by terrorist non-state actors. And in the case of human rights, it would be difficult to deny that major NGOs and civil society actors such as Amnesty International, Human Rights Watch, the International Committee of the Red Cross, Greenpeace and Transparency International have – in terms of their legitimacy and perhaps also performance – presented a challenge to the UN's human rights mechanisms.

Second, there are hegemonic challenges to contemporary multilateral institutions, which relate to the exercise of power (especially American) in an international system which is in some respects unipolar. The US, through its economic and military preeminence, is in a position where it is able to exercise a certain amount of discretion in terms of its support for international organizations. Defense Secretary Donald Rumsfeld stated that one of the most important lessons from the war against terrorism was that "the mission must determine the coalition, the coalition must not determine the mission."[19] With this thinking the US and its allies undertook a war against Iraq in 2003 without the explicit authorization of the UN Security Council. In other areas of multilateralism, the US rejected the International Criminal Court and the Kyoto protocol on climate change, raised the possibility of preventive force outside the UN framework in response to latent security threats, eroded a number of multilateral arms control treaties, and has organized and leads the Proliferation Security Initiative as an alternative arrangement for dealing with illicit transfers of WMD-sensitive material. According to Ikenberry, "America's nascent neoimperial grand strategy threatens to rend the fabric of the international community."[20]

The so-called pattern of US unilateralism has been correctly associated with the malaise of multilateralism, but it is only a partial explanation. US preeminence – which is, in any case, not an unproblematic concept – does not necessarily result in US unilateralism. In turn, unilateralism does not necessarily result in a general decline of multilateralism. Indeed, many of the key institutions of international order established after the Second World War – including the UN and the Bretton Woods institutions – were established, through US leadership, at a time of US preeminence. In addition, according to hegemonic stability theory, it was *declining* US preponderance in the 1970s which was bringing multilateral institutions into question. This suggests that purely structural explanations are inadequate for identifying the relationship between power, leadership, and the maintenance of multilateral institutions.

Having observed all of this, the preeminent position of the US has allowed it to raise legitimate concerns: rigid multilateral institutions cannot hope to be respected indefinitely when their constitutive principles and performance do not meet expectations in terms of legitimacy and effectiveness. The result is that powerful states can afford to circumvent established international organizations in matters related to critical national interests – which is nothing new – and also form alternative and sometimes *ad hoc* coalitions for taking action. According to Ikenberry, America's unilateral strategy is the legacy of a historical suspicion about the value of international agreements: "the United States has decided it is big enough, powerful enough, and remote enough to go it alone."[21]

The hegemonic challenge to multilateralism also relates to growing unease within the US establishment about the sovereign equality principle of international organizations. It is telling that an American task force on UN reform co-chaired by Newt Gingrich and George Mitchell argued that "the challenges and problems faced by the United Nations can be addressed, but only through consistent and concerted action by the world's genuine democracies."[22] This sense of judgment is also reflected, for example, in John Bolton's observation that the US "will not assume that a country's formal subscription to UN counterterrorism conventions or its membership in multilateral regimes necessarily constitutes an accurate reading of its intentions."[23] The presumption of sovereign equality based upon international law – always a questionable norm in practice – is eroding further. Yet the idea that the US has sidelined formal multilateral organizations is spurious, as we shall see. US foreign policy does not reflect simplistic patterns (immediately after 9/11, for example, Joseph Nye suggested – against the conventional wisdom – that the US tone towards multilateralism had softened as the government considered its response to the new challenge[24]).

Third, there are normative challenges to multilateralism which concern the way that decisions are made and implemented in international organizations. There are two dimensions to this. First, established multilateral organizations arguably do not meet standards of accountability and transparency which are considered legitimate in the twenty-first century, at least amongst democratic societies. This is a problem because international organizations are playing an increasingly prominent role in people's lives. A range of public practices and policy decisions have been transferred to the international level, and this raises a number of pressing normative issues which did not apply to the more narrow Westphalian origins of multilateralism. The state sovereignty basis of multilateral legitimacy is no longer sufficient in an era of popular sovereignty and democracy. This requires some elaboration.

Traditionally, ideas of political legitimacy are bounded within the state. Legitimacy in governance is usually conceived in the nature of the relationship between the government and the governed. Justice and political legitimacy bestow the right to govern and define the loss of this right in the context of the value-system and norms of a particular political community. Values and standards vary across the world, but by most definitions of political legitimacy certain foundational criteria must be met: consent, accountability, and the rule of law. In the domestic context this is embraced by the practices of democracy, and the "collective good" is defined and upheld through this process within a given political community.

There are many problems in applying ideas of political legitimacy to the international arena. The basis of political community, within which legitimacy must be constituted, is difficult to conceive at the international level. There is a far greater diversity of value systems so the roots of political legitimacy are elusive. Yet with the profile of international organizations increasing in people's lives there is a pressing need to apply more rigorous ideas of legitimacy to the normative goals and operating procedures underpinning many international organizations. At a time when leadership and governance within states require legitimacy based upon democratic credentials and democracy is expanding across the world, similar principles are increasingly being applied to the international "level" and to international organizations. In fact, democracy and legitimacy increasingly are concepts which extend beyond the domestic polity, partly as a condition of globalizing ideas and interaction amongst societies. Traditionally, the concept of legitimacy did not extend beyond the domestic arena and a different set of norms governed international relationships. This tradition has evolved into a democratic deficit in many organizations. Even in the case of those organizations which can wield enormous leverage upon the domestic policies of some states and exert a significant impact upon the lives of many millions of people, there is little transparency or public input into their policy and decision-making – or at least this is the perception. Why should international organizations be exempt from democratic accountability, transparency, public participation and judgments of legitimacy? In the absence of satisfactory answers to these questions, we have criticisms of unelected, unaccountable and sometimes inefficient international bureaucracies. As a result of this, according to Ruggie, there is a "domestic blowback" against international organizations, especially in the US.[25] In the field, also, the UN is facing stiff competition from NGOs, many – although not all – of which are seen as more flexible and in touch with local needs, and less prone to political and bureaucratic constraints.

On a related level, the consensus and majoritarian bases of decision-making of some international organizations have also been questioned with respect to issues of legitimacy. It cannot be taken as a given that all governments, in international organizations, represent their people. Why, then, should a democratic country or a group of democratic countries be obliged to act – or constrained from acting – on critical issues according to the rules of an international organization in which non-democratic states have a vote? According to the existing rules of many multilateral organizations, the status quo – or inactivity – is acceptable if agreement to act through consensus or majority according to the rules of procedure cannot be achieved, even in situations of emergency. As Keohane observes, this is no longer acceptable in the face of genocide or with the risk of terrorism combined with weapons of mass destruction.[26] If international organizations cannot act in response to the most pressing global problems, then their legitimacy is questioned, even if they are following their rules of procedure. Their procedural legitimacy has come into conflict with their performance legitimacy. International organizations have moved far beyond the Westphalian idea of merely regulating "high politics" amongst states, and expectations – or demands – for their performance and constitutive legitimacy have increased accordingly. It has often been accepted that formal multilateral organizations, as imperfect as they are, were legitimate relative to the feasible alternatives. This is no longer a given.

A further normative challenge relates to the constitutive values upon which international organizations, for historical reasons, are based. Many contemporary forms of institutionalized multilateralism – exemplified in the Bretton Woods organizations – reflect a particular normative heritage based upon liberal values such as the nation-state, liberal democracy and liberal human rights, and above all, market economics and the integration of societies into free trade. However, this liberal outlook is problematic, and the "liberal peace" presumption of multilateral organizations has been challenged both theoretically and on the ground in many countries. Liberal democracy, liberal human rights, and the integration of societies into economic globalization have not taken root everywhere, and have, according some observers, created or exacerbated social conflict. There is, therefore, resistance to the values upon which established forms of multilateralism are based. As international politics intrudes increasingly into societies, international organizations have demonstrated that multilateralism is not value-free. Multilateralism has become entwined with fundamental social and political choices regarding such issues as human rights, governance and democracy, and the balance between the market and welfare. This has inevitably been controversial.

Thus, in summary, we see the challenge to the values and institutions of multilateralism not only as a result of a particular distribution of power, but also systemic factors: the nature of power, the nature of security and of threats to international security, the actors which have an impact upon international peace and security, the international norms which regulate the behavior of actors in the international arena, and the nature of the state. In terms of norms, the reality is that the world is diverse; not all the values that "universal" multilateral organizations project and promote – or even impose, according to some observers – are accepted as truly universal.

Leading states may be less willing to bear the costs and obligations (and restrictions) of maintaining certain multilateral institutions in the face of declining effectiveness, especially in the area of international security. Smaller states feel alienated by the elitist and power political forms of multilateralism which deny representation, even though they rely heavily on their participation in international organizations. Citizens and non-state actors are frustrated by what they see as a lack of accountability and transparency in multilateralism. As a result, confidence in many of the institutions and values of multilateralism is waning in the early twenty-first century. When the effectiveness of multilateral arrangements as well as their constitutive principles fail to meet performance expectations and contemporary norms, their legitimacy is in doubt. For many scholars, this calls for a revised – and critical – view of multilateralism which goes beyond state interaction and which questions many of the normative foundations of conventional multilateralism.[27] In turn, this critical view calls for a "new multilateralism," which is not premised upon states alone but which embraces structural change and bottom-up forces, and does not accept the bases of world order as inevitable or permanent.[28]

International institutions in crisis? International relations theory

In November 2003 United Nations Secretary-General Kofi Annan observed that "The past year has shaken the foundations of collective security and undermined confidence in the possibility of collective responses to our common problems and challenges." Many scholars and policy analysts shared his view, for good reason. Yet in 1982 Secretary-General Pérez de Cuéllar similarly wrote of a "crisis in the multilateral approach."[29] His predecessor Kurt Waldheim observed that the forces of change a decade earlier "were destroying the credit of the United Nations and might ultimately even tear it apart."[30] Observers have been quick to conclude that specific international organizations or the values and institutions of multilateralism more generally are in crisis or fundamentally flawed. The current sense of "crisis," at the beginning of the twenty-first century, is shared by analysts of different ideological and theoretical predispositions, and seems to be a "truly" historical turning point. But how do we know? What does a "crisis" mean in terms of a specific international organization or multilateralism in general? How are scholars of international relations to objectively judge if an international organization – or multilateralism more broadly – is in "crisis"? Can such a judgment be based upon a systematic methodology, rather than just intuition?

International relations (IR) theory provides some thoughts on these questions. The subject of IR seeks to describe and explain the relationships between actors in international politics. The subject seeks to identify and explain change, identify patterns and trends, and explain how actors (states, individuals, international organizations, non-governmental organizations, multinational corporations) relate to each other and to the world as a whole. There are two main types of theories of IR. Some are basically explanatory: they attempt to explain or describe the details of international politics within a coherent model. They attempt to explain how and why actors such as states behave as they do, and predict certain phenomena within certain circumstances. Amongst these theories, some are limited to specific scenarios – such as how the balance of power, deterrence or reciprocity operate between states, or why "democratic peace" exists between liberal states – while meta-theories provide a much broader range of explanations for international politics. Other IR theories are normative: they are concerned with questions of justice and ethics in international politics, and how the world should be. It is essential to bear in mind this distinction when addressing the role of international organizations and multilateralism generally. A difficulty with much scholarship on international organizations – and for some reason, particularly the UN – is that there is sometimes confusion between describing the world as it really is (explanatory theory), and how we would like it to be (normative theory). This confusion significantly weakens UN scholarship.

Liberal internationalist theory argues that cooperation, progress, shared values and community are possible in international relations. It sees sovereign states as the main actors, in an "international society" which can, given the right conditions, have parallels with peaceful domestic society. Rules, laws and norms exist and help to regulate relationships between states and contribute to the shared values of an international society. Human beings are basically "good" and potentially "social," and therefore states can also be so, as a collective expression of human nature in a free society. In the right circumstances – democratic states where the citizens are free to express and pursue their aspirations, and where basic standards of human welfare are met – states will be fundamentally peace-loving and will develop principles to govern inter-state relations. International law, international organizations and norms will underpin stability and cooperation because a stable system is seen to benefit everyone. In particular, liberal internationalism maintains the Kantian position that economic cooperation amongst democratic societies results in international peace and stability – the "democratic peace." Change can occur peacefully and according to international law, as people express their desire for peaceful relationships between countries. War is seen as avoidable because states recognize that war disrupts the system, disrupts cooperation, and is morally wrong.

Within the liberal internationalist perspective, in the absence of ideal-type liberal democratic states, peace and security are based on the idea of collective security. The security of each state is guaranteed by the community of states; an attack on one state is seen as an attack on all states, so security is a collective responsibility. If one state is aggressive, other states will cooperate to defeat that aggression. The League of Nations and the United Nations were both founded on the principles of rules and international law in an expression of collective security. Indeed, liberal internationalism – sometimes called "idealism" – is often associated with mainstream thinking after the First World War. The horrors of that conflict led to a widely held belief that international politics needed to be regulated in order to reflect the aspirations of humankind, which are basically peaceful. Since the end of the Cold War there has been a revival of interest in liberal internationalism.

Sources & manifestations of multilateral malaise 23

The idea of democracy and market economics spreading a "zone of peace," and the growing importance of international organizations, has underscored this. The idea of an international "society" similarly gained renewed support.

There are, of course, many problems with this Kantian vision. To have a stable society, either globally or within one country, there must be cooperation amongst the units – either states or people – based upon a common outlook and shared values. Rules must be obeyed by consensus and believed by the members of the society to benefit everyone. In many domestic situations this works. But at the international level states have a different outlook, based upon their perception of their interests. Some may wish to change the system by force and may reject the rules.

The realist model of IR emerged in part as a theoretical response to the limitations of liberal internationalism. Realism is premised upon state-centricity, hierarchy based on power, and the balance of power. The behavior of states reflects a preoccupation with power politics, the defense and promotion of the national interest, and the demands of survival in an anarchical international environment. International relations is therefore characterized by conflict resulting from a clash of interests and the struggle by states to acquire power. Realism, in becoming the prevalent theoretical model of IR in the second half of the twentieth century, claimed that liberal internationalism failed to explain the hostility of the 1930s, the Second World War, and the Cold War.

The realist model therefore is based on a different, less optimistic view of human nature and the international system. In fact it sees *no* international society or community: it sees anarchy. Accordingly, international politics is based on the need for states to survive and increase power in an anarchical system. There is no international morality or effective international law apart from that which the most powerful states support or impose. There is no world government, no society, and so no protection apart from that which states can provide for themselves. States exist in a condition of insecurity and this "security dilemma" causes them to adopt defensive or aggressive positions, depending on the way in which they interpret threats. Therefore, conflict and struggle are inevitable; they can be managed, but not eliminated. Conflict occurs between states which are satisfied with the present situation (the *status quo*) and those states which want to change/revise the international order in line with their interests. Peace and stability are seen to exist only as a result of a balance of power and deterrence. States only cooperate to gain advantage: they participate in the UN agencies not for the collective good of mankind, but to benefit themselves.

Some realists see the international system as a Hobbesian state of nature: with no government, people naturally seek to dominate, and so with no world government, states will seek to dominate. As Glennon argues, "The first and last geopolitical truth is that states pursue security by pursuing power. Legalist institutions that manage that pursuit maladroitly are ultimately swept away."[31] Classical realists contend that this derives from the nature of humankind, as inherently selfish and aggressive.[32] In contrast, neorealists – also called structural realists – argue that the anarchic structure of the international system determines the behavior of states in this way.[33] All realists are deeply sceptical of efforts to formulate workable norms and rules governing international order or the use of force. The Report of the Secretary-General's High Level Panel on Threats, Challenges and Change argued that: "The maintenance of world peace and security depends importantly upon there being a common global understanding, and acceptance, of when the application of force is both legal and legitimate."[34] Realists reject the idea that such a common global understanding can be achieved. A recent contribution to the literature on the UN suggested that "The Iraq war was a multiple assault on the foundations and rules of the existing UN-centered world order."[35] Realists would reject the idea that world order was, is, or ever could be centered upon the UN.

Within this anarchy, stability and peace can only exist if states agree to manage conflict or if there is a balance of power: states will be satisfied with the situation because they know that they cannot change it without risking their own destruction. The balance of power in the nineteenth century after 1815 and during the Cold War, for example, maintained a certain stability that realists argue had little to do with international law. Realism obviously sees international organizations as tools or instruments of the most powerful members. According to this, "The United Nations is not and cannot be a political actor in a world of sovereign states."[36] Indeed, the aspirations of the UN charter are "lofty idealism"[37] – and the reality is "power politics in disguise."[38]

A more recent theoretical tradition of relevance to multilateralism is neoliberal institutionalism (or simply institutionalism), introduced earlier in this volume. This tradition borrows from both the liberal internationalist and realist approaches. It accepts anarchy amongst states and power politics as fundamental for understanding international politics but argues that shared values and needs can emerge and the responses to these can become institutionalized.

The starting point of realism and neoliberal institutionalism is the "problem of anarchy." States rationally pursue their interests in an anarchical international system. Their interests remain static in nature and are not meaningfully conditioned by the nature of their interaction with other actors; rather, they are pre-formed, defined by the nature of the international system. For the realists – especially the neorealists – this inevitably results in a zero-sum struggle for power and survival which often results in conflict. Moreover, neorealists argue that this is not altered by political changes within states, such as democratization. As Waltz argued, "the structure of international politics is not transformed by changes internal to states, however widespread the changes may be."[39] Interests and identities are determined by the nature of the international system. Neoliberal institutionalists, in contrast, argue that self-interested states can and must cooperate as a result of interdependence, and therefore seek regularized forms of cooperation such as regimes and organizations in order to reduce transaction costs and have confidence in reciprocal agreements. But for both schools of thought, states are rational egoists with static interests which are dictated by the anarchic nature of international politics and not altered by interaction with other actors.

This proposition is challenged by a further theoretical movement called constructivism, which is of great relevance to multilateralism. This is not a single unified theory, but a number of propositions are central to the various strands of the approach. The underlying argument is that interests, identities and therefore relationships of states or other actors are socially constructed. That is, interests are not predetermined, but rather they are formed and evolve largely as a result of interaction with other actors. Interests, identities, relationships – and therefore the behavior of actors – can therefore change. The system is not a deterministic given – it is socially constructed. Constructivism embraces a vision of change, and challenges the solely materialistic theories of international relations. Thus, "the building blocks of international reality are ideational as well as material."[40] According to constructivists, key tenets of realism and institutionalism can be challenged. For example, the central structural mainstay of realism is anarchy, which – either in a permissive or causal sense – results in self-help and power politics. This can be interpreted as socially constructed, and therefore can change. Alexander Wendt has famously argued that "anarchy is what states make of it": "self-help is an institution, one of the various structures of identity and interests that may exist under anarchy."[41] Threats are constructed, rather than being natural or inevitable.

The constructivist approach to international relations has interesting things to say about the contribution of multilateralism to international politics. States cooperate through a range of international regimes and organizations – this is a demonstrable fact – and on the basis of this, constructivists suggest, norms reflecting shared values amongst states can emerge. Evolving – and potentially more friendly – relationships can form on the basis of successful cooperation. Relationships can potentially be transformed. Multilateral arrangements are a manifestation of this process, but in turn, they act as a vehicle for this – they can promote it. A consideration of cooperation in West Europe since the Second World War, which has largely defied realist theory, appears closer to a constructivist approach.

There are many questions regarding the fundamental significance of international organizations in international politics, and IR theories attempt to supply many of the answers: is the international system moving from "anarchy" to "society" through international organizations? Do international organizations bring order to international politics? Are international organizations actors in their own right, or instruments of their most powerful members? Is the sovereignty of states being challenged or undermined (or modified) by international organizations? With the growing number and greater depth of international organizations, is foreign policy shifting away from traditional forms of "hard" (military) power to "softer" forms of power?

This volume does not seek to resolve all of these questions and its theoretical engagement will be specific rather than comprehensive. Its theoretical orientation is essentially institutionalist in nature: it assumes that power is the ultimate arbiter of international politics and states are the principal (but not sole) actors; and that states have a shared interest in maintaining rules and regularity in their interactions, reducing transaction costs, collectively addressing problems which cannot be effectively tackled unilaterally, and maintaining certain norms on issues such as sovereignty, non-intervention and human rights. Multilateral arrangements – whether informal institutions or formal organizations – are one of the means by which states meet these requirements. Multilateral arrangements are not independent from the actors that constitute them or the driving force of international politics, but international institutions are fundamentally important to understanding international politics, and institutions are sometimes formalized as multilateral organizations. The modest claim here, then, is that multilateral organizations play a role in international relations as instruments through which states can formalize – and thus strengthen – certain norms. The question of "crisis" therefore concerns whether established multilateral organizations and regimes – such as the UN, conventions on weapons of mass destruction, conventions on terrorism – are able to effectively address the tasks which member states entrusted to them within this institutionalist understanding, and whether particularly difficult challenges – such as nuclear proliferation, terrorism, state failure, and civil war – pose challenges which existing multilateral values and institutions seem unable to effectively address.

So, "crisis" refers first to specific formal multilateral institutions, rather than the whole concept of multilateralism. A multilateral arrangement may be objectively judged to be in crisis if it is ineffective and/or obsolete in its current form and with respect to current performance, and is consequently losing diplomatic support and funding; if there is the expectation that the institution is permanently flawed in its existing formulation and requires fundamental revision in its normative and operating principles in order to gain or regain effectiveness; or if a completely new and alternative arrangement is required to achieve the necessary policy objectives. Put more elaborately, a multilateral arrangement is in crisis in the following circumstances:

- The constitutive principles upon which the arrangement is founded and operates are consistently challenged by the activities and declarations of its leading members. Thus, key members – and/or a numerically significant proportion of members – pursue relevant policy objectives at odds with, and/or outside the framework of, the organization, regime or institution.
- There is an epistemic consensus that the values and institutions of a particular form of multilateralism are no longer effective or legitimate, and that the multilateral arrangement consistently fails to achieve the principal objectives for which it was created.
- There is an epistemic consensus that the ineffectiveness and illegitimacy of a particular multilateral form are permanent as long as the constitutive principles of the organization remain the same.
- Multilateral institutions are challenged by significant alternative arrangements which perform the same task, to which member states transfer their diplomatic attention and material resources.

Why might a multilateral regime or organization be in "crisis"?

- Most obviously, if the mission of a multilateral arrangement is simply no longer necessary or viable according to formal or informal criteria recognized by member states. An example of this could be the UN Trusteeship Council after all former colonial territories became independent.

28 Sources & manifestations of multilateral malaise

- Decision-making processes are, or become, out of step with the balance of power in international politics. This can involve a leading member state declining in relative power and being less willing to accept an increasingly unattractive cost-benefit equation and "free riders." The opposite tendency can involve a shift towards unipolarity in economic and/or military power, whereby a single state is perceived to be preeminent and free from the constraints of multilateralism when such constraints are deemed unacceptable.
- The balance of interests *within* an international organization changes as a result of new or changing membership, introducing irreconcilable conflicts. The best example here comes from the United Nations General Assembly in the 1960s and 1970s, as a result of the influx of developing countries which embraced an agenda of structural revisionism, seeking to use the UN as a vehicle for changing rules governing international economics. The crisis was resolved by the eventual submission of the General Assembly majority.
- The attitude of powerful states turns against a multilateral organization for ideological reasons – through a change of government, for instance – and such states withhold diplomatic and material support. There were signs of this from the US administration under President Ronald Reagan and then under President George W. Bush.
- The constitutive principles upon which the organization or regime was founded and operates are challenged by changing norms or the breakdown of norms. For example, the growing prominence of terrorist organizations and the perceived threat of weapons of mass destruction in the hands of terrorists or "rogue states" have arguably eroded the UN Charter norms regulating the use of military force in international politics (that is, only in self-defense or within the collective security framework of the UN).
- Multilateralism fails to adapt to changing circumstances and challenges; the constitutive principles and policies of the organization are no longer appropriate to deal with the challenges with which the organization is faced. For example, the state-centric and national interest-orientation of many international organizations has been questioned with regard to dealing with transnational challenges such as contagious diseases.

In turn, if a significant number of key international institutions are in crisis and a common cause or manifestation appears to run through these crises, then it may be meaningful to think in terms of a broader crisis of multilateralism. At this level of the debate there really is

Sources & manifestations of multilateral malaise 29

disagreement about whether established multilateral organizations and regimes are in "crisis" or whether they simply reflect the "normal" realities of international power politics. Many authors – realist, liberal internationalist and institutionalist alike – echo the attitude of the UN Secretary-General: the UN is at a "fork in the road" and facing success or failure, and that it is not "business as usual" for formalized multilateralism.[42] Ruggie, for example, argues that the UN's political role in the world, and the broader idea of global governance, face *unprecedented* challenges from the erosion of the UN's capacity to maintain international peace and security, the erosion of the UN's collective legitimization, and the power and ideology of the US.[43]

This volume, while sharing some of these concerns, does not uncritically accept that there is a crisis of multilateralism. Instead, it argues for a more nuanced approach which describes the problems of multilateralism in the twenty-first century as inherent in the nature of the international system. As Weiss observes, the tumult that shakes the UN and many other formal multilateral arrangements "is the essence of international relations, not an aberration."[44] Focusing on a number of illustrative policy areas, this volume considers which challenges can be absorbed within a process of multilateral evolution, and which must logically give way to new multilateral values and institutions.

2 The United States, power, and multilateralism

Multilateralism – its forms, effectiveness and limitations – is inseparable from power in international relations, in all its manifestations. For this reason, a great deal of attention has been paid to the attitudes and actions of the US, as the world's preeminent military and economic power, because these directly influence the prospects of international organizations and other multilateral arrangements. There is a claim, popular after the Cold War, that the problems of multilateralism are a logical outcome of the present distribution of international power, and specifically US power. According to this view, American power enables that country to act unilaterally, and this is inherently in tension with multilateralism. There does appear to be a trend towards unilateral action in US foreign policy across a wide range of issues; perhaps even a "growing unilateral disengagement."[1] Since the end of the Cold War, this trend has been observed in US policies towards international arms control processes, the use of military force, human rights, the natural environment, and international criminal justice. Most alarming for some, the US has presented a strategic doctrine of preventive force – using military force to prevent the emergence of hostile threats, even before they become imminent – at odds with the established norms regulating the use of force in international affairs. This chapter considers the US approach towards – and impact upon – multilateralism. It illustrates that there is not a simple US unilateral disengagement from multilateral arrangements, but rather three discernible patterns: the US is reducing its support or even withdrawing from a limited number of formalized multilateral arrangements; it is also using persuasion and coercion to promote its interests in multilateral settings; and it is creating new multilateral arrangements when it perceives it is necessary.

A number of factors help to explain these patterns, which must be understood in conjunction with each other: American power, the changing international security environment, and America's perception of its historic exceptionalism and its unique place in the world. First, America's preeminent economic and military power means that the US is more able than other states to pursue its foreign policy unilaterally or operate outside established multilateral arrangements. There is general agreement that the "unipolar moment" has endured.[2] American supremacy in all factors of hard power is beyond question. America's GDP was US $12.5 trillion in 2005. In the same year, according to the Stockholm International Peace Research Institute, US military expenditure was US$ 478 billion, approximately 48 percent of the world total.[3] US "soft power" – the ability to achieve objectives by attraction rather than coercion – is also compelling, although underutilized according to some analysts.[4] President George W. Bush is quite candid in terms of military superiority: "We must remain a military without peer."[5] American preeminence does not, of course, automatically result in American antipathy towards multilateralism or a general malaise in multilateralism.[6] On the contrary, the history of international organizations has demonstrated that the US has been a leader in envisioning, creating and maintaining international organizations and regimes. The UN and many of its agencies, including the Bretton Woods organizations, and innumerable other forms of multilateralism were established under US sponsorship and leadership. Paradoxically, perhaps, this was often unilateral US sponsorship and leadership. In addition, while today many observers suggest that preeminent US power is enabling – or perhaps motivating – the country to ignore or undermine some institutions, in the past theorists of international relations argued on the contrary that *declining* US power resulted in declining support for multilateral institutions and regimes.

Therefore, US behavior towards international organizations – including declining support – is not an inevitability resulting from US power. US power does help to explain the history of US ambivalence towards international regimes and organizations. However, the *ideology* of US unilateralism – which comes from a certain understanding of power and American values – is also important in understanding the policy of the US towards multilateral institutions. Indeed, some observers have noted a pattern: paradoxically, while the US has taken the lead in creating and maintaining international organizations and regimes, it has subsequently withdrawn or weakened its support from a number of these. According to Krisch, this has become more pronounced since the end of the Cold War, and it suggests a gap between the US role in making international law –

creating obligations for others – and its willingness to be constrained itself.[7]

A second dimension is America's perception of a changing security environment. This has led many in Washington to believe that the security of the US – which is unique in its global interests and responsibilities – can only be assured if the country retains the right to use its power unilaterally and without the constraints of multilateral commitments. Most importantly, especially after 11 September 2001, a powerful element in the US administration has become preoccupied with the threat of weapons of mass destruction in the hands of apocalyptic terrorist organizations or rogue states.[8] This perception assumes a fundamental transformation in international politics and strategy. During the Cold War the US faced a distinct, comprehensible threat which could be deterred and which shared a belief in the rules of stability and the balance of power. "Mutual Assured Destruction" dictated that the US and the Soviet Union would exercise restraint and had an interest in containment, not in attempting to defeat the adversary. Maintaining the balance of power through arms control and massive counter-strike capacity generated a certain stability. Secretary of Defense Donald Rumsfeld argued that containment, deterrence and the balance of power are obsolete in the face of the transformation brought on by the war on terror and the threat of rogue regimes with weapons of mass destruction: "the Cold War is over, the Soviet Union is gone – and with it the familiar security environment to which our nation had grown accustomed."[9] President Bush put it vividly in his 2002 state of the Union address: "Thousands of dangerous killers, schooled in the methods of murder, often supported by outlaw regimes, are now spread throughout the world like ticking time bombs – set to go off without warning."[10] It is notable that, beyond the narrow neoconservative clique in Washington, this belief reflects mainstream opinion in the US political establishment. A key bi-partisan study of US interests in the UN formed the following conclusion about the strategic transformation: "Terrorism and the proliferation of nuclear, biological, and chemical weapons are deadly threats that have come together in the twenty-first century to create the world's worst nightmare. They have become the most acute security challenge facing the United States and the international community."[11]

The reality is that many in the US political establishment – and certainly the neoconservatives – have little or no faith that formal multilateral arrangements can alone address this new "nightmare." The most radical thinkers argue that the UN failed the test of Iraq, leaving "the intellectual wreckage of the liberal conceit of safety through international law administered by international institutions."[12] For neoconservatives, then, multilateralism is unrealistic and naïve – and even dangerous – because it complicates foreign and security policy by generating constraining commitments and diverts attention away from critically important challenges. The perception of many observers is that the so-called "multilateralists" have a lack of credibility on the use of force in defense of US interests.[13] The conservatives, or so-called unilateralists, strike a more attractive note in the context of contemporary American politics. In response to complaints that the US acted outside the framework of the UN in its military action in Serbia in 1999, Bolton responded: "We did not need the Security Council's permission to act. Besides, the Security Council was paralyzed and therefore useless for our purposes."[14] Heinbecker suggests that "US attitudes have arguably never been so contemptuous."[15]

Third, the historic exceptionalism of the US in part explains American ambivalence towards international organizations: "a deeply felt and authentically American belief that the United States should not get entangled in the corrupting and constraining world of multilateral rules and institutions."[16] Edward Luck asks, "Why have Americans again and again been the first to create international institutions and then the first to forsake them?"[17] The reasons for this are multiple. The birth of the US reflected a split from the imperial machinations of Europe. Its history has reflected a tension between the leadership of the US in global affairs and a reluctance to be overly committed to the formal structures of international cooperation. The liberal, individualist history of the American psyche may have played a role in this too, characterized by an aggressive independence and at times even isolationism. This has led to the perception that American values and institutions are unique, and can never be subjugated to external sources of authority. This has always been latent but has become pronounced due to the preeminence of US power and the perception of a particularly hazardous international security environment.

The US ambivalence towards formalized multilateralism – and especially the UN – has a long history, and it is interesting to note the reflections of John Bolton – appointed by President Bush as US Permanent Representative at the UN in 2005 – on this because it gives an interesting and candid view of the conservative mentality towards the UN (and multilateralism more broadly):

> During the 1960s and 1970s anti-Western and anti-American UN General Assembly majorities regularly and enthusiastically trashed

our values. Led by the Communist bloc, those dictatorial or authoritarian governments mocked democracy through resolutions in the General Assembly and other UN bodies in an attempt to advance a thoroughly anti-democratic agenda. They assaulted America's world leadership and integrity in resolutions condemning US foreign policies, year after year after year. They attacked our friends and allies ... They undermined economic liberty and global prosperity by endorsing Soviet-backed policies such as the New International Economic Order, a socialist dream of forcing redistribution of wealth to the Third World. And, all the while, the UN bureaucracy grew and grew, just like a coral reef – no planning, no system, no goal, yet blessed with apparently eternal life.[18]

In the 1960s and 1970s a number of historical processes transformed the UN into something quite different from that which was created in 1945 and something increasingly at odds with key actors in international politics, especially the US. These historical changes are still important in understanding the antipathy which exists towards multilateralism in some quarters in the US. The influx of new UN members, as former colonial territories became independent, alienated the organization from the West as the organization became embroiled in North-South tensions and revisionist "Third World" campaigns. Thus, what has been called the "minilateralist"[19] or the "club model"[20] of international organizations – whereby an exclusive collective of powerful states created post-war multilateral arrangements with their own worldview and interests in mind – was coming under strain and increasingly challenged. The new "Third World" majority – to use the terminology of the time – found a voice in the UN organs and agencies through a sense of solidarity and shared plight. Because of their numerical superiority and bloc voting developing countries could exert considerable leverage upon the agenda and decisions of UN organs. This "radically altered the entire character of the United Nations."[21] The new majority demanded economic redistribution and egalitarian systemic changes exemplified by the formation of the UN Conference on Trade and Development and the proposed New International Economic Order. These initiatives, and the militant spirit in which they were proposed, were the antithesis of the prevalent free market thinking of the West. The combative US position was epitomized at the time by UN Representative Daniel Patrick Moynihan, who denounced the organization as a "dangerous place" – a vehicle for undemocratic forces and communists to mount diplomatic attacks against the West and to set an anti-US tone in international politics.[22]

Disillusionment with multilateral organizations on the part of much of the West, and in particular the US, meant that the UN was often peripheral to the foreign policy of major powers in the 1960s and 1970s. The Vietnam War, the maintenance of superpower *détente*, arms control, the Middle East peace process, and many crises of decolonization, are examples of critical issues pursued or left outside the UN. The relative decline of US hegemony had, according to many analysts, underpinned the growing antipathy of the US towards multilateralism. The collapse of fixed exchange rates and the soaring oil price increases of 1973 exacerbated the atmosphere of discord and US disillusionment. Observers noted that "at the White House, where Nixon and Kissinger were the architects of American foreign policy, there was little regard for the United Nations."[23] While Nixon's memoirs hardly mention the UN, Kissinger's clearly suggest that the UN was an instrument at his disposal for the pursuance of his own agenda.[24]

This skepticism towards the UN and some other multilateral organizations continued into the 1980s, exacerbated by an upsurge of Cold War hostility and the continuing "Third World" discontent and militancy. Major actors – and most importantly the US – circumvented the UN at critical moments, and proxy Cold War conflicts in the developing world were impervious to constructive intervention by the organization. Some of the analysis of the period shows parallels to the tone of debate in the twenty-first century. In the words of Taylor and Groom, the organization "was on the sidelines and penniless.... The United Nations framework itself had become dilapidated and in gross need of reform. In short, a great experiment was in danger of failure."[25] Anthony Parsons experienced that environment as the British Representative to the UN, observing that by the mid-1980s "the UN was in deep trouble, perhaps at the lowest ebb in its history ... The UN had reached the bottom after a long fall from the pinnacle of exaggerated expectations which had characterized its creation."[26] In the Western imagination, international organizations seemed "out of control."[27]

The agenda of the New Right in the 1980s, epitomized by President Reagan and US Representative at the UN Jeane Kirkpatrick, was combative and provided a foretaste of the post-Cold War neo-conservative ideology. According to Franck, in "the space of 40 years, the United States had gone from believing that the United Nations should and could do anything, to believing that it should and could do nothing."[28] From a systemic perspective, the Reagan approach reflected declining northern commitment to universal multifunctional organizations.[29]

Haas applied the concept of regime decay to the declining-hegemony thesis to explain the waning capability of the organization in conflict management.[30] The indignation of the US towards the UN reflected the end of American dominance and of western cultural universalism – and the frustration that the US was still shouldering the heaviest financial burden for the organization.

In addition to holding individual states accountable for their errant behavior at the UN, the US – and to a lesser extent the United Kingdom – imposed a number of economic sanctions and withdrew or restricted their diplomatic support of agencies which manifested the worst excesses. The US withdrew from the ILO between 1977 and 1980 and from UNESCO in 1985, and refused to sign the 1982 Law of the Sea Convention. The 1985 Kassebaum Amendment involved a significant reduction of the US share of assessed contributions. The 1985 Sundquist Amendment threatened to withhold some of the US contribution to secretariat salaries. If Israel was expelled, suspended, denied its rights or credentials, the US would suspend its own participation and reduce its contribution. Finally, the US withheld funds from specific UN activities which were disapproved of, such as support for the PLO, SWAPO, and the preparatory commission for the implementation of the Law of the Sea Commission.[31] As Bolton has suggested, "Since the UN had turned away from its principal founder, it is no wonder that the United States turned away from the UN."[32]

In some corners of the US, this attitude, in its twenty-first century guise, is conveyed quite forthrightly. Extremist viewpoints are not characteristic of US policy, but as a caricature they do reflect a conservative undercurrent which exists in Washington and has influence. A brief survey illustrates some interesting views. According to neo-conservatives, the mission of the UN and formal multilateralism more generally is clear: it is a means for the rest of the world – much of which does not meet basic standards of democracy and human rights – to constrain US power by attempting to tie the country into dubious legal obligations. So the "whole point" of the "multilateral enterprise" is to "reduce American freedom of action by making it subservient to, dependent on, constricted by the will – and interests – of other nations."[33] This is seen as a natural response to US preeminence: America is beyond peer in its power, and the only means available for other countries which resent or feel threatened by this is to promote the norm of multilateralism. Other realist observers are concerned about constraints upon US freedom of action: "the loss of American independence and flexibility caused by becoming wrapped around the UN axle."[34] Ruggie suggests that the US is experiencing the domestic blowback of global governance: "the very success of strategies to promote the internationalization of universal norms and standards into America's domestic political and legal spheres has triggered growing political opposition, and has raised a far more serious intellectual challenge than liberal internationalism has ever faced."[35]

Arch-conservatives also detest what they claim is the "perverse moral relativism" of the UN based upon membership according to sovereign statehood: "false equality among nations" whereby "Any nation, pseudo-nation, or thugocracy, such as Iran under the mullahs, can be a member."[36] For these conservatives, it is simply unacceptable that countries – including undemocratic, communist or "rogue states" – should have leverage over US policy: it is "corrosive moral equivalence."[37] It is equally reprehensible that the US is beholden to international regimes of any kind which do not share the values of the US. Indeed, Newt Gingrich suggested that "the fact that the UN has no democratic preconditions for membership limits America's ability to render the UN's infrastructure and its decisions compatible with American values and interests."[38] At the same time, conservatives lament the "double standards" which take place at the UN: the relentless attacks against Israel while the human rights abuses of Arab states and China are ignored, and the obstruction of US membership of the UN Commission on Human Rights while Sudan and Libya were elected. According to a former US Deputy Undersecretary of Defense, today's UN is a place:

> where good is evil, right is wrong, and every dictator and despot is given the same rights and privileges as the leaders of free nations. For the United States, the UN is a quagmire of diplomacy in which wars can be lost but not won, alliances can dissolve but not be formed, the birth of nuclear terrorism is being watched but not aborted, and no adult supervision is imposed on a Third World playground where anti-Americanism is the favorite game.[39]

We see more restrained elements of this view even in the official US proclamations which are characterized by a confidence – which is almost absolute – about justice in international politics. President Bush told the UN General Assembly that the world is divided "between those who seek order, and those who spread chaos; between those who work for peaceful change, and those who adopt the methods of gangsters; between those who honor the rights of man, and those who deliberately takes the lives of men and women and children without mercy or shame."[40] There was little to disguise the unspoken implication of this message: it is not only individuals who can be divided in this way, but also sovereign state members of the UN General Assembly. Secretary of State Condoleezza Rice, when referring to the human rights mechanisms of the UN, cautioned that the organization "should never – *never* – empower brutal dictatorships to sit in judgment of responsible democracies."[41] The idea that the General Assembly has "unique legitimacy" is therefore abhorrent to many American conservatives.[42] The social-welfare tone of some of the UN's initiatives has also been at odds with the "small government" thinking of many American conservatives who believe that as much as possible should be left to the responsibility of states.[43]

It is important also to keep in mind that conservative attacks upon "multilateralism" in the US derive from a domestic political agenda: Republicans portray "liberals" and Democrats as pandering to multilateralism, compromising American independence, and the "abdication of American leadership."[44] In this way, political debate in the US, at its most hysterical, comes close to using the expression "multilateral" as a slur. The image of UN corruption and inefficiency feeds this. The most high profile example was the oil-for-food scandal. This scandal implicated some UN officials – along with private companies and some national officials – in financial impropriety in connection with the program which allowed Iraq to export a certain amount of oil in the 1990s in return for food and other supplies to mitigate the terrible humanitarian impact of UN sanctions. While UN Secretary-General Kofi Annan was himself not guilty of fraud, the independent inquiry into the scandal headed by Paul Volcker pointed to serious management failures in the UN Secretariat, including by the Secretary-General and the Deputy Secretary-General.[45] Conservative critics found much in this scandal with which to question whether the international civil service is able to meet the standards of accountability and transparency expected of a public service in the twenty-first century.

A further theme that has grown from the idea of US exceptionalism and preeminence is that multilateralism forms part of a movement – or even a conspiracy – to promote a multipolar world as a means of constraining US power. It is no secret that political leaders around the world – and notably in Europe – would prefer a multipolar world in which the US has to contend with checks and balances upon its power. The issue of multilateralism has therefore become embroiled in a deeper debate about the trans-Atlantic relationship and competing visions of world order in the US and Europe. While the US is increasingly skeptical about multilateralism, European powers are seen as defending multilateral values as inherently good, and even as a means of responding to US hegemony.[46] Most pointedly, there is a widely held impression that France has, since the late 1990s, sought to lead multilateral initiatives in order to counter American unilateralism. It is worth quoting Kagan at length:

> It is time to stop pretending that Europeans and Americans share a common view of the world, or even that they occupy the same world. On the all-important question of power – the efficacy of power, the morality of power, the desirability of power – American and European perspectives are diverging. Europe is turning away from power, or to put it a little differently, it is moving beyond power into a self-contained world of laws and rules and transnational negotiation and cooperation. It is entering a post-historical paradise of peace and relative prosperity, the realization of Immanuel Kant's "perpetual peace." Meanwhile, the United States remains mired in history, exercising power in an anarchic Hobbesian world where international laws and rules are unreliable, and where true security and the defense and promotion of a liberal order still depend on the possession and use of military might.[47]

While these views are simplistic and perhaps extreme – and are contested[48] – they are qualitatively characteristic of conservatives generally in the US. And it is not only conservatives who associate the difficulties of multilateralism and global governance with transatlantic friction; Ruggie argues that "any European 'pro-UN' posture that consists mainly of a desire to use the organization as a fulcrum from which to balance the United States not only will prove futile, but also finish off what's left of the UN's political role."[49]

The terror of 11 September 2001 compounded the perception of US exceptionalism and the sense of a changed security environment. According to Dobbins, "Before September 11, 2001, the moderate, conservative and neoconservative elements of the Bush administration's policy had been in rough balance. The 9/11 attacks changed all this. They stimulated an immediate and understandably unilateralist impulse to retaliate."[50] In turn, the attacks also convinced many in the US that American preeminence – especially military – must be maintained at all costs. The implications of this are the following.

The US is less committed to respecting state sovereignty and the legalist equality of state sovereignty, especially related to sensitive security issues. For example, in this view, some states simply cannot be trusted with weapons of mass destruction and their commitments to abide by international arms control mechanisms are not sufficient assurance of their good intentions. In addition, if states provide a haven for terrorists – or are unable to prevent their territory from being used for this purpose – they effectively forfeit their legal rights to territorial inviolability.

There is a strategic shift in the US – elaborated in Chapter 3 – away from reliance upon deterrence and towards the use of force preventively and outside the legal framework of the UN, to "take the battle to the enemy, disrupt his plans, and confront the worst threats before they emerge."[51]

The pattern of US behavior also implies a "general depreciation of international rules, treaties, and security partnerships."[52] Most pointedly, the US political establishment, at the beginning of the twenty-first century, does not accept that the UN Security Council is the ultimate arbiter of the use of force in international relations or the Secretary-General's idea of the "unique legitimacy" of the UN in dealing with threats to international security.[53] In reality, the US rarely has – if ever – genuinely embraced these ideas, whatever the party in government. President Jacques Chirac argued that "Multilateralism is the key, for it ensures the participation of all in the management of world affairs. It is a guarantee of legitimacy and democracy, especially in matters regarding the use of force or laying down universal norms."[54] US thinking and practice – both contemporary and historical – reflects a fundamental rejection of this idea, and not only amongst the neoconservatives. The commitment, in the words of President Bush, to maintain "military strengths beyond challenge" underscores all of this.[55] Moreover, the general depreciation of multilateralism is, according to some, not only as a result of US sabotage, but also a result of declining international confidence in the US as the global hegemon.[56]

This also suggests that the idea of the legitimacy of multilateralism has shifted. Ruggie argued that "multilateral diplomacy has come to embody a procedural norm *in its own right* ... in some instances carrying with it an international legitimacy not enjoyed by other means."[57] The US has certainly not dispensed with this. However, there is a distinct understanding in US policy circles that legitimacy derives more from outcomes – and the extent to which outcomes are convergent with US interests – than from process and procedures. This is a function of American exceptionalism as well as its preponderance of power. Multilateralism and consensus are no longer – if they ever were – seen as an end in itself, but rather a means to an end. As Secretary of State Condoleezza Rice observed, "we will need to be judged by how effective we are, not just by the forms that we use."[58] This contrasts distinctly with the words in President Chirac's speech to the General Assembly, in which he asserted that "there is no alternative to the United Nations."[59] Bolton offers perhaps the most accurate evaluation of American thinking on the UN and perhaps all multilateral arrangements:

> It can be a useful tool in the American foreign policy tool kit. The UN should be used when and where we choose to use it to advance American national interests, not to validate academic theories and abstract models. But the UN is only a tool, not a theology. It is one of several options we have, and it is certainly not invariably the most important one.[60]

A bi-partisan US Congressional task force on UN reform clearly reflected the idea that existing multilateral institutions are not sacrosanct: "Without fundamental reform, the United Nations' reputation will suffer, reinforcing incentives to bypass the UN in favor of other institutions, coalitions, or self-help."[61]

However, it would be wrong to assert that the US has simply turned away from the UN or multilateralism in general. The US does recognize the value of multilateral approaches – both *ad hoc* and formal – in promoting its interests. The US seeks, through persuasion and sometimes coercion, multilateral channels that are convergent with US interests, and may create new or alternative forms of multilateralism to better fit its values and needs when necessary. For example, President Bush's 2002 speech at the General Assembly – which set up the war against Iraq a few months later – was replete with references to UN efforts in order to seek to put the confrontation with Iraq into the UN context, citing the Security Council no less than 16 times. Indeed, rather than being simply unilateral, the Bush administration has sought to demonstrate how existing international organizations are deficient: "Will the United Nations serve the purpose of its founding, or will it be irrelevant?"[62] Some conservatives describe this as "pseudo-multilateralism" – the US essentially acts alone, but seeks to hide its activities behind the façade of multilateralism.[63] A better analysis is that the US does value multilateralism, but that it is, in some limited areas of foreign policy, pursuing alternative multilateral approaches amongst likeminded states which circumvent the complications and strictures of conventional international organizations. By 2006 the US was confronting the limits of its power, embroiled in two foreign wars and confronted by two nuclear crises. Neoconservatives acknowledge the need for allies in addressing these challenges. The importance attached to the UN Security Council by the US in 2006, for example, in addressing the nuclear ambitions of Iran and North Korea illustrates this.

The US approach to multilateralism is conditioned by ideological and cultural factors and the country's power; it can bend the rules of the institutionalist bargain without undermining international regimes because, in most instances, other states still have to go along. Hegemonic powers establish international orders which reflect their worldview and interests, especially after structural/systemic conflicts. This process occurred with the end of the Cold War but without the obvious disjuncture of 1919 or 1945. The US will support multilateral arrangements which reflect its interests and worldview; it may challenge those which do not, especially when they diverge from US interests to an intolerable extent. The US hegemony will continue to be both benign (providing public goods) and coercive (forcing compliance). The US is likely to continue to support institutions of order and also free riders, but is much less tolerant to challengers and spoilers. This will have implications for formal multilateral structures – such as the UN – which reflect a wide range of political interests on the increasingly spurious basis of sovereign equality.

3 Collective security and the use of force

This chapter analyzes the role of formal multilateral organizations – especially the UN – in international security and particularly in regulating the use of armed force by states. A number of questions are addressed: does a legal, or rule-based, framework regulate the use of military force? If such a framework existed, was it undermined by the war against Iraq of 2003 and the doctrine of the preventive use of military force? In 2003 French President Jacques Chirac demanded: "It is the role of the Council to set the bounds to the use of force. No one is entitled to assume the right to utilize it unilaterally and preventively."[1] A distinctly different tone emerged from a bipartisan US Congressional study on the UN: "Our actions are usually more effective when they are taken in concert with others. At the same time, the United States can, and sometimes must, act independently if collective efforts cannot be achieved or are ineffective."[2] Do conflicting views such as these illustrate a fundamental rupture in international order?

It comes as little surprise that a renowned realist such as Michael Glennon would argue that "no rational state will be deluded into believing that the UN Charter protects its security";[3] or that Richard Perle would proclaim "the intellectual wreckage of the liberal conceit of safety through international law administered by international institutions."[4] It is perhaps more meaningful when such a staunch defender of multilateralism as John Ruggie would state that the UN "lacks the capacity to act predictably on its core mission: to save succeeding generations from the scourge of war."[5] Legalists, too, bemoan the erosion of norms regulating the use of force. For one eminent international lawyer, the question is not whether the UN-based system has been undermined – for it surely has – but how to respond: "Should one help to create a new legal regime based on the conduct of those who were violating the existing order? Or should one rail against the violators, at the mortal risk of being thought cranky, 'irrelevant,' or even 'unrealistic'?"[6]

Two main lines of enquiry will be pursued in this chapter and Chapter 6: whether a rule-based system of collective security amongst states of widely different levels of power and interests, in an anarchic international environment, is viable; and whether the constitutive actor of traditional ideas of collective security – the state – is a viable unit of analysis in light of the impact of non-state actors, civil war, state failure, and other "non-traditional" forms of insecurity which afflict people: that is, whether there is a "'lack of fit' between collective security institutions and contemporary problems."[7] This chapter addresses the first line of enquiry, and Chapter 6 addresses the second.

The overarching argument of this chapter is that collective security and the rules regulating the use of military force were not destroyed by the war against Iraq in 2003 or strategic ideas of preventive or unilateral military force. This argument is based upon three related observations. First, these rules never in reality constituted a perfectly viable system. International law regulating the use of force – as with other areas of policy – has always been violated but it essentially remains intact because most states, generally, support a norm which proscribes aggression. It is unrealistic to assume that the UN Charter could constitute an absolute constraint on state action. Yet states do not need to have full confidence in the UN for their security in order for the UN to have some relevance to their security needs. Few states – and certainly, few major powers – have full confidence; but this does not make the UN immaterial. Traditionally, multilateralism in the security field takes the form of alliances and self-help; in contrast, UN-based collective security seeks to maintain a universal non-discriminatory system. This is inherently much more demanding. A breach of "norms" regulating the use of force does not suggest that the norms are permanently undermined and no longer operable. Second, despite Iraq, there has been a decline in the use of force between states since the end of the Second World War. Third, the diplomatic attention given to the UN Security Council prior to the use of force against Iraq – and with reference to subsequent threats to international peace and security – suggests that states place significance upon international rules in how they respond to perceived threats. In this respect, the UN has been described as "the forum of choice for debating and deciding on collective action requiring the use of military force."[8]

Collective security

In 2003 the US and its allies undertook a war against Iraq without the authority of the UN Security Council and in spite of the explicit opposition of a number of Council members (and a much wider proportion of the UN membership). The US justified its policy with reference to a number of claims, raised at different times before and after the war. It claimed that Iraq was in violation of Security Council resolutions dating back to the settlement of the Gulf War in 1991 and thus posed a threat to regional security; that Iraq sought to illegally procure weapons of mass destruction; that the regime of Saddam Hussein was responsible for atrocities against the people of Iraq; that Iraq supported and promoted international terrorism; and that regime change in Iraq would introduce a democratic force into the region which would, through a demonstration effect, contribute to stability and progress. Many countries contested these claims at the time and the evidence that has emerged since 2003 appears to support the critics.

According to Tucker and Hendrickson, the US undermined its long-held commitment to international law, its acceptance of consensual decision-making, its reputation for moderation, and its identification with the preservation of peace.[9] Aside from arguments relating to the US justification to go to war – which are widely regarded as being flawed – and the reputation of the US, there has also been broader discussion on the impact of the war upon the "rules" governing the use of force in international politics. Thakur suggested that "Iraq has the potential to reshape the bases of world order in fundamental, profound and long-lasting ways."[10] Krause claimed that there is a "crisis of collective security."[11] Realist scholars argue that collective security is not in crisis since 2003 – rather, it has always been a mirage; stability and peace, where they exist, are brought by some combination of hegemony, the balance of power, and deterrence.

A look at history is necessary to bring this debate into perspective. For its supporters, the UN Charter model of collective security was certainly a revolution in international relations in 1945. The security of each state was to be guaranteed by the community of states; an attack on one state was an attack on all states, to be repelled by all states, and so security became a collective responsibility. The use of military force, unless in self-defense, collective self-defense, or under the authorization of the UN Security Council, would constitute aggression and be illegal. In turn, credible assurances were to exist to give confidence to states – and especially weaker states – that their security would be guaranteed by the commitment of other states to come to their aid if they are a victim of aggression. The UN Charter attempts to legalize this principle, investing in the Council the ability to decide when aggression has occurred, and the responsibility to authorize a response to aggression, including the use of military force.

A number of conditions must exist for an ideal system of collective security to function. Its members must accept the concept that peace is indivisible: that aggression anywhere is a threat to every state. They must also be willing and able to support collective security by assisting in the response to aggression, through military force if necessary, whenever and wherever it occurs. The members must essentially accept the status quo in terms of territory and the norms of international relations. An ideal collective security system is also more likely to function when there is some distribution of power internationally rather than a situation of unipolarity or hegemony. Finally, a mechanism or regime – such as the UN Charter – is necessary to formalize and operationalize the system of collective security.

A blanket prohibition of aggression in international affairs is a radical departure, and a look at history will illustrate how the norm against the use of force has grown stronger. Certainly, regulating the use of military force in international relations has been a perennial challenge since distinct human communities began pursuing regularized contacts amongst each other. In the modern era – when the notion of international relations emerged in the European context – the historic landmarks of diplomacy and international politics primarily focused upon issues of territory and restraint in the use of force amongst the great powers, based upon an intentional balance of power. However, since international politics became formalized, the use of force has been something that has been regulated amongst the leading powers, but generally reserved as a tool for dealing with lesser states and colonial territories, and not prohibited as a matter of moral repugnance. Indeed, the use of military force has generally been accepted in international relations, until the twentieth century, for maintaining stability amongst great powers, responding to challenges to hegemons or balance of power systems, or putting down rebellions inside states which might threaten the order.

The Peace of Westphalia of 1648 brought an end to the Thirty Years' War and led to the norms of sovereignty, independence and exclusive territoriality. However, it did not seek to introduce a general prohibition of the use of military force. Indeed, henceforth, the use of force continued, albeit primarily in the name of political rather than religious interests. The celebrated period of the balance of power amongst the Great Powers following the fall of the Napoleonic empire similarly sought to maintain order and stability – and the regimes – of the great powers in Europe: Austria (after 1867 the Austro-Hungarian Empire), France, Britain, Prussia (after 1871 Germany) and Russia. This was less about prohibiting the use of military force as a moral evil than maintaining the equilibrium of a balance of power which would bring stability and keep certain parties in power. It did entail constraints upon the use of force, of course, because this was an essential part of reciprocal recognition of the sovereign territory of the great powers. However, the use of military force against lesser powers – client states – to respond to transgressions, or to respond to revolutions was acceptable as long as it did not undermine the balance of power amongst the leading states. Indeed, it could even be welcomed by the client states if it helped to preserve conservative regimes in power.

This system was manifested in a variety of diplomatic forms which reflected the great power status in the balance of power. The Treaty of Chaumont (1814) was an alliance against Napoleonic France. The Quadruple Alliance of 1815 formalized relations between the four Great Powers of the anti-France coalition. The rehabilitated France was recognized in 1818 with the new five-power concert which maintained the balance of power. Between 1822 and 1913 there were 26 conferences which sought to maintain stability amongst the great powers, secure the privileged elites against challengers, maintain the regimes of these powers, and maintain agreement on territory and territorial changes. The great powers had an interest in recognizing – and not challenging – the status of each other. It did not stop the use of military force against lesser European powers or the violent pursuit of empires in other parts of the world.

The First World War destroyed the great power system and led to a widely held belief – amongst publics as well as political leaders – that war was not something that should or could be "managed" by great powers, but should be avoided entirely. The industrial scale of the Great War and the manner in which the violence of conflict penetrated deep into the psychology of many leading states represented a genuine change in attitudes towards war. The League of Nations was the first experiment in collective security; it was also global in aspiration, with an original membership of Argentina, Australia, Belgium, Bolivia, Brazil, Canada, Chile, China, Colombia, Cuba, Czechoslovakia, Denmark, El Salvador, France, Greece, Guatemala, Haiti, Honduras, India, Italy, Japan, Liberia, Netherlands, New Zealand, Nicaragua, Norway, Panama, Paraguay, Persia, Peru, Poland, Portugal, Romania, Siam, South Africa, Spain, Sweden, Switzerland, United Kingdom, Uruguay, Venezuela, and Yugoslavia. Twenty-one countries subsequently joined. The League, at least in theory, sought to prohibit aggression by international law; members states committed themselves to respect "the territorial integrity and existing political independence of all Members of the League" against "external aggression" (Article 10). Article 16 stated that "Should any Member of the League resort to war in disregard of its covenants ... it shall *ipso facto* be deemed to have committed an act of war against all other Members of the League." This was an attempted embodiment of Woodrow Wilson's "fourteen points" for world peace; point 14 suggests: "A general association of nations should be formed on the basis of covenants designed to create mutual guarantees of the political independence and territorial integrity of States, large and small equally."

The League of Nations is best known for its failures, however. Japanese aggression in China, Italian aggression in North Africa, German aggression in Europe, and finally the Second World War occurred in violation of the League Covenant. Seventeen members withdrew, and one was expelled. A number of organizational weaknesses hampered the organization, but its true crisis must be seen as an extension of the turmoil of inter-war international relations. This saw a struggle between *status quo* powers – such as France and Britain – and dissatisfied revisionist powers which sought to challenge the norms and rules of the international system, such as Italy, Japan, Germany, and the Soviet Union. Within this, the League was a part of the "illusion of peace" which masked a deep conflict.[12] It is worth going into some detail because of the parallels some observers have drawn between the fate of the League of Nations and the UN at the time of the war against Iraq in 2003.[13]

The interpretation of most historians is that Britain, France and to a lesser extent the United States, were attempting to operate an unrealistic hegemony-concert and keep Germany, Italy, Japan and the Soviet Union under control. The League, as the institutionalization of this post-war system, became embroiled in an international order which proved to be unviable. The system did not weaken Germany enough because the Versailles treaty, which ended the First World War, was not fully enforced. Britain and the US wanted to bring Germany back into mainstream international politics – accepting that the economic health of Europe depended upon the integration of Germany – as long as it did not represent a threat. When the Western countries did begin to become worried about Germany's rearmament and recovery, because they had fed the illusion of peace to their publics, it was difficult for them to take serious defensive measures. At the same time, the Western countries had signed a treaty that created enormous grievances in Germany. So, according to many, the worst thing possible happened: the Versailles Treaty injured Germany, but allowed her to become strong again and challenge perceived injustices committed against her. The post-war system similarly failed to accommodate or sufficiently contain the aspirations of Japan and the Soviet Union and also – although less significantly – Italy.

The League depended upon the majority of states – and certainly the most powerful ones – supporting a system of collective security with a common outlook on the rules governing international order. However, after the First World War, powerful states shared no such outlook, and some rejected the "rules" and sought to change the system by force. Other states did not wish – or were not able – to support the system of collective security enshrined in the League covenant. Therefore the League was secondary in importance to, and at odds with, the underlying power political dynamics, the underlying instability, and the deterioration in relations which marked the period.[14] It was a textbook example that an international normative system does not, and cannot, bring stability if it does not reflect – or is out of step with – the underlying power political order.

The UN regime for international peace and security was, in principle, a continuation of earlier ideas of collective security: the use of military force would be prohibited unless in cases of self-defense, collective self-defense, or under the authorization of the UN Security Council. The UN would take effective collective measures for the prevention and removal of threats to the peace, and for the suppression of acts of aggression or other breaches of the peace. As the Charter states, it would also bring about by peaceful means, and in conformity with the principles of justice and international law, the settlement of international disputes which might lead to a breach of the peace. The UN members committed themselves to certain rules and standards of behavior, which were to represent an end to the balance of power politics and the system of alliances which were seen to have caused wars in the past. Security was to be a collective responsibility: aggression would be defeated by the international community through the UN. In addition, relationships and interaction between states were to be managed and regulated. So, in principle, the UN sought to end power politics by establishing a system of collective security. In theory this was a radical agenda: sovereign equality of states, and the settlement of disputes by peaceful and just means, would indeed constitute a departure from the past. Yet the UN Charter was not a completely liberal internationalist treaty. Its structure clearly reflects power in international relations, most obviously in the form of the Permanent Five Security Council concert.

The new multilateralism covered all forms of international interaction. The Bretton Woods institutions (the General Agreement on Tariffs and Trade, the International Monetary Fund, and the World Bank) were established to manage international economic and trade relations. Existing functional agencies and those which were newly created were brought under the UN system. So, the UN was supposed to represent a system for peace and the management of international activities through international law.

The death of collective security?

Realists now argue that we are seeing exactly the same process that occurred in the 1930s with regard to the League of Nations, although less dramatically. According to Glennon, "although the UN's rules purport to represent a single global view – indeed, universal law – on when and whether force can be justified, the UN's members (not to mention their populations) are clearly not in agreement."[15] According to this argument, the international normative system – especially rules regarding the use of force – does not reflect, and is out of step with, the underlying power political order and threats to security. In particular, in an environment of US preeminence, mass destruction terrorism, and weapons of mass destruction, realists argue that the concept of collective security – always a façade – has lost all semblance of legitimacy. Therefore, states will not feel bound by the rules. The war against Iraq in 2003 was the proof of this new reality.

The problem with the realist argument is that it assumes that collective security has to work effectively all the time in order for it to be a viable concept. Some of the claims of a crisis of international order seem to be based upon the presumption that the UN system of collective security worked effectively until the US-led coalition invaded Iraq in 2003. But this is clearly not the case. In reality, of course, few states – and certainly, very few major powers – have full confidence in the UN for their security. But this does not make the UN irrelevant to their security or international security more generally. The UN may influence how states pursue their security needs even if they (at least those capable) reserve the option of unilateral force in the last resort, or maintain security alliances. As a historical comparison, the nineteenth-century concert system could not contain all of the ambitions of the great powers, but this did not mean that it completely ceased to exist – rather that it could not work effectively in all circumstances. The UN, as Adam Roberts suggests, is "damaged but not destroyed" as a framework for reaching decisions on the use of force.[16]

In fact, if we consider the use of military force outside the framework of the UN to mean the erosion of the UN system of security, then the UN is not doing so badly. There has been a perceptible decline in absolute numbers of all types of war, both civil and international. This is reflected in data from various authoritative sources.[17] Uppsala University's Conflict Data Project observed that: "the number of armed conflicts remains lower than at any time since the early 1970s."[18] In terms of inter-state war, most analyses suggest that after the Second World War there was not any radical pattern or trend, but in the post-Cold War era the trend has definitely been in decline. Most sources trace the start of the decline from the 1970s.[19] Different analyses may present different results on conflict trends (largely as a result of differing definitions of conflict) but the notable analyses support this conclusion: that the incidence of inter-state conflict has declined, and the decline since the end of the Cold War seems even more pronounced. Version 3.0 of the Correlates of War Inter-State War data set identifies the major inter-state wars during the Cold War period as: the First Kashmir (1948/9), Palestine (1948), Korean (1950–3), Russian-Hungarian (1956), Sinai (1956), Assam (1962), Vietnam (1965–75), Second Kashmir (1965), Six Day War (1967), Israel-Egyptian (1969–70), "Football War" (1969), Bangladesh (1971), Yom Kippur (1973), Turkish-Cypriot (1974), Vietnamese-Cambodian (1975–9), Ethiopian-Somalian (1977–8), Ugandan-Tanzanian (1978–9), Sino-Vietnamese (1979), Iran-Iraq (1980–8), Falklands (1982), Israel-Syria-Lebanon (1982), Sino-Vietnamese (1987), and Gulf War (1991). The frequency and magnitude of wars (in terms of materials deployed and battlefield fatalities) since the end of the Cold War has declined, despite the 1999 Kosovo and 2003 Iraq conflicts.

This does not, of course, suggest that the absence or presence of war alone is a reflection of the success or failure of the UN framework regulating the use of armed conflict. The wars against Iraq in 2003 and Serbia in 1999 occurred without Security Council authorization and outside of the normal rules of self-defense. This is why they – and especially Iraq – are considered as harbingers of doom for the UN Charter. But it is the role of the UN vis-à-vis any particular conflict, and not simply the presence and absence of conflict, which has a bearing on the validity and feasibility of the UN and collective security. So the invasion of Kuwait by Iraq and the war against Iraq in 1991 is not considered to be evidence of the weakness of the UN-based system of international security. On the contrary, because the 1991 war was authorized by Security Council resolutions it is ostensibly seen as bolstering the collective security role of the UN.

Nevertheless, this does not mean that incidences of inter-state war in general are irrelevant to the question of the status of rules governing the use of military force in international affairs. A system of collective security has its value in *deterring* aggression – and in the framework of the UN Charter, also encouraging states to pursue peaceful means of settling disputes – and not only in *responding* to aggression. And so the clear decline of absolute numbers of inter-state wars – despite the political magnitude of the war against Iraq in 2003 – shows that something is having the effect of reducing war amongst states. Institutionalists and Kantians might argue that this demonstrates the strengthening of norms proscribing aggression and emphasizing the peaceful resolution of disputes. Realists would counter that the balance of power, deterrence, and hegemony combined to keep inter-state conflict down in a world of "competition for power and shifting national interests."[20]

More tangible evidence concerning the viability of the UN regarding the use of force is to consider patterns in actual state behavior since 1945 – not only wars, but the use of force in general. In this period there has been a decline in the incidence of war and in the use of military force in violation of UN principles, especially since the end of the Cold War. These trends hold true both overall and in relation to the behavior of important states in the international system, including the US. The High Level Panel Report puts this into historical perspective, observing that states often violated the rules governing the use of force during the Cold War – yet since that time the desire for viable rules has grown.[21]

The strategic doctrine of preventive military force appears to present a more serious blow to the UN-based regulation of the use of force. The preeminent global power – the US – has openly presented a doctrine which questions the validity and legitimacy of the existing legal rules governing the use of military force in international relations. States have long reserved the right of military force in order to preempt an imminent military strike against them, and this is generally accepted under the international law of self-defense. However, the strategy of using military force, without the authorization of the UN, to *prevent* the emergence of a potential threat is generally considered to be an illegal violation of norms which protect territorial integrity and proscribe aggression. The National Security Strategy of the US, published in September 2002, was therefore highly controversial. In the foreword, President Bush stated that America would act against "emerging threats before they are fully formed."[22] This was not just a short-term reaction against the devastation of 9/11; the 2006 National Security Strategy reiterated the preventive doctrine.[23]

The preventive doctrine argues that the Cold War strategy of deterrence, based upon the threat of retaliation, is not a viable means of defense against rogue states and their terrorist clients. The option of anticipatory and preemptive action to forestall threats, before dangers gather, is therefore a necessary response to the contemporary realities. The Strategy states that:

> For centuries, international law recognized that nations need not suffer an attack before they can lawfully take action to defend themselves against forces that present an imminent danger of attack. Legal scholars and international jurists often conditioned the legitimacy of preemption on the existence of an imminent threat – most often a visible mobilization of armies, navies, and air forces preparing to attack. We must adapt the concept of imminent threat to the capabilities and objectives of today's adversaries.[24]

Many commentators have reacted with alarm to this strategy, and argued that it is in direct conflict with the UN framework regulating the use of force – in self-defense or at the request of the Security Council – because it allows the US to employ unilateral military force when it alone believes that it is necessary to respond to an emerging threat. Thomas Franck has suggested that the preventive doctrine means that the US "is free to use force against any foe it perceives as a potential threat to its security, at any time of its choosing and with any means at its disposal. This would stand the Charter on its head."[25]

The emergence of this strategy as an official policy was the culmination of conservative thinking in the US that had been developing for some time. 11 September 2001 – and the need for a doctrine to deal with the apocalyptic amalgamation of weapons of mass destruction, terrorism and rogue states – brought the strategy to the surface. Iraq can of course be seen in this context, although the US officially argued that UN Security Council resolutions dating back to the 1990 Iraq invasion of Kuwait and the settlement of that war provided continuing authorization for the use of military force against Iraq.

It is interesting that, in their response to the strategy of preventive force, some UN supporters have sought to integrate the concept rather than challenge it legally. The Secretary-General observed, in his report *In Larger Freedom*, that, "Where threats are not imminent but latent, the Charter gives full authority to the Security Council to use military force, including preventively, to preserve international peace and security."[26] Nevertheless, on the basis of the Security Council's performance in the past, even in response to clear cases of large-scale aggression, it is difficult to accept that the UN at present is adequately constituted to authorize preventive force in response to latent threats.

It will therefore not have the full confidence of some key countries over critical issues related to international security, unless it undergoes a radical transformation in its rules of procedure and its definition of "threats to international peace and security."

A more realistic view is that the preeminent power may very occasionally use force preventively but that this is not necessarily on the increase, and that it does not destroy the norms of state sovereignty and non-aggression. And it is certainly not new: unilateral use of force by states has a history since 1945, whether to preventively or pre-emptively forestall an armed attack, or assist nationals, to influence a government in a target country or to alleviate the suffering of civilians. The war against Iraq in 2003 was in part considered to be an affront to the rules governing the use of force because we have grown accustomed to states observing these rules. This, ironically, has the effect of showing how durable those rules remain.

Conclusion

Ziring, Riggs and Plano argue that: "When one country dominates world events and holds a monopoly of world power, the system of collective security is doomed to failure."[27] According to this line of argument, no other state – or even group of states – has the power to present a credible deterrent against the arbitrary use of force by the US. The 2003 Iraq war was the epitome of this; although the US was not the only country which supported the conflict diplomatically or militarily, the coalition of the willing would not have existed without US leadership and the US was not reliant upon any such assistance. Diplomatic opposition to the war was overwhelming, but the US proceeded. Yet Iraq, however politically important – and despite the huge importance attached to that case by some international lawyers[28] – is still not enough to demonstrate a new pattern. In spite of Iraq, the High Level Panel Report suggested that the historical record shows that since the end of the Cold War "the yearning for an international system governed by the rule of law has grown."[29] The UN system of collective security, in reality, never totally replaced the age-old practices of balance of power, spheres of influence, and the whims of hegemony. The UN system exists in parallel, and sometimes vies with these traditional power political forces. Indeed, superpowers have rarely sought Security Council approval for their actions – the fact that the US did seek approval is meaningful.

The High Level Panel Report even suggests that: "The United States decision to bring the question of force to the Security Council reaffirmed not just the relevance but the centrality of the Charter of the United Nations."[30] This might be a little optimistic. Nevertheless, the current debate about whether the war against Iraq, US pre-eminence, and the preventive force doctrine have undermined the UN system of collective security, is somewhat spurious. The war against Iraq in 2003 – and even the preventive strategic doctrine of the US – is not new as a challenge to collective security. As Tharoor has observed, "the United Nations was not created by starry-eyed Kantians; it was established as a response to a Hobbesian world. The UN Charter was the work of the victorious Allies of the Second World War converting their wartime alliance into a peacetime organization."[31] Those states which have the power to consider the unilateral use of military force still seek to avoid the opprobrium of their allies and Security Council censure wherever possible. Suggestions exist to strengthen and rationalize the UN authorization of the use of force – for example building political consensus linked to the seriousness of the threat that the military force is purportedly responding to and the proper purpose of the use of force, which should be a last resort and proportionate to the threat.[32] The norm against aggression and the use of force (except in self-defense) appears anyway to be strengthening, if state behavior since 1945 is an indication. Realists will always argue that this is a function of hegemony, alliances, the balance of power and deterrence, but cannot offer a persuasive explanation as to the decline of war in recent decades.

4 Humanitarian intervention

The previous chapter considered whether the established rules governing the use of military force (only in self-defense, collective self-defense, or with the authorization of the Security Council under Chapter 7 of the UN Charter) are breaking down. The chapter concluded that the rules are not "breaking down" as such; they have never been fully observed, they have often been violated, yet states (even those states which believe they are capable of unilaterally ensuring their own security) have generally sought to maintain them because the costs of the alternatives (deterrence, alliances, unilateral military capacity, hegemony) generally outweigh the benefits. These alternatives are, moreover, beyond the means of most states. In addition, states generally prefer a rule-based system because it provides a measure of predictability in international politics. The chapter conceded that this equation has potentially been upset by the over-riding preeminence of one country: no other state – or even group of states – has the power to present a credible deterrent against the arbitrary use of force by the US. However, there is not enough evidence to suggest that the US will disregard the UN Charter in this way on a repeated basis.

The use of military force to protect human rights is relevant to the debate on the legitimacy of international organizations and multilateralism in two interconnected ways. First, it presents another area where rules governing the use of force, embodied in the UN Charter, have come under question as moral arguments to alleviate widespread suffering have challenged legal restrictions on the use of force. Thus, the idea of humanitarian intervention challenges the inviolability of sovereignty, which is the mainstay of multilateralism. Second, while global organizations – specifically the UN – have a responsibility to respond to the worst abuses of human rights, they have been woefully inadequate in developing a doctrine and the practical means to provide protection for humans in dire circumstances. This represents a serious moral challenge to international organizations. These themes also suggest a paradox: the use of military force for human protection can be controversial when it does occur – as in Kosovo in 1999 – and when it does not occur, as in Rwanda in 1994. In exploring the multilateral dimension to this debate, this chapter concludes that the failure of the UN to marshal a robust response to egregious human suffering brings its legitimacy into question. The chapter therefore challenges the idea that there is an "emerging norm that there is a collective international responsibility to protect."[1]

The use of force for human protection: "humanitarian intervention"

The use of force for human protection, in violation of the sovereignty and against the wishes of the target state – commonly described as "humanitarian intervention" – raises a number of fundamentally important questions. Should coercion – including military force – be employed to prevent or alleviate widespread and appalling human suffering, without the consent of the state in which human rights abuses are taking place? If so, when, how, by whom, and under what authority? And have the answers to these questions changed in the context of recent political, legal and normative developments? In addressing these questions we confront some of the most difficult challenges in the discourse and practice of international relations. Humanitarian intervention problematizes the relationship – and sometimes tension – between the fundamental tenets of order, justice, individual and state sovereignty, legitimacy, law, solidarism, human rights, and obligation. This chapter considers if the so-called emergence of a norm of humanitarian intervention is challenging the established rules regulating the use of military force, and second, whether the role and performance of international organizations in this issue has implications regarding their legitimacy.

If international organizations – and especially the UN – are unable to prevent or alleviate egregious violations of human rights because of the constraints of international law or as a result of their decision-making procedures, is their legitimacy eroded? If there is an (emerging) international norm of humanitarian intervention, what are the implications for state-centric, status quo-oriented multilateralism, which is premised on the foundation of state sovereignty? The idea of humanitarian intervention suggests a growing solidarist norm that Westphalian multilateralism does not embrace. Put most bluntly: if the UN – an organization purportedly dedicated to peace and human rights – is not able to act in situations where innocent humans are victims of genocide or crimes against humanity, how can it be considered legitimate? To refer to an extreme example, Roméo Dallaire's experience as peacekeeping force commander in Rwanda during the 1994 genocide taught him that the politics of responding to humanitarian emergencies at the UN is characterized by indifference, self-interest, racism, and the question of whether there is any strategic or resource value in a region.[2] According to Dallaire, "Member nations do not want a large, reputable, strong and independent United Nations, no matter their hypocritical pronouncements otherwise. What they want is a weak, beholden, indebted scapegoat of an organization, which they can blame for their failures or steal victories from."[3]

Revisiting humanitarian intervention

The relationship between human rights and the institutions of international relations is complex and often dichotomous. Humanitarian intervention represents the most acute test of that relationship. Humanitarian intervention is regarded here as the use of military force, across state borders, to prevent or alleviate egregious and widespread human rights abuses, without the consent – and against the wishes – of the state in which human rights abuses are taking place.[4]

Humanitarian intervention, in breach of the sovereignty of a state, is essentially a violation of both treaty and customary international law. The UN Charter, most notably Articles 2(4) and 2(7), and a number of landmark resolutions, make this clear.[5] Article 2(4) states that "All Members shall refrain in their international relations from the threat or use of force against the territorial integrity or political independence of any state." Article 2(7) preserves the sanctity of "matters which are essentially within the domestic jurisdiction" of states. There are only two derogations from this: the use of force in self-defense (including collective self-defense) and military enforcement mandated by the Security Council (Chapter VII, Article 42). Generally, state practice also reflects the legal weakness of "humanitarian intervention," even in cases when a humanitarian motive may have lain behind the use of force.

At the same time, a number of arguments have been developed in support of a "norm" of humanitarian intervention. First, there is a fairly widely held solidarist belief that widespread and egregious human rights abuse should not be tolerated, even when confined within the borders of a country, and despite the implications this may hold for the sovereignty of such a country.[6] There is thus some acceptance of the principle that, irrespective of international peace and security, grave humanitarian suffering must be addressed by the international community within the framework of the UN, either by right or obligation, even without the consent of the target territory. Second, there is a persuasive case to be made that severe human rights abuses have destabilizing repercussions that are not confined to an individual state, and that therefore severe human rights abuse constitutes a threat to international peace and security. In this context, authorization by the UN Security Council for the use of military force is possible under Chapter VII. This can be called the "international security" perspective. The critical legal question concerns the place of human rights within the UN conception of peace and security, and specifically a possible wider acceptance of the idea that humanitarian suffering on a large scale represents a threat to international peace and security and that there is an obligation to respond to this. There has arguably been such a broadening of the Security Council's interpretation of "threats to international peace and security."

This "international security" approach to humanitarian intervention – based upon the belief that widespread human suffering can represent a threat to the maintenance of international peace and security and therefore can fall under the Security Council's responsibility under Chapter VII – is fairly widely accepted. However, the solidarist claim – that human rights abuses, even without a clear threat to international peace and security, demand Security Council enforcement action – is much less accepted. Humanitarian intervention outside UN authorization is more controversial still.

Since the end of the Cold War we have witnessed events that suggest a selective norm of humanitarian intervention from the "international security" perspective, while the idea of a solidarist norm in practice is much less clear. The Security Council issued resolutions in relation to Iraq, Somalia, Yugoslavia, Haiti, Rwanda, and East Timor that made some link between human rights and international peace and security under Chapter VII authority. But the Kosovo conflict was the event that defined most of all the dilemmas inherent in humanitarian intervention, especially without Security Council authorization. In 1999 NATO used military force in the Federal Republic of Yugoslavia in response, ostensibly, to severe human rights abuses in Kosovo.[7] It was arguably the first time in the contemporary international period that a group of states, acting without explicit Security Council authority, defended a breach of sovereignty primarily on humanitarian grounds.[8] Some states – such as China, Russia and India – expressed outright opposition. Many observers expressed deep unease at the failure to work through the UN but accepted that the suffering in Kosovo had to be addressed.

In the broader context, this meant that a fundamental dichotomy between order/legality and justice had to be tackled. In an address to the UN General Assembly in September 1999, the Secretary-General referred to a "developing international norm in favor of intervention to protect civilians from wholesale slaughter and suffering and violence."[9] He recalled the failures of the Security Council to act in Rwanda and Kosovo, and challenged the member states of the UN to "find common ground in upholding the principles of the Charter, and acting in defense of our common humanity." In his Millennium Report to the General Assembly a year later, he restated the problem: "if humanitarian intervention is, indeed, an unacceptable assault on sovereignty, how should we respond to a Rwanda, to a Srebrenica – to gross and systematic violations of human rights that offend every precept of our common humanity?"[10]

Evolving thought on humanitarian intervention

As a result of a number of incidents since the end of the Cold War – and in particular the Kosovo intervention and Rwanda genocide – there has been a concerted effort to move the debate forward and resolve the dilemmas of this topic. In particular, Rwanda was a shocking episode which forced governments and citizens around the world to reflect upon their own duties towards victims. Roméo Dallaire described the "stinking nightmare of rotting corpses," and the "attempted annihilation of an ethnicity, the butchery of children barely out of the womb, the stacking of severed limbs like cordwood, the mounds of decomposing bodies being eaten by the sun."[11] It is difficult to reconcile the horror of Rwanda with legal and political discourse.

Nevertheless, one way of focusing this discussion is to consider a number of landmarks in conceptual and policy analysis on the topic, produced or sponsored by governments or leading research institutions. The report of the International Commission on Intervention and State Sovereignty (ICISS) entitled *The Responsibility to Protect*, the report of the Independent International Commission on Kosovo, the report prepared by the Advisory Committee on Issues of Public International Law and the Advisory Council on International Affairs (Netherlands), and the report of the Danish Institute of International Affairs, together represent a significant spectrum of academic and policy analysis on humanitarian intervention and may suggest evolving thinking on a number of key issues.

The questions that will be addressed are: is there an (emerging) international norm of humanitarian intervention? What are the implications of this for state sovereignty? Do international political norms and standards of legitimacy indicate a greater willingness for states and international organizations to engage in humanitarian intervention? Does recent state practice indicate that the international legal prohibition of humanitarian intervention (when not authorized by the UN Security Council) may be changing? Is there an evolving notion of "international peace and security" according to the UN Security Council? What criteria should international actors apply to the use of force for protecting human lives – what is the threshold of suffering? The four reports considered here all respond to these questions. They also attempt, with varying degrees of success, to balance and sometimes reconcile the different and often opposing legal, political and moral claims relating to intervention.

The Responsibility to Protect

The Responsibility to Protect, published late in 2001, is the most influential contribution to the humanitarian intervention debate in recent decades.[12] It consciously attempts to take a new approach to humanitarian intervention by suggesting a fresh vocabulary and clear ideas for reconciling conflicting principles. It represents an assertive manifestation of post-Westphalian thinking, political liberalism, and human solidarism. It is about the responsibility of sovereign states to protect their own people from harm, and "the need for the larger international community to exercise that responsibility if states are unwilling or unable to do so themselves."[13] The report rejects the phrase "humanitarian intervention" and a "right to intervene" in favor of "intervention for human protection purposes" and a "responsibility to protect." It thus shifts the focus from the rights of interveners to the rights of victims.

This study, in parallel with the other reports, claims that there has been an evolution of international norms that form the backdrop of the debate. The report observes that the changing international environment has generated "new expectations for action and new standards of conduct in national and international affairs" and that the current debate about intervention for human protection purposes "takes place in a historical, political and legal context of evolving international standards of conduct for states and individuals, including the development of new and stronger norms and mechanisms for the protection of human rights."[14] It argues that a "modern" understanding of state sovereignty is evolving in the context of these changing norms: the world is moving from a territorial-based sovereignty – where those in power control sovereignty – to popular sovereignty, in the context of principles of democratic entitlement and solidarism. Accordingly, "sovereignty implies a dual responsibility: externally – to respect the sovereignty of other states, and internally, to respect the dignity and basic rights of all the people within a state. In international human rights covenants, in UN practice, and in state practice itself, sovereignty is now understood as embracing this dual responsibility. Sovereignty as responsibility has become the minimum content of good international citizenship."[15]

It is worth summarizing the main points of the report.[16] In terms of core principles: state sovereignty implies responsibility, and the primary responsibility for the protection of its people lies with the state itself. Where a population is suffering serious harm, as a result of internal war, insurgency, repression or state failure, and the state in question is unwilling or unable to halt or avert it, the principle of non-intervention yields to the international responsibility to protect. The responsibility to protect embraces three specific responsibilities. First, the responsibility to prevent: to address both the root causes and direct causes of internal conflict and other man-made crises putting populations at risk. Second, the responsibility to react: to respond to situations of compelling human need with appropriate measures, which may include coercive measures like sanctions and international prosecution, and in extreme cases military intervention. Finally, the responsibility to rebuild: to provide, particularly after a military intervention, full assistance with recovery, reconstruction and reconciliation, addressing the causes of the harm the intervention was designed to halt or avert. In terms of priorities, prevention is the single most important dimension of the responsibility to protect: prevention options should always be exhausted before intervention is contemplated, and more commitment and resources must be devoted to it. Military intervention for human protection purposes is an exceptional and extraordinary measure. To be warranted, there must be serious and irreparable harm occurring to human beings, or imminently likely to occur, of the following kind:

- Large-scale loss of life, actual or apprehended, with genocidal intent or not, which is the product either of deliberate state action, or state neglect or inability to act, or a failed state situation; or
- Large-scale "ethnic cleansing," actual or apprehended, whether carried out by killing, forced expulsion, acts of terror or rape.

The use of military force must also strictly adhere to a number of "precautionary principles." First, "right intention": the primary purpose of the intervention, whatever other motives intervening states may have, must be to halt or avert human suffering. Right intention is better assured with multilateral operations, clearly supported by regional opinion and the victims concerned. Second, "last resort": military intervention can only be justified when every non-military option for the prevention or peaceful resolution of the crisis has been explored, with reasonable grounds for believing lesser measures would not have succeeded. Third, "proportional means": the scale, duration and intensity of the planned military intervention should be the minimum necessary to secure the defined human protection objective. Fourth, "reasonable prospects": there must be a reasonable chance of success in halting or averting the suffering which has justified the intervention, with the consequences of action not likely to be worse than the consequences of inaction.

Under what authority can military force be used for human protection purposes? The report states that there is no better or more appropriate body than the United Nations Security Council to authorize military intervention for human protection purposes. Security Council authorization should in all cases be sought prior to any military intervention action being carried out. Those calling for an intervention should formally request such authorization, or have the Council raise the matter on its own initiative, or have the Secretary-General raise it under Article 99 of the UN Charter. The Security Council should deal promptly with any request for authority to intervene where there are allegations of large-scale loss of human life or ethnic cleansing. If the Security Council rejects a proposal or fails to deal with it in a reasonable time, alternative options are: consideration of the matter by the General Assembly in Emergency Special Session under the "Uniting for Peace" procedure; and action by regional or sub-regional organizations under Chapter VIII of the Charter, subject to their seeking subsequent authorization from the Security Council.

A number of observations about the ICISS report can be ventured. It provided a new approach in two ways. First, a key component of the approach is the re-conceptualization of the intervention debate in terms of the responsibility to protect rather than the right to intervene. Is this a substantive step forward, rather than just clever wordplay? Without doubt, the underlying issues are not changed by this change of terminology: it still amounts to the use of military force to protect human rights without the consent of the sovereign authority. The problems will always be the same: reconciling the use of force for humanitarian purposes with the prohibition of the use of force in international politics unless in self-defense or in the interests of maintaining international security. So why does this constitute a "new" approach, as the report claims? The reason is that if the terms of the debate are changed, then the normative framework of the debate can be reappraised, and the polemics of the debate may be circumvented to an extent.

At present, the principles of non-intervention and state sovereignty are privileged above other principles of international law, particularly those relating to human rights. However, the responsibility to protect suggests that sovereignty is as much about upholding human rights as it is about territorial control and inviolability. As a corollary, other tenets of sovereignty (such as recognition by other states) should be conditional upon the state meeting certain humanitarian standards. In addition, the report presents the responsibility to protect in the context of an integral responsibility to prevent and a responsibility to rebuild. The report does not necessarily bring new insights to conflict prevention or post-conflict peacebuilding, but the holistic integration of prevention, protection and rebuilding make up an impressive and compelling argument. This addresses a great need in policy terms. Preventive and post-conflict challenges are woefully under-funded and while humanitarian intervention will always be an attractive topic for analysts, greater benefit would be imparted by more attention to preventing crises and assisting in rebuilding communities.[17]

Reflecting on Srebrenica

The issue of how to respond to humanitarian emergencies is sensitive for the government and public of the Netherlands. At Srebrenica in Bosnia in 1995, 7,000 men and boys were killed when Bosnian Serb forces overran the UN "safe area" guarded by Dutch peacekeepers.[18] The Bosnia experience lies in the background of the report on humanitarian intervention commissioned by the Dutch government and published in 2000.[19] The report – which has as its overriding objective to bring together the moral, political and legal dimensions of humanitarian intervention – has a number of remarkable aspects. It boldly states that even when prohibited by international law, "humanitarian intervention can be justified on political and moral grounds."[20] It thus makes a clear distinction – and illustrates a potential gap – between what is legal and what is legitimate.

The basic message is that humanitarian intervention can be legitimate from a political and moral perspective, and this might in turn presage a gradual evolution of international law. Moreover, it cleverly reverses the logic of the usual legal approach to the issue. Indeed, most people see the idea of humanitarian intervention as potentially threatening to the sanctity of sovereignty and hence, by extension, to international law. On the contrary, the report states that:

> the position of international law may inadvertently be undermined if it does not provide for intervention in cases of flagrant violations of universally accepted human rights ... can the ban on intervention under international law and the ban on the use of force between states be reconciled with the significant developments that have taken place in international law regarding the protection of fundamental human rights?[21]

Thus, more explicitly than the other landmark studies, the Dutch report points out something that is obvious but strangely often overlooked: while international law sanctifies state sovereignty and non-interference, it also embodies a wide array of international human rights obligations. *Both* must be upheld if international law is to be legitimate.

The Dutch report is undeniably progressive. Even its definition of humanitarian intervention takes certain things for granted that many governments might balk at:

> The threat or use of force by one or more states, whether or not in the context of an international organization, on the territory of another state: (a) in order to end existing or prevent imminent grave, large-scale violations of fundamental human rights, particularly individuals' right to life, irrespective of their nationality; (b) without the prior authorization of the Security Council and without the consent of the legitimate government of the state in whose territory the intervention takes place.[22]

The corollary of this is that the report presumes that any action – including the authorization of force for the protection of human rights – authorized by the Security Council is no longer controversial. This is questionable, especially when there is no clear threat to international peace and security as laid down in the UN Charter. In fact the Security Council remains circumspect in authorizing force for purely humanitarian purposes, even when genocide may feature. Many authorities – including most member state governments – still apply the Security Council responsibility for maintaining international peace

66 Humanitarian intervention

and security in the narrow sense and would have problems with the idea that the use of military force for human protection purposes, if authorized by the Security Council, is a settled norm in international relations. Nevertheless, the report presents this liberal internationalist presumption: instead of a justice vs. order dichotomy, "universal respect for fundamental human rights is also seen as a precondition for a stable international order, as an aspect of the 'constitution of the international community.'"[23]

The report concedes that while "there can be no doubt that fundamental human rights are an increasingly important factor in international relations ... this cannot be said to have resulted in a growing willingness to intervene militarily at the global level."[24] Yet its conclusion is strangely paradoxical. Not only that there is:

> currently no sufficient legal basis for humanitarian intervention without a Security Council mandate, but also that there is no clear evidence of such a legal basis emerging. At the same time ... it is no longer possible, in interpreting and applying international law, to ignore situations in which fundamental human rights are being or threatened to be violated on a large scale and the international community is taking no action to stop or prevent this.

Furthermore, it argues that the international duty to protect and promote the rights of individuals and groups has developed into a universally valid obligation that is incumbent upon all the states in the international community, both individually and collectively. In light of the difficulties inherent in reforming the Security Council, therefore, the report even suggests that efforts be made to develop a justification for "humanitarian intervention without a Security Council mandate."[25] Furthermore, "In the event that the competent UN bodies fail to take or authorize action that is perceived as humanly unavoidable, the essential international duty to protect fundamental human rights could constitute the legal ground that justifies deviating from the ban on the use of force as laid down in the UN Charter."[26]

In terms of process, the Dutch report has similarities with *The Responsibility to Protect*. First, the Security Council is the primary (but not only) authority for humanitarian intervention. In the absence of Security Council agreement, "the maximum degree of legitimacy must be obtained by other means."[27] The next step is to submit the matter to the General Assembly via the Uniting for Peace Resolution where a resolution recommending action can be taken by a two-thirds majority. However, even without General Assembly involvement, a group of states that themselves meet international standards of human rights, and preferably in a regional grouping, may be authorized to take coercive action. The threshold for the Dutch report is when "fundamental human rights are being or are likely to be seriously violated on a large scale and there is an urgent need for intervention ... [and where the] legitimate, internationally recognized government is unable or unwilling to provide the victims with appropriate care." As precautionary safeguards, intervention must only be considered if the humanitarian emergency can only be reversed or contained by deploying military resources, if the intervening parties have exhausted all the appropriate non-military means of action. Moreover, humanitarian intervention "must be in proportion to the gravity of the situation"; "must not itself constitute an even greater threat to international peace and security"; and must be "limited to what is necessary in order to attain the humanitarian objective."[28] We see here clear parallels to the "precautionary principles" of the ICISS report.

The clear assertion of the Dutch report is that if the Security Council does not act in response to egregious abuses of fundamental human rights, other states or groups of states may undertake humanitarian intervention. Indeed, the report considers it "desirable to develop a separate justification for humanitarian intervention without Security Council authorization, and one that enjoys broad international support and clearly reflects the increased international significance of human rights."[29] Simultaneously, the report concludes that "current international law provides no legal basis for such intervention, and also that no such legal basis is yet emerging."[30] Therefore, the report is implying that in exceptional circumstances moral necessity can outweigh legal doctrine. There is little discussion of the real consternation that this idea might provoke in countries such as Russia, China and India, and indeed, the Dutch report seems to be consciously directed at "likeminded" states. It specifically encourages agreement in "Western circles" for developing a framework for humanitarian intervention "for their own use."[31] Again, non-Western states might not be comfortable with this idea – for their own use *where*?

Clearly, therefore, unlike the ICISS report, the Dutch paper does not have global pretensions and is willing to find legitimacy within the liberal confines of a certain political mindset. This is surely problematic. There are reasons why there is a UN Security Council veto and they are not all bad: it is a safeguard against action that would be contrary to the interests of major powers, which is essential for maintaining the engagement of major powers in the UN. Of course this means that the UN does not always act as it should, but this is reality. We should not be too quick to circumvent the Council on the basis of perceived humanitarian necessity – it may indeed sometimes be necessary, but drawing up a framework for such a course of action appears to weaken the authority of the UN. Perhaps the approach of the ICISS report is more to the point here: "The task is not to find alternatives to the Security Council as a source of authority, but to make the Security Council work better than it has."[32]

Legal and Political Aspects – Danish Institute of International Affairs

The Danish report, published in 1999, concentrates on political and legal aspects of humanitarian intervention and explores a number of policy scenarios. It concludes that a continuation of the status quo and the development of an *ad hoc* intervention strategy are preferable and most feasible. This means acknowledging and legitimizing the norm of humanitarian intervention in exceptional circumstances and attempting to make it work more effectively and legitimately, but without attempting to institutionalize the norm. Put less charitably, we could say that this report advocates a continuation of ambiguity.

The tone of the legal discussion is close to that of the Dutch report, and equally paradoxical. It affirms "in principle, the exclusive legal authority under international law of the Security Council to take decisions on humanitarian intervention" yet states that "in extreme cases, humanitarian intervention may be necessary and justified on moral and political grounds even if an authorization from the UN Security Council cannot be obtained."[33] Moreover, "A distinction can be made between the legality and the legitimacy ... of humanitarian intervention," and humanitarian intervention can be legitimate on political and moral grounds even when it is not lawful.[34] In common with the Dutch report, the Danish report suggests that "A legal justification asserting a new (emerging) right of intervention may, if supported by a vast majority of other states, lead to the creation of corresponding new legal norms, whereas a purely political-moral justification, as a point of departure, leaves the existing norms unchallenged."[35] It situates its discussion within the relationship between order and justice and has an interesting discussion on this theme:

> it is neither a simple opposition, nor a question that can be "solved" or defined away. A tension remains, even if the two can often be reconciled. In one respect, order is a precondition for justice, in another justice is a precondition for order, and thirdly,

one often has in concrete situations to balance the two against each other and decide how much of one to trade to obtain some of the other.[36]

Like all the reports, this one observes that "the scope of sovereignty has gradually been reduced due to international norms and requirements of democracy, human rights, and minority rights."[37]

More than the other publications, the Danish study situates the discussion in the context of the specific challenges posed by weak and failed states and post-Cold War patterns of conflict. In terms of process, the Danish report departs from the ICISS and the Dutch report on a number of points. Notably, it is more conservative – or perhaps restrictive – in its legal interpretations. First, it argues that the Uniting for Peace Resolution does not provide a legal pretext for transferring an issue related to human rights to the General Assembly if the Security Council is unable or unwilling to take action because the resolution only assumes competence for the Assembly to recommend military action in case of a breach of the peace or an act of aggression.[38] In addition, in analyzing what is meant by a "threat to the peace" with reference to Article 39 of the UN Charter, the Danish report is restrictive. It argues that a threat to the peace "clearly refers to international peace ... It was hardly the intention of the framers of the Charter that internal conflicts and human rights violations should be regarded as a threat to international peace."[39] Moreover, "state practice after the end of the Cold War (1990–99) concerning humanitarian intervention is neither sufficiently substantial nor has there been sufficient acceptance in the international community to support the view that a right of humanitarian intervention without Security Council authorization has become part of customary international law."[40] At the same time, the level of actual opposition seems less, and the *practice* of the Security Council has demonstrated a development and broadening of the notion: the Council thus increasingly "seems to regard a civil war with large-scale human suffering as a threat to international peace in its own right, regardless of its international consequences."[41] This was the case in Somalia and Haiti, where violation of democracy was even addressed through Chapter VII of the UN Charter as a threat to the peace. Thus, we have witnessed a "dynamic change" in the concept of international peace, albeit only in extreme, unique and exceptional circumstances.[42]

The Danish report is again similar to the other three regarding the procedure of intervention. Rather than asserting a threshold or strict criteria for the use of force, it identifies "possible criteria for humanitarian intervention": where serious and massive violations of human rights and international humanitarian law occur – specifically genocide, crimes against humanity and war crimes – and a state is unwilling or unable to prevent such abuses; when the Security Council fails to act; and when diplomatic and non-military measures of coercion have been exhausted.[43] Intervention must employ only necessary and proportionate force; the scale, duration and purpose of intervention must be only the minimum necessary to achieve the humanitarian objectives. Thus, "the challenge is to keep open the option for humanitarian intervention without Security Council authorization in extreme cases, without jeopardizing the international legal order."[44]

The Independent International Commission on Kosovo

The report of the Independent International Commission on Kosovo, published in 2000, is somewhat different from the other three in that it focuses upon a specific case: NATO's controversial use of force against Yugoslavia in 1999. With striking similarity to the other reports – especially the Dutch and Danish studies – the Kosovo report hinges upon the distinction and the gap between law and legitimacy. The Kosovo Commission concluded that the NATO military intervention was "illegal but legitimate."[45] It explicitly suggests that there is a need to close the gap between legality and legitimacy and formulate a "principled framework for humanitarian intervention" which would be adopted by the General Assembly.[46] This would take the form of a Declaration on the Right and Responsibility of Humanitarian Intervention, "accompanied by UNSC interpretations of the UN Charter that reconciles such practices with the balance between respect for sovereign rights, implementation of human rights, and prevention of humanitarian catastrophe."[47] If this was not ambitious enough, the report calls for the amendment of the UN Charter, to incorporate these changes "in the role and responsibility of the United Nations and other collective actors in international society to implement the Declaration."[48]

In terms of the threshold criteria and operational guidelines again we find similarities with the other three reports, although with less precision. The two triggers of humanitarian intervention are: severe violations of international human rights or humanitarian law on a sustained basis; and state failure that results in great human suffering. In terms of procedure, the "overriding aim of all phases of the intervention involving the threat and the use of force must be the direct protection of the victimized population"; and "The method of intervention must be reasonably calculated to end the humanitarian catastrophe as rapidly as possible, and must specifically take measures to protect all civilians, and to preclude any secondary punitive or retaliatory action against the target government."[49] Here we can see the experience of Kosovo reflected in the rationale, where humanitarian intervention resulted in a reversal of fortunes – the remaining Serb population in Kosovo suffered the wrath of Albanian Kosovo militants once the Yugoslav military control over the territory had been eliminated.

Before military force is used for protecting human rights, there must be a "serious effort" to find a peaceful solution and all non-military means must have been exhausted. The use of force should not be unilateral but based in some form of multilateral authority.[50] This is a departure from some of the other reports, which do not feel that a multilateral intervention is necessarily more legitimate than unilateral (when outside the UN Security Council). Curiously the Kosovo report also states that "There should not be any formal act of censure or condemnation of the intervention by a principal organ of the United Nations, especially by the International Court of Justice or the UNSC."[51] This seems rather unsatisfactory: either Security Council authorization is necessary, or it is not. If Council authorization is not achieved, it seems disingenuous to claim legitimacy from the *absence* of censure. Of course that is exactly what NATO did with the defeat of the Russian draft resolution on 26 March 1999, but to suggest a codification of such a procedure would seem to dilute the UN's duty to take positive action itself.

In terms of establishing a framework within which the international community can more effectively address the dilemmas of humanitarian intervention, the Kosovo Commission report is the most ambitious. It states that "ideally, the Charter must be amended to enhance the role of human rights in their own right within the system for collective security."[52] This would make it possible for the Council to invoke violations of human rights and humanitarian law as a basis for action: the Council "would consequently no longer have to stretch reality to invoke the notion of 'threat to the peace' in every case, and would also have greater difficulty standing by and doing nothing."[53] The report puts forward the suggestion to insert references to human rights in existing articles of the UN charter – for example in Articles 1, 24, 39 – that would allow the Security Council to take a clear leadership role in responding to grave threats to human rights. The report concedes that such an amendment would be extraordinarily difficult. The Kosovo report also remarks upon the pre-conflict and post-conflict responsibilities of the international community, but without integrating them into a holistic framework of international action as the "Responsibility to Protect" study does so well.

Consensus for normative progress?

Together, these four studies bring together an impressive weight of academic and policy thinking on the issue of humanitarian intervention. Collectively, to the extent that they share common positions in response to some of the most critical challenges of humanitarian intervention, they also carry evidence of a significant level of consensus towards this subject.

All four publications assert that in extreme cases it may be necessary to employ military force, across state borders, to prevent or alleviate egregious and widespread human rights abuses, without the consent – and against the wishes – of the state in which human rights abuses are taking place. All four claim that Security Council authorization is critical to the use of military force for human protection purposes. In situations where humanitarian crises are threatening international peace and security, the studies are in agreement that Security Council action under Chapter VII is legitimate and in fact a responsibility. In terms of egregious human suffering that does not necessarily constitute a threat to international peace and security, the reports are less emphatic but generally support the idea that the Council still has a responsibility to act. Thus, the studies find consensus in a broadening of the notion of international peace and security and threats to it.

This is an interesting reaffirmation of political liberalism and the doctrine that human welfare ultimately underpins the stability of political institutions. The reports support the assumption that we are gradually moving beyond – or at least problematizing – the "justice versus order" – binary and that in fact, to a large extent, justice underpins order in the international system. The reports are all underpinned by a human solidarism – the belief that we have duties to people in other countries, and that our own integrity as global citizens rests in part upon an acknowledgment of these duties – and the corollary argument that human rights norms and laws should be strengthened. In connection with this, the reports are premised upon an evolving – perhaps post-Westphalian – notion of state sovereignty that is unambiguously conditional upon responsibilities towards citizens. As some of this borrows from classical humanist thought, it might therefore be more correct to think in terms of a "*re*-emergence" of a norm of humanitarian intervention.

In the absence of Security Council authorization for humanitarian intervention the reports highlight a perennial conundrum – the disjuncture that can exist between legality and morality in extreme situations – without offering a solution. International law does not support a norm of humanitarian intervention outside Security Council authority, but political and moral arguments may bring legitimacy; thus the dilemma of humanitarian intervention is not solved. All four studies, either explicitly or implicitly, argue that in extreme cases humanitarian intervention may be necessary and justified on moral and political grounds even if authorization from the UN Security Council cannot be obtained. The reports do make some progress in suggesting how the international community might attempt to move beyond the *ad hoc*, inconsistent nature of humanitarian intervention, and thereby enhance the legitimacy of military coercion for humanitarian reasons when it is necessary. Thus, the studies seek to clarify the circumstances under which intervention is necessary, the procedure that should be followed in order to ensure that alternative non-military options have been exhausted, and operational steps and safeguards that optimize the legitimacy and effectiveness of the use of force. There is a growing consensus on basic criteria and threshold for intervention: these can be regarded as genocide, crimes against humanity and other serious violations of international humanitarian law.

The studies, like much commentary on this issue, sometimes confuse the distinction between empirical description and normative prescription. That is, the distinction between describing what *is* reality and what *should be* reality is blurred. The assumptions regarding sovereignty reflect this. According to *The Responsibility to Protect*, sovereignty brings with it responsibilities towards the needs and rights of citizens. It would be nice to believe this. However, responsibilities towards the needs and rights of citizens are in fact not a prerequisite for state sovereignty. There are many states that do not meet this standard and their sovereignty is never doubted internationally, with the exception of the most shocking cases. For most of the post-war period "humanitarian intervention" was very rarely invoked as a pretext for violating sovereignty. Even in the cases in the 1990s where the UN Security Council took action under Chapter VII – Iraq, Somalia, Haiti, former-Yugoslavia, Kosovo, East Timor – the Council stressed the unique and exceptional nature of the situation, stressed the importance of the sovereignty and territorial integrity of the target state, and tried as far as possible to word the resolution so that the action was being taken with the consent of the target states (as in Iraq and East Timor).

State practice and international law suggest that the principle of non-intervention and the conventional external notion of sovereignty are quite alive and well, even if alternative ideas are emerging. The ICISS report states that "no one is prepared to defend the claim that states can do what they wish to their own people, and hide behind the principle of sovereignty in so doing" – perhaps so, but many societies experience serious human rights abuse and most states acquiesce in the face of this. Even in the face of the worst atrocities in the 1990s – including Rwanda and Bosnia – the response of the international community was decidedly half-hearted. Can we believe that the situation has changed so much since then? Lesser but still terrible human rights abuses are a daily occurrence in many states without the demonstrable weakening of their sovereignty or any lessening of the international recognition of their sovereignty. Norms may change, and of course no one will claim that sovereignty is an inviolable barrier behind which human rights can be wantonly abused – but that does not mean that the international community is prepared to positively act on a "modern" form of sovereignty conditioned by the need to meet certain standards of human welfare. In their idealism perhaps, some of the reports pin their hopes on the General Assembly to act in the face of Security Council inaction, without any reason to presume that a majority in the Assembly would necessarily be any more willing to authorize the use of force.

These studies suggest that there is an emerging (perhaps reemerging) norm of humanitarian intervention based upon political and moral necessity. However, the task of reconciling this norm with the structures of the contemporary international system – such as international law, sovereignty and political expediency – still lies ahead. Nevertheless, the *Responsibility to Protect* has entered the lexicon of international politics at the normative level. The sections of the High Level Panel relating to state sovereignty clearly echo the theme: "the obligation of a State to protect the welfare of its own people and meet its obligations to the wider international community."[54] As a corollary, the report also acknowledges that this responsibility to protect conditions modern ideas of sovereignty; in situations where a state is unable or unwilling to fulfill basic standards of human rights, that responsibility may shift to the international community.[55]

A further key report of the UN is the Secretary-General's reform report *In Larger Freedom*, which also strongly endorses the "responsibility to protect" concept. The report states that: "the time has come for Governments to be held to account, both to their citizens and to each other, for respect of the dignity of the individual, to which they too often pay only lip service."[56] It continues,

If national authorities are unable or unwilling to protect their citizens, then the responsibility shifts to the international community to use diplomatic, humanitarian and other methods to help protect the human rights and well-being of civilian populations. When such methods appear insufficient, the Security Council may out of necessity decide to take action under the Charter of the United Nations, including enforcement action, if so required.[57]

Many will correctly observe that such diplomatic niceties do not have a great deal of meaning in reality, and the intergovernmental UN Summit Outcome of 2005 watered down the messages of the High Level Report and the Secretary-General's *In Larger Freedom*. However, these reports, and even the Summit Outcome, go beyond the usual UN banalities in their promotion of human security ideas. Above all, the explicit endorsement in the Summit Outcome of the responsibility to protect is a great leap forward for the UN member states. The Summit Outcome declares that states have a responsibility to protect their populations from genocide, war crimes, ethnic cleansing and crimes against humanity. The international community also has a responsibility in the provision of this protection, including collective action and coercion under Chapter 7 of the UN Charter "should peaceful means be inadequate and national authorities are manifestly failing to protect their populations."[58]

Conclusion

Does the so-called emergence of a norm of humanitarian intervention challenge the rules governing the use of force? At the normative level there is a case for arguing this, since it has become uncontroversial to claim that sovereignty and territorial inviolability are conditional upon the fulfillment of basic human rights and needs. The "Responsibility to Protect" is the embodiment of this claim, and this has been reflected in the statements of many states and international organizations. A number of Security Council decisions since the end of the Cold War have reflected this evolving thinking.

However, in terms of actual state action – the real indicator of new norms – it is necessary to be much more cautious about a norm of humanitarian intervention. While the idea of a "Responsibility to Protect" has been accepted by member states, both individually and at the UN, state practice and UN decision-making demonstrates the vast gap between statements and actual state behavior. Widespread and egregious human rights abuses took place in Rwanda, the Darfur region of Sudan, the Democratic Republic of the Congo, Uganda, Chechnya, and Somalia, amongst others, without meaningful intervention. Other smaller scale conflicts and cases of state failure in which serious human rights abuses have occurred suggest that the responsibility to protect has yet to become a settled norm.

Thomas Weiss argues that state sovereignty, the preeminence of power politics, and the reality of US power all prevent progress on this issue and multilateral institutions are simply unable to provide human protection in many critical situations. He argues that the "humanitarian intervention fashion" of the 1990s now seems like ancient history, and the political will for humanitarian intervention has evaporated.[59] The High Level Panel Report suggests that "there is a growing acceptance that while sovereign governments have the primary responsibility to protect their own citizens from such catastrophes, when they are unable or unwilling to do so that responsibility should be taken up by the wider international community."[60] However, there is no consistent evidence to support this conclusion which appears to express a normative desire rather than an empirical description of reality. Forsythe argues that humanitarianism reflects a perennial – and unresolved – tension between nationalism and cosmopolitanism in an international system which allows an "inconsistent humanitarian impulse" at best.[61] He suggests that the only hope of overcoming this is a transformation in attitudes: morally, when humankind accepts that deprivation and suffering of others diminishes our own humanity; and in terms of expediency, when decision-makers realize that chaos and suffering elsewhere can threaten their own security.

The institutionalist logic of multilateralism – based upon reciprocity, regularity and burden sharing – does not operate with respect to state response to grave human suffering in terms of creating a *system* to aid innocent civilians in dire need. Even when state leaders are genuinely moved by egregious human rights abuses the political, material and human costs of intervention, whether unilateral or through an international organization, potentially outweigh the benefits. Moreover, reciprocity does not function in this realm. States which are capable of mounting military operations would generally discourage the prospect of other states intervening at their own discretion into the affairs of other states because of the potential which exists for a clash of national interests. States may accept the case for intervening for human protection purposes in specific circumstances, such as Kosovo in 1999. However, this is always through a conjunction of many factors, and never purely humanitarian. A general norm of responsibility to protect does not exist. States are not willing to accept a norm which would obligate them to undertake risky operations in unforeseen circumstances. Their support for such operations will always be contingent upon the specific circumstances of each case, and not a commitment to a general rule. By definition, this is not multilateralism, which requires commitment, even to unforeseen circumstances in a particular policy area. Some states are wary of a norm of humanitarian intervention because they fear the possibility, however remote, that the principle could be held against them.

The gap between legality and legitimacy in terms of the use of military force to alleviate terrible human suffering is a challenge to the moral legitimacy of international organizations. There is a discrepancy between the principles and goals to which states commit themselves through their membership, and their willingness to uphold these principles. However, it is not necessarily a functional challenge to multilateralism. Paradoxically, if states are generally unanimous in *not* actually implementing the responsibility to protect, then this idea does not threaten the fabric of an international organization, since the majority of members agree to the rules of the game, however disingenuous or perverse these seem. There was, sadly, no rush to abandon the UN in response to its failure to stop genocide in Rwanda or widespread violence in Darfur, which would have represented a crisis for the organization. This can be compared to the issue of the use of force over Iraq, which came closer to constituting a crisis: France stated that it would veto any resolution authorizing the use of force, the US took the decision to go to war without a further Security Council resolution and argued that the UN risked becoming irrelevant if it failed to address the realities of contemporary security challenges, and many states believed that the war eroded the authority of the UN.

In cases of grave human suffering, such a standoff is rare, and consensus on inactivity is more common. Therefore, a crisis in multilateralism connected to the use of military force for human protection is not a serious difference of opinion amongst states – because most states do not in reality support an operationalization of a consistent principle of a responsibility to protect – but rather a moral crisis in that multilateral organizations cannot compel their members to uphold the values they have committed to.

5 Weapons of mass destruction

Multilateral arrangements to regulate the development, stockpiling, transfer and use of weapons of mass destruction (WMD) – nuclear, chemical and biological weapons – are under sustained challenge. This challenge has brought into doubt some of the foundations of conventional arms control, the bargaining process amongst states which seeks to balance strengths and interests. At the heart of this challenge lies the military preeminence and ideology of the US, changing strategic demands, technological developments, arms control verification and enforcement loopholes, and the erosion of the norm of nuclear non-proliferation. This chapter examines the impact of these factors upon the regulation of WMD and evaluates the extent of the challenge to multilateralism in this area.

Existing multilateral arrangements have had a reasonably good history in regulating WMD in recent decades. By 2004, only 10 countries were believed to have, or be close to having, nuclear weapons, compared to 16 in the 1980s and 21 in the 1960s.[1] However, a number of norms and regimes have showed signs of unraveling since the 1990s. The actions of a number of states have demonstrated the limitations of multilateral arms control arrangements. North Korea withdrew from the nuclear Non-Proliferation Treaty (NPT) in 2003 and tested a suspected nuclear device in 2006. India and Pakistan tested nuclear weapons and publicly became nuclear weapon states. Iraq was able to pursue a program of WMD before UN pressure forced it to desist, and South Africa acquired nuclear weapons in the 1980s before giving them up. Moreover, Libya had an advanced program of WMD before deciding to halt its progress. It also transpired that a clandestine network to transfer nuclear information emanated from Pakistan. A standoff with Iran showed that a country which was not legally in violation of its non-proliferation obligations can become the source of intense concern when fears arise that it is developing a military use of nuclear materials under the guise of a civilian nuclear program. The NPT review conference of 2005 ended in deadlock, "with competing agendas, widespread distrust, and no consensus on next steps for stopping the spread of or elimination of nuclear weapons."[2] The UN World Summit Outcome in 2005 made no progress on non-proliferation. The Conference on Disarmament is, according to at least one analyst, "becoming an international disgrace" because of ineffectiveness.[3] A number of other treaties or initiatives are stalled, have failed, or are in serious doubt, including efforts at space arms control, negotiations on a biological weapons verification protocol, the Comprehensive Nuclear Test Ban Treaty (CTBT), and the fissile material cut-off treaty (FMCT).

These episodic concerns are symptomatic of deeper problems relating to multilateral arms control of WMD. The trade-off which lies at the heart of the NPT regime – the obligation of nuclear weapons states to disarm and provide peaceful nuclear technology to non-nuclear states, and the obligation of non-nuclear states to refrain from developing nuclear weapons – is under severe strain. This weakens the legitimacy of the regime and increases the risk of countries rejecting the norm of non-proliferation. In addition, there are serious concerns that weaknesses in the NPT regime allow states to develop nuclear materials and technologies without being in breach of the NPT, enabling them to withdraw from the treaty and move to weaponization if they desire. The NPT and other WMD regimes suffer from a serious compliance problem: they do not contain sufficient safeguards against violation, or sufficient means to ensure transparency or verifiability. At the same time, existing regimes do not provide sufficient early warning in the event that states or non-state actors are developing WMD, they do not demand sufficient transparency and verification, and they do not permit action until the situation may be too late. Other agreements, such as the Anti-ballistic Missile treaty, were created in a vastly different strategic environment.

The strategic environment has evolved. Existing regimes were created to manage WMD amongst viable states, based upon deterrence and the acceptance of stability and verifiability. The twenty-first century agenda includes the threat – however remote – of non-state actors acquiring and using WMD, and of weak or reckless states using or illicitly supplying WMD information or materials to non-state groups. The US believes that its adversaries are seeking WMD to counter US conventional superiority, and that "terrorist groups are seeking to acquire WMD with the stated purposes of killing large numbers of our people."[4] The perception of important decision-makers, especially in the US, is that many existing multilateral arms control regimes cannot credibly deal with "rogue states" or terrorist organizations. According to the US National Strategy to Combat Weapons of Mass Destruction, "the US approach to combat WMD represents a fundamental change from the past" requiring the US to "promote new agreements and arrangements that serve our nonproliferation goals."[5] From this perspective, "the old ways of pursuing arms control are mostly obsolete ... a new arms control framework designed for a new world is urgently needed."[6] The European Union strategy against the proliferation of WMD, expressing commitment to existing multilateral regimes, is distinctly different in tone.[7]

The use of military force – especially amongst countries which possessed WMD – was not a viable option during the Cold War as mutually assured destruction underpinned stability, especially amongst nuclear states. However, in this evolving strategic environment the use of military force to regulate the development, stockpiling, transfer and prevention of the use of WMD – against a state harboring or providing WMD technology to terrorist groups, or rogue states intent on developing WMD, for example – is no longer inconceivable.

The most powerful states – and particularly the US – are reducing their support for certain multilateral WMD regimes, moving towards a unilateral approach to their needs. The US, for example, withdrew from the Anti-Ballistic Missile treaty, preferring to invest in missile defense. Similarly, the Proliferation Security Initiative – a coalition of states acting to impede illicit WMD-related trade to and from states of concern and terrorist groups – represents a departure from existing arms control approaches. According to one WMD expert, the Republican administration of George W. Bush has been "particularly unilateralist and obstructionist in respect of multilateral activity pertaining to WMD."[8]

From a functional perspective, what is needed is a re-envisioning of multilateral arms control agreements to address changing strategic demands, technological developments, and arms control verification and enforcement loopholes. In particular, multilateral arms control arrangements must be more effective in deterring, and giving early warning of, treaty violations. They must also address the challenges of WMD-capable states which are outside key arms control instruments. The erosion of the norm of nuclear non-proliferation also needs to be urgently reversed. In addition, the credibility of verification mechanisms for international non-proliferation agreements must be strengthened.

Multilateral arrangements for WMD

The key multilateral WMD instruments are the NPT, the CTBT, the 1993 Chemical Weapons Convention (CWC) and the 1972 Biological Weapons Convention (BWC). These have verification mechanisms: the International Atomic Energy Agency (IAEA), the Comprehensive Nuclear Test Ban Treaty Organisation (CTBTO), and the Organisation for the Prohibition of Chemical Weapons (OPCW). Other important treaties include the Anti-Ballistic Missile (ABM) Treaty, Intermediate-Range Nuclear Forces Treaty, International Code of Conduct against Ballistic Missile Proliferation, Limited Test Ban Treaty (LTBT), Missile Technology Control Regime, Open Skies Treaty, Outer Space Treaty, Peaceful Nuclear Explosions Treaty (PNET), Physical Protection of Nuclear Material Convention, Seabed Arms Control Treaty, and the Threshold Test Ban Treaty (TTBT).

Major regional treaties include the African Nuclear Weapons Free Zone Treaty (Treaty of Pelindaba), the Latin America Nuclear Weapons Free Zone Treaty (Treaty of Tlatelolco), the South Pacific Nuclear Weapons Free Zone Treaty (Treaty of Rarotonga), and the 1994 US-North Korean Agreed Framework.

A number of UN bodies are mandated to deal with WMD issues. The Conference on Disarmament (CD) was established in 1979 as the single multilateral disarmament negotiating forum of the international community. The First Committee of the UN General Assembly considers a range of security and disarmament issues and adopts non-binding resolutions. The UN Disarmament Commission (UNDC) is a specialized body that allows in-depth deliberations on specific disarmament issues and generates concrete recommendations. In addition, within the UN Secretariat the Department of Disarmament Affairs promotes the goal of nuclear disarmament and non-proliferation and the strengthening of the disarmament regimes in respect to other WMD. There is also an Advisory Board on Disarmament Matters, established in 1978 to advise the Secretary-General on arms control and disarmament. The United Nations Institute for Disarmament Research (UNIDIR) conducts research on disarmament and security with the aim of assisting with disarmament efforts. Finally, the Security Council is the UN organ which has the primary responsibility for the maintenance of international peace and security. As such it has the responsibility to respond to any WMD issue which is a threat to peace and security. The Council also has a specific role in relation to other organizations; the IAEA, for example, may submit reports to the Council for consideration and further action. This chapter will deal with challenges presented by global WMD regimes.

NPT

The NPT entered into force in March 1970 with the objective of preventing the spread of nuclear weapons. The key component of the treaty is that the five nuclear weapons states – the United States, Russia, China, France, and the United Kingdom – commit to pursue general and complete disarmament, while the non-nuclear weapons states agree to forgo developing or acquiring nuclear weapons. Article 6 commits nuclear weapons states to "pursue negotiations in good faith on effective measures relating to cessation of the nuclear arms race at an early date and to nuclear disarmament, and on a Treaty on general and complete disarmament under strict and effective international control." The NPT also prohibits the transfer of nuclear weapons material and requires non-nuclear weapons states to accept safeguards – administered by the IAEA – for the verification of their NPT treaty obligations. The treaty does not affect the "inalienable right" of state parties to develop research, production and use of nuclear energy for peaceful purposes. It also supports the "fullest possible exchange" of such nuclear-related information and technology between nuclear and non-nuclear weapons states. The treaty provides for a review conference every five years and a decision after 25 years on whether the treaty should be extended. The 1995 review conference extended the treaty indefinitely and the 2000 review conference adopted the "13 steps" to establish clearer targets in line with the commitment of nuclear weapons states to disarm. However, the 2005 review conference ended in acrimony, with little agreement on substance.

The NPT is almost universal in membership – 189 states-parties – with India, Israel, and Pakistan remaining outside the treaty. In 2003 North Korea announced that it was withdrawing from the treaty, but since it did not fully follow the procedures for withdrawal, the precise legal situation regarding North Korea's membership is unclear. However, most observers would agree that North Korea is, de facto, no longer a member, and its nuclear test in 2006 made this discussion irrelevant. Despite the criticism that the treaty is flawed, it remains the most widely supported treaty on WMD. Yet the strains are obvious. They result from states which are a party to the NPT but in violation, nuclear capable states which are outside the regime, non-state actors and in particular terrorist organizations, and weaknesses in the regime which make it vulnerable to further breakouts.

First, the trade-off which lies at the heart of the regime – the commitment of nuclear weapons states to disarm and provide peaceful nuclear technology to non-nuclear states, and the commitment of non-nuclear states to refrain from developing nuclear weapons – is in danger of collapse. Nuclear weapons states emphasize non-proliferation but ignore disarmament. Moreover, a number of nuclear weapon states are actively overhauling their arsenals or – in the case of the US – developing aggressive nuclear postures. These maintain nuclear readiness and reject the idea of unambiguous negative security assurance to non-nuclear states. They also countenance first strikes, preemptively if necessary.[9] The likelihood of American nuclear primacy in the near future – the ability to destroy an adversary's nuclear forces, eliminating the possibility of retaliation – underscores the fact that disarmament is very far from the minds of US policy-makers.[10] For nuclear weapons states, the benefits of retaining nuclear weapons outweigh the costs, such as the censure of non-nuclear weapons states or the risk that non-nuclear states will withdraw from the treaty and pursue a nuclear weapons program. Nuclear weapon possession brings with it accoutrements of great power status – including prestige, military power and bargaining power – and it also provides a hedge against future uncertainties.

During the Cold War, an era of massive retaliation and mutually assured destruction, nuclear weapons were the mainstay of deterrence amongst nuclear weapons states. Despite the taboo against their use in the post-Cold War world, nuclear weapons states are unwilling to forgo an advantage in the event of uncertainty. Classical deterrence is not dead; it is an overstatement to suggest that: "The days of cold war arms control are gone for good."[11] Genuine apprehension exists between the US, China and Russia and the utility of nuclear weapons as a deterrent remains common sense and completely uncontroversial amongst the elites of those countries. But the real uncertainty is mainly formed by the possibility that other countries could acquire WMD – not only nuclear weapons – in response to which a credible nuclear deterrent remains necessary. The conventional military superiority of nuclear weapons states – especially the US, Russia and China – represents a formidable deterrent in itself against "rogue states" acquiring WMD. But as long as the possibility exists for unforeseen nuclear proliferation, there is no compelling incentive for nuclear states to disarm.

The development of smaller, tactical nuclear weapons by the US suggests that American strategists do plan for the scenario of using nuclear weapons if necessary. Its refusal to declare no first use of nuclear weapons or non-use against non-nuclear weapons states underlines this. Lesser nuclear weapons states – such as the UK and France – have seen their conventional military capacity decline comparatively and thus cling on to the nuclear deterrent as a means of maintaining their great power status. Britain's official position is that as long as a potential enemy has a nuclear weapon Britain should retain the capacity. Nuclear weapons states outside the NPT regime – Israel, India, Pakistan and possibly North Korea – have obvious incentives to maintain nuclear capacity in light of the security predicaments each perceive. The impact of this is multifold. First, from the perspective of non-nuclear weapons states Article 6 of the NPT is not credible; the position of the nuclear states represents a blatant double standard: "It is truly remarkable how those who worship at the altar of nuclear weapons condemn others wishing to join their sect as heretics."[12] For many, this double standard is symptomatic of a broader structural injustice in international politics.[13]

The acrimony which resulted from this double standard paralyzed the NPT review conference of 2005. The standoff between non-nuclear states pushing for disarmament and the US taking the lead in resisting any commitment to disarmament also obstructed any progress on nuclear arms control in the Summit meeting of the UN in 2005, which marked the organization's 60th anniversary. In addition, the position of the nuclear weapons states clearly demonstrates the continued utility of nuclear weapons. Nuclear weapons states justify their continued possession of such weapons – in breach of the NPT – on the basis of their own security needs, yet deny the same privilege to non-nuclear weapons states on the basis that it would be a threat to international stability and security. Arguably, the lesson of this has been that certain states – such as India, Pakistan and North Korea – felt that the security benefits offered by the regime were outweighed by pursing their own WMD programs. India and Pakistan could also claim that the norm of non-proliferation was not legitimate. The danger, therefore, is that non-nuclear states will "rebel" against the norm of non-proliferation.[14] Even if that does not happen, the legitimacy of the nuclear weapons states which pursue non-proliferation is surely damaged.[15]

The unhappiness of non-nuclear states and the lack of credibility of Article 6 does not necessarily mean that the NPT will disintegrate. There are incentives for non-nuclear states to remain within the regime and not to defect. Withdrawing from the NPT and going nuclear – or developing a nuclear weapons program clandestinely from within the NPT – has its hazards. The taboo against nuclear proliferation is still strong, resulting in the prospect of sanctions, pariah status, or even military invasion. The case of Iraq illustrates this; a lesson apparently appreciated by Libya, which publicly renounced WMD in a celebrated case of redemption. Moreover, it is questionable whether the legitimacy problems of the NPT regime – and in particular the failure of Article 6 – have directly led to any defections. The cases of India, Pakistan and Israel – which are not members of NPT – and North Korea – which has withdrawn – might be better explained by the particularly sensitive security predicament in which each finds itself, rather than as a result of the legitimacy problems of the non-proliferation regime. Almost all states would be similarly motivated if they had the capacity. Nevertheless, the legitimacy problems of the regime may have been one factor amongst many for states which face a particular security predicament and which have the capacity to pursue a nuclear weapons program, for which the incentives of pursuing nuclear weapons outweigh the costs. The fear is that other states in a similar situation may find similar incentives. The report of the High Level Panel on Threats, Challenges and Change stated that:

> the nuclear non-proliferation regime is now at risk because of lack of compliance with existing commitments, withdrawal or threats of withdrawal from the Treaty on the Non-Proliferation of Nuclear Weapons to escape those commitments, a changing international security environment and the diffusion of technology. We are approaching a point at which the erosion of the non-proliferation regime could become irreversible and result in a cascade of proliferation.[16]

Second, the NPT regime may allow states to develop nuclear materials and technologies without being in breach of the NPT, enabling them to withdraw from the treaty and move to weaponization without much additional effort if they desire. Thus, a number of states can be considered virtual nuclear weapons states: they have the capacity and have undertaken the preparations for the development of nuclear weapons and could promptly move to weaponization as soon as the incentives outweigh the costs. The NPT allows civilian nuclear activities – such as enriching nuclear materials for peaceful energy purposes – the results of which can be diverted to military purposes. This possibility is intolerable to the major sponsors of the non-proliferation regime – and in particular the US – and places the credibility of the regime in doubt. The apparent North Korea nuclear test in October 2006 – following its withdrawal from the NPT in 2003 – was an illustration of such a worst-case scenario.

The confrontation between Iran and various international actors in 2003–6 provides an example of a more general concern that states might seek a civilian nuclear energy program in order to create a military option. In 2003 the IAEA reported that Iran had hidden a uranium enrichment program for 18 years. Iran insists that it is pursuing a peaceful program of nuclear energy – an "inalienable right" under the NPT. Many states – and particularly the US – do not accept the prospect of Iran pursuing any nuclear activities which could in the future be channeled into a military program. Iran's technical violations – an undeclared enrichment program in the past – provided the basis for such opposition. The IAEA asked Iran to commit itself to a permanent cessation of all enrichment activities and Iran refused. There are also a number of other peculiarities which opponents of Iran have seized upon: Iran's vast oil reserves would seem to provide more than enough energy for the country into the future, although its refining capacity remains weak. In addition, Russia offered to enrich fuel on behalf of Iran, but this proposal has not found support in Iran.

The principal concern of the US and Western Europe is in reality not Iran's technical violation, but rather that a state with which they have had difficult relations, in a sensitive geographic region, might seek to have the option of developing nuclear weapons in the future. The standoff with Iran was caused by Iran's failure to disclose uranium-enrichment activities, not the enrichment activities themselves. The fact that Iran and the US are implacable enemies, and the US officially counts Iran as a sponsor of international terrorism, are also central to the confrontation between the international community and Iran. The possibility, however remote, that the country might develop a nuclear capacity and then be in a position to withdraw from the NPT and move towards weaponization, is unacceptable for the US, even if the NPT regime allows peaceful nuclear programs for energy purposes. Indeed, Iran's failure to declare its activities allowed the US to focus the spotlight on Iran, but even if Iran had been transparent – in line with IAEA and NPT guidelines – it is highly likely that the US would still not have been comfortable with a civilian nuclear program in Iran.

The response of the IAEA was rather piecemeal for two years after the crisis began in 2003 and this raised strong criticism in the US. Finally, the Board of Governors decided in February 2006 to issue a resolution which recalled "Iran's many failures and breaches of its obligations to comply with its NPT Safeguards Agreement and the absence of confidence that Iran's nuclear program is exclusively for peaceful purposes resulting from the history of concealment of Iran's nuclear activities."[17] That resolution also referred the concerns of the IAEA to the Security Council, which is a significant step as the Council has the authority to impose sanctions against Iran. In turn, at the end of March 2006 the President of the Security Council issued a statement which expressed, on behalf of the Council, "serious concern" that "the IAEA is unable to conclude that there are no undeclared nuclear materials or activities in Iran."[18]

The lack of a verifiable mechanism to ban the production of fissile material – and enforce a ban – is a conspicuous weakness in the nuclear non-proliferation regime. While the IAEA resolution and its referral to the Security Council were welcomed by the US, the US continued to have reservations about the performance of the IAEA and the NPT. In particular, from the perspective of their critics, there are serious doubts that these regimes can prevent states such as Iran from pursuing clandestine nuclear weapons programs. The unlikely specter of unilateral action – including military force – was widely discussed but not ruled out by Washington. The precedent of Israel's military strike against Iraq's Osirak nuclear reactor in 1981 formed the backdrop to the repeated assertions of US political leaders in 2005 that Iran must not be allowed to develop nuclear weapons.

The US position on Iran, according to many observers, exaggerates the dangers of that country. Repeated statements by US officials indict the country as part of an axis of evil and assert that Iran must not be able to develop nuclear weapons. These statements appear to build a political case which pre-judges Iran and promote the impression that Iran is demonstrably seeking to develop WMD in breach of international law. The Board of Governors of the IAEA, while clearly expressing concern in 2006, did not make the determination that Iran is actively pursuing nuclear weapons. The US position also obviously represents a double standard when one considers that Israel, India and Pakistan – all in varying degrees allies of the US – have developed nuclear weapons. Although all three are outside – and thus not in violation – of the NPT, the proliferation of nuclear weapons is a dangerous development. The cooperation of the US with India for the exchange of civilian nuclear technology has also been regarded as an endorsement of India's move towards the development of nuclear weapons. The danger of an Iranian nuclear weapon program is real, and the clandestine activities to enrich uranium are a source of suspicion, as the IAEA Board of Governors observed. Nevertheless, the conclusion drawn by many observers is, therefore, that allies of the US may be permitted to develop nuclear weapons (or at least would suffer less opprobrium), while states which find themselves seriously at odds with the US may not even be able to pursue a civilian nuclear program.

Whatever the truth regarding Iran, the case illustrates that the NPT and other WMD regimes suffer from a serious compliance problem: they do not contain sufficient safeguards against violation, or sufficient means to ensure transparency or verifiability. In short, the signature of states may not engender confidence that they are fully meeting their obligations, or that they will not withdraw from the regime. The legally binding nature of WMD regimes is questionable; "rogue states" and non-state groups are not bound by legal regimes, and non-state groups may well not be deterred by the prospect of retaliation. At the same time, existing regimes do not provide sufficient early warning to indicate that states or non-state actors are developing WMD, they do not demand sufficient transparency and verification, and they do not permit action until the situation may be too late. As the High Level Panel Report notes, "Almost 60 States currently operate or are constructing nuclear power or research reactors, and at least 40 possess the industrial and scientific infrastructure which would enable them, if they chose, to build nuclear weapons at relatively short notice."[19]

Problems with the ABM treaty and regimes regulating nuclear testing are also symptomatic of the challenges facing the non-proliferation regime. The treaty entered into force in October 1972. It was negotiated between the United States and the Soviet Union as part of the Strategic Arms Limitation Talks, and prohibited Washington and Moscow from deploying nationwide defenses against strategic ballistic missiles. The ABM treaty states that limits on anti-missile defense would be a "substantial factor in curbing the race in strategic offensive arms." The rationale of the ABM treaty was peculiar to the Cold War logic of stability through mutual assured destruction. Without national defenses, each superpower remained vulnerable, deterring both sides from launching a first strike because each faced massive retaliation and its own destruction. Vulnerability strengthened the credibility of mutual deterrence and thus strengthened stability. An effective missile defense would have been destabilizing because each would have reduced the confidence of the other side in its retaliatory capacity, which would have increased the risk of a first strike. The ABM treaty also reflects the logic that limits on defensive systems would reduce the need to build greater offensive weapons to overcome any defense that the other might deploy.

In December 2001, President George W. Bush announced that the United States would withdraw from the ABM Treaty, one of the "last vestiges" of the Cold War. Bush stated that the treaty "hinders our government's ability to develop ways to protect our people from future terrorist or rogue-state missile attacks" and it was defunct because the relationship between the US and Russia now represented mutual cooperation, not mutual assured destruction.[20]

Few would deny that the ABM Treaty rested upon strategic and political calculations which became significantly less viable after the end of the Cold War. Moreover, the perceived danger of WMD in the hands of "rogue states" has become tangible in the US. However unlikely it is from a strategic perspective that a country would attack the US with missiles, and despite the double standards at work in the US condemnation of WMD proliferation, there is a sense that a treaty established upon the calculations of 30 years ago is not strategically or politically viable for the twenty-first century. Of course, the pre-eminent military position of the US allowed it to arrive at this determination.

The future of the NPT regime is also linked to the CTBT. In 1999, the US Senate rejected the CTBT and no US administration has since then asked the Congress to reconsider the issue. This means that the treaty is unlikely to attract sufficient ratifications to enter into force, and thus a binding global legal prohibition on nuclear testing will not take effect. Most countries do, however, observe a voluntary moratorium. In April 2006, the total number of signatories of the treaty was 176 and it had been ratified by 132 states. The CTBT will formally enter into force only after 44 designated "nuclear-capable states" have deposited their instruments of ratification with the UN Secretary-General. India, Pakistan, and North Korea – among the 44 nuclear-capable states – have not signed, and only 34 states have ratified the treaty. UN Secretary-General Kofi Annan said, in a speech to the UN General Assembly, that "The longer its entry into force is delayed, the more likely that nuclear testing will resume. Were this to happen, it would be a major setback in non-proliferation and nuclear disarmament efforts."[21]

There are a number of export control regimes which are also relevant to the nuclear non-proliferation regime, as well as other types of WMD. The Missile Technology Control Regime (MTCR), for example, was established in April 1987 and aims to limit the spread of ballistic missiles that could be used for nuclear, biological and chemical attacks. The voluntary regime requests its members – 34 in 2006 – to restrict their exports of missiles and related technologies capable of carrying a 500-kilogram payload at least 300 kilometers or delivering any type of WMD. The MTCR has apparently had some success in slowing or stopping several missile programs, but a number of countries – especially India, Iran, North Korea, and Pakistan – continue to strengthen their missile programs.[22] The Nuclear Suppliers Group (NSG) is a group of 45 nuclear supplier countries which seeks to prevent the misuse of civilian nuclear exports. The NSG, established in 1974, has focused mainly on the challenge of proliferation amongst states, but notably in 2002 it agreed to revise its guidelines to prevent and counter the threat of diversion of nuclear exports to nuclear terrorism. The proposed Fissile Material Cut-off Treaty is an attempt to impose limitations upon the total amount of nuclear material in existence, in the interests of preventing proliferation. However, in 2004 the US announced that they did not support the treaty because of verification concerns.

Chemical weapons

Chemical weapons represent a special challenge in the area of WMD. The clandestine production of toxic or incapacitating chemicals – unlike nuclear weapons – can be hidden within civilian chemical production because of the dual-use nature of many of the materials and processes involved. The CWC is a multilateral treaty, of unlimited duration, that bans chemical weapons. The convention opened for signature in 1993 and entered into force in 1997. The CWC prohibits developing, producing, acquiring, or transferring chemical weapons. It is administered by the OPCW, which monitors members' activities which may relate directly or indirectly to chemical weapons. This monitoring, which involves inspections of member states' facilities, is based upon declarations submitted by state parties themselves. The CWC requires state parties to declare their chemical weapons stockpiles, chemical weapons production facilities, relevant chemical industry facilities, and other weapons-related information. This must be done within 30 days of the convention's entry into force for the state parties.[23]

The convention provides for on-site activities to give assurances of compliance. There are routine inspections of chemical weapons-related facilities and chemical industry facilities to verify declarations. More interestingly, there are "challenge inspections": all state parties have a right to request an on-site challenge inspection of any facility or location in the territory of any other state party for the purpose of clarifying and resolving any questions concerning possible non-compliance, and to have this inspection conducted anywhere without delay.

In response to possible non-compliance, the OPCW can request state parties to satisfy any concerns which may exist. The Executive

Council can, in cases of "particular gravity and urgency," bring the issue directly to the attention of the UN General Assembly and the Security Council. As with referrals by the IAEA, the Council can take a range of steps, including requesting compliance, the imposition of sanctions, or other action under Chapter VII. The CWC currently has 175 state parties. Eleven signatory states – including Israel – have not yet ratified. Key non-signatories include North Korea and Syria, both of which are accused by the US of having chemical weapons programs.

The multilateral management of chemical weapons presents particularly difficult challenges and it is certainly more difficult to administer with confidence than nuclear weapons. Chemical weapons are particularly difficult to manage for a number of reasons. The dual-use nature of many of the precursor materials – for military and civilian purposes – makes clandestine chemical weapons programs difficult to detect. The relatively cheap cost and simplicity of producing chemical weapons – especially compared to nuclear weapons – and the availability of know-how put these weapons within the reach of many countries. Clearly a reliable delivery system is necessary for any weapons to have utility. Nevertheless, chemical weapons are certainly within the means of states which would never be in a position to pursue a nuclear weapons program. Missile proliferation, combined with the prospect of chemical weapons, therefore present a significant threat. In terms of non-state challenges and terrorism, the problem also includes unorthodox means of delivery.

Countries are able to (and indeed have been known to) pursue clandestine chemical weapons programs. Alternatively, states have made preparations for chemical weapons production while not taking the final step – and thus avoid violating international conventions – but nevertheless providing the option for developing chemical weapons if they perceive it to be necessary. Chemical weapons arms control traditionally reflected the agreement that such weapons are abominable and the overwhelming logic that everyone benefits from a reciprocal commitment not to use chemical weapons. The premise of this conventional wisdom is being increasingly questioned. Some states see chemical weapons as a viable deterrent. The US, in particular, believes that "rogue states" and non-state groups (principally terrorist organizations) either alone or in collaboration with each other, constitute an acute chemical weapons threat.

The CWC has performed well amongst state parties. The OPCW inspects military and industrial sites in dozens of countries to ensure compliance. OPCW membership now embraces over 95 percent of the world's population and 98 percent of the relevant global chemical industry, a notable achievement in a relatively short span since the establishment of the organizations in 1997. There has been a rapid increase in participation by states in the Convention. The OPCW conducted over 2000 inspections during its first eight years – although none of them challenge inspections.[24] Nevertheless, there are still challenges: declared stockpiles remain, dating from the Cold War, and there is a possibility that undeclared stockpiles exist, despite the on-sight inspections of the OPCW. A number of chemical weapons-capable states – such as Syria, Egypt, North Korea and Israel – remain outside the chemical weapons prohibition regime. In addition, terrorist organizations are clearly not signatories of the CWC, nor do they feel constrained by it.[25]

Biological weapons

Biological weapons spread pathogens which cause diseases that attack humans, animals, or food crops. They present acute challenges for prohibition because it is difficult to monitor their production and stockpiling since their production can be hidden within legitimate civilian procedures. Indeed, as with chemical weapons, states have generally refrained from their use primarily through a fear of retaliation in kind.

The Convention on the Prohibition of the Development, Production and Stockpiling of Bacteriological (Biological) and Toxin Weapons and on their Destruction (BWC) was concluded in 1972. States party undertake never to develop, produce, stockpile or acquire biological agents or toxins, or weapons, equipment or means of delivery designed to use such agents or toxins for hostile purposes or in armed conflict. The convention also prohibits any transfer of biological weapons materials and also allows any party to lodge a complaint with the Security Council if it believes another party is in breach of its obligations. The convention has been patently violated. The Soviet Union, a state party, maintained a large offensive biological weapons program after ratifying the BWC. Iraq, a signatory state, had a biological weapons program which was uncovered by the UN Special Commission on Iraq after the Gulf War. In November 2001 the United States publicly accused Iraq and North Korea of violating the convention, and expressed doubts about Iran, Libya, Syria and Cuba.

The chemical and biological treaty regimes are aided by complementary multilateral arrangements. The Australia Group, established in 1985, is a voluntary, informal, export-control arrangement through which 38 countries, as well as the European Commission, coordinate their national export controls to limit the supply of chemicals and biological agents and equipment to countries and non-state entities suspected of pursuing chemical or biological weapons.

Adapting to changing demands and realities

The key WMD regulations are clearly under some strain. The NPT regime is challenged by a lack of credibility in its disarmament requirements, and by a weakness which renders it unable to satisfactorily monitor or verify compliance (especially amongst nuclear-capable states). According to the High Level Panel, there is a danger of a "cascade" of nuclear proliferation.[26] The loophole of the NPT regime will continue to widen as more states develop nuclear energy programs in the future and the number of nuclear-capable states increases.[27] The ABM treaty was premised upon strategic logic which is hard to justify in the twenty-first century. The regulation of chemical and biological weapons, although widely supported, suffers from a lack of verification.

In terms of nuclear weapons, existing regimes were created to manage WMD amongst viable states, based upon deterrence and the acceptance of stability and verifiability. The political environment is quite different from that which existed when many multilateral arms control arrangements were negotiated. The premise of states as the unit of analysis, the acceptance of international legal commitments, and voluntary verification mechanisms have all come under strain. After 9/11, concerns over proliferation – especially amongst states considered by the West to be outside the mainstream of the international community – and the potential for mass destruction terrorism have increased the sense of anxiety. Nevertheless, new initiatives within the existing multilateral implementing organizations – such as the IAEA and the OPCW – have been active in addressing unconventional challenges such as transfers of WMD to non-state groups. Still, existing arms control approaches are based upon the presumption of rational, viable states, while the contemporary – and future – challenge is more likely to be associated with weak or failed states.

States have used the UN to take the lead – and bring together various multilateral regimes – in strengthening multilateral approaches to WMD in changing circumstances. Resolution 1540, adopted by the UN Security Council in April 2004, is one such example. It explicitly recognizes the risk that non-state actors – meaning terrorist groups – may acquire nuclear, chemical and biological weapons and stipulates actions which must be undertaken by member states to prevent this. The resolution was explicitly adopted under Chapter VII of the UN Charter, which deals with mandatory obligations necessary for the maintenance of international peace and security. Failure to comply therefore constitutes a threat to international peace and security. The resolution presents a range of requirements to prevent the transfer of any WMD materials to non-state groups, and prevent non-state actors from manufacturing WMD. It requires the establishment of domestic controls to prevent proliferation, and measures to account for and protect WMD materials. Recognizing that some states may lack the capacity to fully implement these measures, the resolution encourages other states to provide assistance where necessary. The resolution requires member states to submit a report on measures taken to implement the resolution and has been hailed as a landmark initiative. The reporting requirement, the Chapter VII authority and the specific prohibition on all assistance to non-state groups make the resolution actionable and substantive. After the efforts of the US and the UK to frame the war against Iraq in 2003 as a response to Iraq's violations of Security Council resolutions, Resolution 1540 is highly significant. The implication is that the US would insist upon a UN response to states which it believed had violated the resolution, and if that did not happen – as in the case of Iraq – it might feel legitimized to act outside the UN.

The reality today appears to be that the key issue is *who* has nuclear weapons. American hegemony and sense of exceptionalism play a role in its skepticism towards some multilateral WMD regimes. There is a conservative argument that the UN – and other legalist forms of multilateralism – is flawed because of the "moral equivalence" implied by sovereign equality, which has implications for formalized multilateralism in general. This represents a deep ideological cleavage. Many commentators and political leaders bemoan the "double standards" of the US in targeting Iran and Iraq for purportedly developing WMD while ignoring (or even abetting) Israel's possession of nuclear weapons. Indeed one could argue that the UK or France – which have failed to actively pursue disarmament – are just as in breach of the NPT as Iran, but few people would claim that a nuclear UK would make them feel more insecure than a nuclear Iran. Conservative political elites in the US openly reject the idea that all states are equal in legitimacy or threat. For American conservatives, "A fisheries treaty with Canada is something real. An Agreed Framework on plutonium processing with the likes of North Korea is not worth the paper it is written on."[28] Moreover, the North Korean nuclear test in October 2006 provided a further challenge to nuclear non-proliferation which appeared to confirm the worst fears regarding the weaknesses of the regime.

6 Civil war, state failure and peacebuilding

Most violent conflict since the Second World War has been intra-state: civil war, state failure and low-intensity violent conflict. The impacts associated with these phenomena include the direct human costs – death, injury, human rights abuse, forced migration – the destruction of infrastructure, and the destruction of societal institutions. Civil wars and situations of state failure also contribute to international insecurity, in the form of refugee flows, the trafficking of arms and narcotics, and the spread of insurgencies. Civil wars and weak states can also form the bases for terrorist planning, recruitment and organization, with implications for regional and international security. Civil war and state failure are therefore primary challenges in international politics and for international organizations. Yet the history of multilateral efforts – including those of the UN – to prevent and resolve civil wars and build peace after conflict shows a mixed record. This chapter considers whether the failures of international organizations such as the UN in preventing and resolving civil conflict – as a humanitarian as well as a security challenge – undermine the legitimacy of multilateralism in this area. Three main themes are explored: the functional effectiveness – or lack thereof – of the UN's approach to civil war; the normative stance of the UN, which has traditionally been based upon ideas of impartiality and neutrality; and the "liberal" value system which accompanies international peacebuilding efforts.

Contemporary forms of conflict – sometimes described as "new wars" – defy the conventional models of conflict and security reflected in the UN Charter. Despite the obvious challenges posed by such conflict to the values of the UN and the international society of states, the capacity for traditional institutionalized models of multilateralism to prevent or address civil war is questionable. This raises a number of questions. Does the international community – through the UN – have a coherent doctrine with which to address civil war and state failure? Do civil wars represent a challenge to the legitimacy of international organizations? Are the difficulties encountered in preventing and responding to civil war a result of the structural, legal or political characteristics of international organizations? Do the values which are reflected in the approach of international organizations, based upon the "liberal peace," offer a viable approach to resolving civil conflict which is rooted in social and economic problems? In particular, is the promotion of market economics and democracy – now considered almost sacrosanct in building peace – viable? Can the theoretical tenets of multilateralism – based upon reciprocity, indivisibility and non-discrimination – suggest incentives for states to become involved in building peace in conflicted societies in a consistent and effective manner?

Civil war and state failure: "new wars"

Since the end of the Cold War there has been a great deal of scholarship on civil war. This has generated a range of propositions regarding the causes and sources of conflict, the relationship between natural resources and conflict, the political economy of conflict, and the role and potential of external actors in resolving conflict and building peace.[1] A number of observations are common within this scholarship. Most wars in recent decades have been intra-state rather than inter-state, and a number of patterns dominate: ethno-nationalist insurgency, political-ideological insurgency, resource conflict, ethno-nationalist separatist conflict, social conflict, irredentist conflict, warlord insurgency, and inter-clan political conflict. These conflicts are often characterized by state failure and social breakdown, and a breakdown of public authority which blurs the distinction between public and private combatants, and between combatants and civilians. They also display competition over natural resources and illegal commercial activities, and conflict between private armies and criminal warlords, often organized according to some form of identity. Ethnic and religious conflicts are more characteristic of contemporary wars than political ideology. Analysts often suggest that civilian casualties and forced human displacement are dramatically increasing as a proportion of all casualties in conflict, and that civilians are deliberately targeted as an object of war. Atrocities and ethnic homogenization are key hallmarks of contemporary conflict.

Since the 1990s many analysts have argued that this reality is not captured by mainstream approaches to conflict and security in international relations, approaches which are also embodied in most forms of multilateralism. International security has traditionally been defined as military defense of sovereign territory; defending territory against, and deterring, "external" military threats. The vocabulary of this field is characterized by its Cold War origins: the security dilemma, deterrence, containment, balance of power, retaliation, absolute and relative gains, zero-sum and non-zero-sum games, arms races, and security regimes. In terms of security studies, the traditional approach is defined by Stephen Walt: "security studies may be defined as the study of the threat, use, and control of military power. It explores the conditions that make the use of force more likely, the ways that the use of force affects individuals, states and societies, and the specific policies that states adopt in order to prepare for, prevent, or engage in war."[2] This has generally focused upon the military – rather than social, economic, or cultural – aspects of violence, and the unit of analysis has generally been the state. In the study of international relations, this is a central focus of the realist school which is preoccupied with an anarchic state system whose chief characteristic is a perennial competition for security based upon (primarily military) power. While changes may occur inside states, the system remains a self-help, anarchic, hierarchical arena that conditions or even determines the behavior and attitudes of the actors. National security therefore is the imperative of defending territory against external military threats. Although the UN Charter was certainly not designed to exclusively deal with the military and state-centric threats to security, this conventional security conception is apparent when reading the Charter.

The contrast between the reality of contemporary forms of violent conflict and the traditional model of international security led a number of scholars to argue that it is now possible to think in terms of "contemporary" or "modern" conflict, and particularly civil war, as a departure from "earlier" forms of conflict. This argument holds that "One of the most dramatic ways in which the post-Cold War world differs from the Cold War international system is in the pattern of violence that has been developing."[3] Moreover, "The new wars can be contrasted with earlier wars in terms of their goals, the methods of warfare and how they are financed."[4] In terms of the main protagonists and units of analysis of "new wars," the basic argument is that inter-state wars have declined in number relative to civil wars; or even that we are seeing the "end of old-fashioned war between states."[5] A common expression of this idea is presented in the report of the International Commission on Intervention and State Sovereignty: "The most marked security phenomenon since the end of the Cold War has been the proliferation of armed conflicts within states."[6] Violent civil conflict is generally linked with a social environment that implicates a range of non-state as well as state actors. The weakening or undermining of the state is central to this environment, sometimes seen in the context of economic forces and globalization which erode state capacity, authority, and the provision of public goods. In turn, a pattern of violence by private – often criminal – groups emerges in this vacuum of state authority and power, often associated with ethnic allegiances, and often vying over natural resources or criminal opportunities. Thus, according to this argument, the context of contemporary wars is generally within, rather than between, states, although usually with regional consequences.

The global context is the decline of bipolar power and into this vacuum the (re)emergence of identity politics and criminality. The key actors are insurgency groups, criminal gangs, diaspora groups, ethnic parties, international aid organizations, mercenaries, as well as regular armies. One of the most interesting, perhaps counter-intuitive, observations of this literature is the idea that international aid and intervention by the "international community" exacerbates new wars: "mafia-style economies and protracted internal warfare are often a result of international interventions which are actually claiming to foster the establishment of market structures and democracy."[7]

The social and economic context of new wars is characterized by weak or failed states, a collapse of the formal economy, and rivalry between criminal groups over natural resources or illegal commercial activities. Globalization is an important component to the political economy of new wars, and the starting point is that "the age of globalization is characterized by a gradual erosion of state authority" and accompanying "violent war economies."[8] As Kaldor puts it, "the processes known as globalization are breaking up the socio-economic divisions that defined the patterns of politics which characterized the modern period. The new type of warfare has to be understood in terms of this global dislocation."[9] Thus, neoliberal economic forces have resulted in a weakening of state capacity and a weakening of the provision of public goods. So, "the 'failure' of the state is accompanied by a growing privatization of violence ... the new wars are characterized by a multiplicity of types of fighting units both public and private, state and non-state, or some kind of mixture."[10]

In the most extreme cases, the state itself is criminalized as it becomes little more than a means to exploit state revenue and natural resources. Competition for control of the state is a competition for control over the power to exploit. The decline of state legitimacy and power gives rise to rivalry amongst non-state actors and the distinction between public and private authority is blurred. Within this context, violence is effectively privatized as the state's control and monopoly over violence declines as an extension of the erosion of state capacity: "The new wars occur in situations in which state revenues decline because of the decline of the economy as well as the spread of criminality, corruption and inefficiency, violence is increasingly privatized both as a result of growing organized crime and the emergence of paramilitary groups, and political legitimacy is disappearing."[11] This is a "globalized war economy": fighting units finance themselves through plunder and the black market or through external assistance. These are sustained through violence so "a war logic is built into the functioning of the economy."[12] According to Duffield this logic is self-sustaining and rational, rather than an expression of breakdown or chaos.[13]

Much of the new wars literature has argued that economic motives and greed are a primary underlying driving force of violent conflict. Indeed, the violence itself creates opportunities for entrepreneurship and profit; the continuation of violence rather than military "victory" is often the objective. In this context Keen has suggested that:

> Conflict can create war economies, often in the regions controlled by rebels or warlords and linked to international trading networks; members of armed gangs can benefit from looting; and regimes can use violence to deflect opposition, reward supporters or maintain their access to resources. Under these circumstances, ending civil wars becomes difficult. Winning may not be desirable: the point of war may be precisely the legitimacy which it confers on actions that in peacetime would be punishable as crimes.[14]

This has been put into the context of globalization by other analysts, which "creates new opportunities for the elites of competing factions to pursue their economic agendas through trade, investment, and migration ties, both legal and illegal, to neighboring states and to more distant, industrialized economies."[15] Some authors specifically relate civil war in certain societies to the intensification of transnational commerce in recent decades, drawing a distinct picture of conflict in the late twentieth century.[16] Paul Collier argues that "economic agendas appear to be central to understanding why civil wars start. Conflicts are far more likely to be caused by economic opportunities than by grievance."[17] Not surprisingly, there is evidence that many civil wars are therefore caused and fuelled not by poverty but by a "resource curse."[18]

In sum, globalization represents two processes in the new wars thesis. It underpins changes in the state – particularly an erosion of state authority and public goods – which can make societies vulnerable to conflict. Second, globalization generates increased opportunities for economic motives in civil war as a result of transborder trade, both legal and illegal.

The social and economic context is also closely linked to the primary motives of protagonists and combatants in conflict. The new wars literature focuses mainly on economic and identity-based motives. Snow suggests that "new internal wars" seem "less principled in political terms, less focused on the attainment of some political ideal ... these wars often appear to be little more than rampages by groups within states against one another with little or no ennobling purpose or outcome."[19] Indeed, the lack of clear political objectives, and the absence of a discernible political ideology to justify actions is a common theme of new wars analysis. Kaldor suggests that "The goals of the new wars are about identity politics in contrast to the geo-political or ideological goals of earlier wars."[20]

The new wars thesis also makes certain claims regarding the social, material and human impact of conflict, including patterns of human victimization and forced human displacement. This includes absolute numbers of fatalities and displaced people, deliberate or inadvertent targeting of civilians, and the relative proportion of combatant to civilian casualties. The literature on new wars is unanimous in the view that "an unhappy trend of contemporary conflict has been the increased vulnerability of civilians, often involving their deliberate targeting."[21] Thus, new wars are characterized by the deliberate targeting and forcible displacement of civilians as a primary objective of violence, and the "importance of extreme and conspicuous atrocity."[22] Systematic rape as a weapon of war, ethnic cleansing, the use of child soldiers, and a high proportion of civilian to combatant casualties are prominent features of these civil wars. This is often explained as a function of the changing context of violent conflict: that is, the objective of combatants is not necessarily victory over a rival political force or agenda, but the continuation of violence itself. As Snow points out, "In places like Bosnia, Somalia, Liberia, and Rwanda, the armed forces never seemed to fight one another; instead, what passed for 'military action' was the more or less systematic murder and terrorizing of civilian populations."[23]

The Carnegie Commission on Preventing Deadly Conflict described the "strategies and tactics that deliberately target women, children, the poor, and the weak," claiming that "In some wars today, 90 percent of those killed in conflict are non-combatants, compared with less than 15 percent when the century began."[24] A number of analysts concur with this.[25] In terms of forms of warfare, "Behavior that was proscribed according to the classical rules of warfare and codified in the laws of war in the late nineteenth century and early twentieth century, such as atrocities against non-combatants, sieges, destruction of historic monuments, etc., now constitutes an essential component of the strategies of the new mode of warfare."[26] The UN High Commission for Refugees "State of the World's Refugees Report" follows a similar line of argument in terms of forced human displacement, which is closely related to victimization in times of war. It suggests that there have been "changing dynamics of displacement" and describes "the changing nature of conflict."[27] It observes the "devastating civilian toll of *recent* wars," stating that "in the post-Cold War period, civil wars and communal conflicts have involved wide-scale, deliberate targeting of civilian populations."[28] The UNHCR states that "Refugee movements are no longer side effects of conflict, but in many cases are central to the objectives and tactics of war."[29] Again, amongst many academics, a common theme is that "the global dynamics of flight and refuge are changing" in the context of the "changing nature of conflict."[30]

The data presented by the UNHCR appeared to support this by the end of the 1990s. As of 31 December 1999 the total number of people "of concern" to the UNHCR – comprising refugees, asylum seekers, returned refugees, and internally displaced persons – was over 22 million. The estimated number of refugees by region, 1950–99, shows an almost perfectly linear increase in refugees from 1951 to the end of the century.[31] Kaldor concludes that "the distinctions between external barbarity and domestic civility, between the combatant as the legitimate bearer of arms and the non-combatant, between the soldier or policeman and the criminal, are breaking down."[32]

The reality of "new wars"

Cases of "new wars" abound. The Bosnian civil war in the 1990s was a quintessential example. The fighting was characterized by forced human displacement, severe human rights violations, ethnic cleansing, paramilitary groups, and national or ethnic identity politics. The environment was characterized by the collapse of the formal economy and public authority, and the exploitation of this environment by organized criminal groups. Conflicts in Burundi, Sierra Leone, Chechnya, Somalia, Afghanistan, Nigeria, Cambodia, Liberia, Congo, and Angola, amongst others, reflected to differing degrees some combination of these factors in the 1990s.

However, as I argue elsewhere, the distinction between "contemporary" forms of conflict and wars of earlier times is exaggerated and in some instances does not stand up to scrutiny, especially when drawing upon historical material.[33] In particular, the extent to which contemporary forms of organized violence reflect new patterns in terms of actors, objectives, human impact, and the political economy and social structure of conflict, is questionable. Moreover, the tendency in the new wars scholarship to identify common patterns in "contemporary" civil conflicts ignores important differences amongst them. Much of this is not new; all of the factors that characterize new wars have been present, to varying degrees, throughout the last 100 years.

In terms of the incidence of types of wars throughout the twentieth century and into the twenty-first century, civil war has always been more frequent than inter-state war. Moreover, most sources indicate that both inter-state and civil war has shown a marked decline since the early 1990s.[34] Uppsala University's Conflict Data Project suggests: "the recent decline in armed conflict after the end of the Cold War has now brought the probability of a country being in conflict to a level corresponding to the end of the 1950s and lower than at any later time during the Cold War."[35] The new wars thesis argues that patterns of victimization and human impact are peculiar to the late twentieth century, and are worsening. However, there is little evidence to substantiate this claim. Atrocities have been a feature of all wars – both civil and inter-state – throughout the twentieth century and earlier, although certain *types* of violent conflict have reflected higher levels of deliberate civilian victimization. Similarly, forced human displacement – both collateral and deliberate – has also long been a feature of violent conflict, and ethnic cleansing is not peculiar to the wars of the 1990s.

Nevertheless, the literature on the "new wars" provides a service in explaining patterns of contemporary conflict and especially in drawing attention to the social and economic aspects of conflict and the relationship between security and development. It also focuses attention upon the shortcomings of the institutionalized multilateral approaches to conflict, which are based upon a state-centric rationale.

The UN's record

The UN Charter is largely premised upon a conventional peace and security challenge: preventing and addressing war between autonomous sovereign states. According to a narrow reading of the Charter, member states are not obliged to act unless a situation is deemed to be a threat to international peace and security. This has not prevented

UN involvement in civil wars, but it has made the involvement selective and sometimes ambivalent. It has also arguably led to questionable results. Two schools of thought have emerged regarding the structural capacity – or incapacity – of the UN in relation to the challenges of civil war and state failure. Paul Heinbecker asserted that "a glaring contradiction" exists between the most basic purposes of the UN, to save succeeding generations from war, and the UN's tenet of state sovereignty, since most contemporary wars occur within states.[36] In contrast, others argue that the Charter provides a sound basis for addressing current and future security challenges.[37]

The history of the UN certainly illustrates the challenges of civil war. The UN did not take a major role in the post-colonial conflicts in Africa (Angola, Mozambique, Sudan, Ethiopia, Nigeria-Biafra, Rwanda, Burundi), Asia (India, Pakistan, Bangladesh, Sri Lanka, Vietnam, Indonesia, Cambodia, Laos) and the Middle East. Similarly, in Latin America (for example Nicaragua, Colombia, Guatemala, El Salvador, Argentina and Chile), while there was more UN involvement, it was only after many years of violence. After the Cold War, conflicts in Sierra Leone, Somalia, Chechnya, Afghanistan, Iraq, the Democratic Republic of the Congo, Rwanda and Bosnia – amongst others – largely defied the UN as an effective peacemaker, at least for some years.

Yet during the Cold War it was not the legal limitations of the UN Charter which obstructed the organization from playing a significant role, but rather the politics of the Cold War and the lack of political will of members to commit themselves to involvement in civil wars. However, member states did have an interest, on occasions, in containing civil conflicts and preventing them from escalating, or preventing them from drawing in superpower involvement which could have more threatening implications.

The Security Council, especially after the Cold War, has become increasingly involved in civil wars. Peace operations were introduced into many conflicted or post-conflict situations, such as Bosnia, Croatia, Macedonia, East Timor, Cambodia, Tajikistan, El Salvador, Guatemala, Haiti, Sierra Leone, Angola, Central African Republic, Congo, Liberia, Mozambique, Namibia, Rwanda, and Somalia.

However, the record, in terms of building peaceful stable societies, has been mixed. The UN Secretary-General wrote in 2005 that: "Our record of success in mediating and implementing peace agreements is sadly blemished by some devastating failures. Indeed, several of the most violent and tragic episodes of the 1990s occurred after the negotiation of peace agreements ... Roughly half of all countries that emerge from war lapse back into violence within five years."[38] In the

1990s, one principal reason for this poor record was the approach adopted by international peacekeeping. Peacekeeping evolved during the Cold War as a mechanism to contain conflict mainly but not exclusively between states, in order to bolster a cease-fire agreement and give confidence to conflict settlement efforts. It was also a mechanism which would help to prevent a conflict from spreading and threatening regional or international security.

Occasionally, peacekeeping forces were also introduced to facilitate the withdrawal of an intervening power. The first United Nations Emergency Force (UNEF I, 1956–1967), for example, was established to secure the cessation of conflict, including the withdrawal of France, Israel and the United Kingdom from Egyptian territory after the Suez War. After the withdrawal, it served as a buffer between the Egyptian and Israeli forces. UNEF II was established in October 1973 to support the cease-fire between Egypt and Israeli, following the war, and control the buffer zones established under those agreements. The UN Operation in the Congo (ONUC) was established in 1960 after independence plunged the country into civil war. It sought to ensure the withdrawal of Belgian forces, to assist the Government in maintaining law and order and to provide technical assistance. ONUC subsequently sought to maintain the territorial integrity of the Congo.

So called "classical peacekeeping" was based upon a number of principles: it should be impartial and neutral in relation to the interests of the local parties, it must have the consent of the host government, and it must use force only as a last resort and in self-defense. Peacekeeping during the Cold War represented an important form of innovation. However, when the same normative principles were applied to pacify civil wars after the Cold War the results were dubious in settings such as Bosnia, Somalia, Haiti and Rwanda.

There was certainly a conscious effort to adapt peacekeeping operations to the changing circumstances. Typically, post-Cold War UN peace operations have involved peacekeeping, peacemaking and peacebuilding. In accordance with wider conceptions of peace and human security these activities are also considered increasingly within a comprehensive model. As the Secretary-General proclaimed, "[t]he second generation of peace-keeping is certain to involve not only military but also political, economic, social, humanitarian and environmental dimensions, all in need of a unified and integrated approach."[39] After the relative success of UN operations in facilitating the end of Cold War conflicts in El Salvador and Nicaragua, the UN became involved – perhaps too hastily – in situations of civil conflict elsewhere in the world where the same resolve for peace did not exist.

UN involvement in civil wars has had enormous political and practical hazards – especially if fighting is still occurring – which have effectively invalidated traditional peacekeeping principles. The commitment and consent of the parties may not be stable. The parties are factions rather than states, and may still be involved in a struggle: their attitude towards the UN will be a result of what they believe they can achieve from the UN operation, and that may change from day to day. Their cooperation will vary, their consent may be withdrawn, such as in Cambodia, the former Yugoslavia, Angola and Somalia. Armed groups are not subject to the international instruments of leverage and sanction that states are, so their accountability and respect for the "blue helmet" will be less. The UN is not dealing with regular armies, as was generally the case with the classical interpositional model of peacekeeping, but with irregulars and militias, and sometimes renegade and independent forces. The legal regime of a status of force agreement may be worthless, and traditional rules of engagement – based on self-defence in the last resort – may not be suitable.[40] The domestic political situation is invariably less stable than that of peacekeeping at the border. Moreover, the impartiality of the UN is put under severe threat as intervention invariably contributes something to the local power balance.[41] These factors have increased the political and practical hazards of involvement in civil conflict. As a result, a reassessment of UN peace operations led to a climate of caution in the Security Council after the immediate post-Cold War experimentation in the early 1990s.

The UN involvement in the former Yugoslavia epitomized the complexities and the political and practical hazards of multifaceted peace operations in conflicted societies. The involvement of the UN began with an attempt to support the Serb-Croat cease-fire in Croatia, and following that, it widened and deepened to other areas. This involved preventive activities in Macedonia, peacemaking in support of a search for a negotiated settlement, an extensive range of peacekeeping tasks, efforts to bring to trial those guilty of war crimes, a major humanitarian operation, and the first steps towards reconstruction. In Bosnia the mandate of the organization was "to help alleviate the consequences of the conflict, particularly by providing humanitarian relief to suffering civilians, and to facilitate in various forms the efforts of all parties to reach a negotiated solution."[42] Beginning with an effort to assist the distribution of humanitarian relief, the mandate of the UN Protection Force (UNPROFOR) snowballed with the passing of endless resolutions – many under or alluding to Chapter VII – which had little practical or political effect on the ground. This credibility gap between the resolutions and the will to support them frustrated and imperilled peacekeepers and the position of the UN in general. The ill-fated safe haven concept, designed to protect six chiefly Muslim areas, was perhaps the starkest manifestation of this. UNPROFOR never had the political or military support to respond effectively to the continuous violations of the areas.

In 1995, the operation reached a turning point and its flaws were blatant. Unable to protect civilians yet mandated to protect safe areas, the presence of lightly armed peacekeepers on the theoretical basis of impartial intervention prevented the possibility of more forceful measures because of their vulnerability to reprisal. Some have bluntly questioned the concept of an impartial involvement, claiming that the UN made the situation worse and a long-term solution more elusive, damaging the reputation and legitimacy of the organization.[43] To many people the experiences of UNPROFOR supported Rosalyn Higgins' observation that the provision of ancillary relief and peacekeeping without a cease-fire was a "totally unrealistic mandate" and "doomed to failure."[44] As the Brahimi Report would later reflect, in too many cases peacekeepers "tended to deploy where conflict had not resulted in victory for any side, where a military stalemate or international pressure or both had brought fighting to a halt but at least some of the parties to the conflict were not seriously committed to ending the confrontation."[45]

Bosnia was undoubtedly a part of the learning process, alongside other cases which were questionable in their outcomes – or outright failures – such as Burundi, Rwanda, Somalia, and Haiti. We can therefore put the difficulties experienced in the early 1990s into perspective. However, problems have continued, beyond the so-called "post-Cold War" period. While the UN has continued to experience difficulties or questionable results in certain cases – such as Afghanistan, Haiti, Iraq, and East Timor – other conflicts have defied significant UN involvement, such as Sudan. The reasons for this remain essentially the same: although civil wars can now easily be construed as a threat to international peace and security and thus a clear case for UN involvement can be made, member states are often reluctant to commit sufficient attention and resources to support a meaningful peacebuilding effort.

It is important to put this record into perspective, of course. The High Level Panel Report points out the "unprecedented success" of the UN, arguing that the increased involvement of the UN in civil wars since the end of the Cold War has coincided with a sharp decline in the number of such wars.[46] It argues that "In the last 15 years, more civil wars were ended through negotiation than in the previous two centuries in large part because the United Nations provided leadership, opportunities for negotiation, strategic coordination, and the resources needed for implementation. Hundreds of thousands of lives were saved, and regional and international stability were enhanced."[47]

Moral impartiality and neutrality

During the Cold War UN peace operations were premised upon the principles of neutrality, impartiality and the consent of the sovereign government and other parties. In situations where peacekeepers formed an interpolating line between national armies which had agreed to a cease-fire and to the presence of the UN, this made sense and was necessary. However, a continuation of these principles in situations of civil conflict has come close to undermining the legitimacy of the UN on a number of occasions.

In the course of the Bosnian civil war, the UN bore witness to a series of atrocities committed against non-combatants by all sides, culminating in a massacre of Bosnian Muslims in the UN "safe haven" of Srebrenica in 1995, where approximately 7,000 men and boys were killed. The UN had the authority to request air power but had consistently demonstrated unwillingness to use force. The reasons for this were legitimate: its own personnel on the ground were ill-prepared to confront the superior forces of the Serbian irregulars, and to do so would have jeopardized the safety of peacekeepers. In addition, their legal mandate was ambiguous concerning the use of force. There were also concerns that the use of force would disrupt the supply of humanitarian assistance and threaten the fragile peace process of which the UN was a supporter. We know also, of course, that many member states did not support a more robust approach by the UN; as Weiss wrote, with reference to Bosnia, the UN is "a convenient forum for governments to appear to be doing something without really doing anything substantial to thwart aggression, genocide, and forced movement of peoples."[48] The judgment of history is, however, that none of these reasons excused the organization – including senior secretariat staff – from taking a more robust stance and protecting fundamental human rights.

A similar case occurred in Rwanda. Signs that a genocide was being prepared in the country were apparently ignored in New York. Senior UN secretariat staff members failed to act upon critical signs, instead putting faith in a questionable peace process which they did not want to disrupt.[49] The report of the independent inquiry into the actions of the UN during the 1994 genocide in Rwanda concluded that "The failure by the United Nations to prevent, and subsequently, to stop the genocide in Rwanda was a failure by the United Nations system as a whole."[50] The fundamental failure was the lack of resources and political commitment devoted to Rwanda, and the persistent lack of political will by states to act. In accepting the report, Secretary-General Kofi Annan – who, at the time of the Rwanda genocide, was UN Under-Secretary-General for peacekeeping – responded:

> All of us must bitterly regret that we did not do more to prevent it. There was a United Nations force in the country at the time, but it was neither mandated nor equipped for the kind of forceful action which would have been needed to prevent or halt the genocide. On behalf of the United Nations, I acknowledge this failure and express my deep remorse.[51]

The UN – both the member states and the secretariat – learned from this experience. The landmark Brahimi report, for example, argued that peacekeepers must in all instances be given a robust mandate and the means to implement it, and they cannot be "impartial" in the face of gross violations of human rights. As the report notes, "No failure did more to damage the standing and credibility of United Nations peacekeeping in the 1990s than its reluctance to distinguish victim from aggressor."[52] Srebrenica and Rwanda represented an enormous blow to the legitimacy of the UN, and the implications of this have not been resolved.

While there was an ongoing learning process concerning the limitations and past mistakes in addressing conflict, and a better understanding of how future operations should be approached, this does not mean that the debate about the effectiveness and legitimacy of the UN's role towards civil wars is closed. The lack of agreement in the UN regarding civilian casualties (or even genocide) in the conflict in Sudan, and the resistance of the government of Sudan to a UN presence in 2006 suggested that fundamental problems remain regarding the UN's capacity to prevent or stop civil war. The time it took before the UN was effectively engaged in the Democratic Republic of the Congo after a five-year civil war was also discouraging.

Liberal peace

A further challenge for multilateralism in addressing civil wars concerns the values upon which international organizations base their peacebuilding approaches and activities. Many cease-fires and peace agreements in civil wars are initially unsuccessful or give way to renewed, and often escalated, violence. An emerging debate is exploring whether the collapse or endangerment of peace processes in recent years – in cases such as Burundi, Rwanda, East Timor, and Afghanistan – might be in part explained by the values of international peace processes which follow the values of the "liberal peace."[53] The liberal peace embraces democracy, human rights, market values and the integration of societies into globalization, self-determination and the idea of the state. Most internationally sponsored peace processes can be characterized by these values, which are assumed to be integral to modern, stable societies. This assumption also reflects a broader political wave of opinion. A number of states have placed a great deal of national foreign policy emphasis upon the promotion of democracy as a means for spreading peace within societies and internationally. While the "democratic peace thesis" has attained empirical validity in terms of peaceful relations between states, the "liberal peace" is now promoted conceptually and in policy circles as a panacea for peace and development within states.

However, the liberal peace is problematic. Democracy (in terms of liberal democracy), human rights (especially when emphasizing civil and political rights), market values, the integration of societies into globalization, self-determination and the idea of the state are not necessarily universal values. Moreover, the liberal peace is not necessarily appropriate for post-conflict or divided societies. Indeed, democracy and the market are arguably adversarial or even conflictual forces – suitable in liberal Western societies, but not universal. Therefore, so-called peacebuilding and post-conflict peacebuilding are not normatively neutral concepts, and this raises important questions concerning the role of international organizations in attempting to end civil conflict. In some circumstances, some of the values may be at odds with the attainment of sustainable peace. For example, a neoliberal economic agenda may exacerbate social and economic tensions. Democracy promotion may exacerbate political conflict and sectarian divisions. As Paris has observed, "the process of political and economic liberalization is inherently tumultuous: It can exacerbate social tensions and undermine the prospects for stable peace in the fragile conditions that typically exist in countries just emerging from civil war."[54]

Moreover, the manner in which the components of the liberal peace are being promoted is, arguably, not evenhanded and certainly loaded in favor of the market and not social justice, and in favor of stability rather than human rights and accountability. Peace processes themselves are not always equitable or "fair."

Some aspects of contemporary conflict management associated with the liberal peace – including the role of international financial institutions, NGO work, and some aspects of humanitarianism – may in fact be contributing to certain types of conflict, especially when conflicts are driven by a "war economy." Some analysts have even considered whether international organizations – which promote liberal economic values, globalization, and democracy – are inadvertently complicit in fomenting contemporary civil wars which are rooted in social and economic factors. Tirman, for example, argues that economic and political globalization is promoted and enabled by multilateral institutions. Therefore, incidences of instability and organized violence linked to social and economic factors in market-based countries raise troubling questions for multilateralism.[55] In the push for open markets multilateral institutions such as the International Monetary Fund and the World Bank have insisted on certain economic and political reforms in developing countries that may in fact have induced instabilities that are conducive to civil war.

Troubling questions are emerging regarding the value system which underpins the approach of the international community towards peacebuilding – and which imbues international organizations. Is the liberal peace being promoted in societies in which it may not be entirely appropriate for social, cultural, or economic reasons? Or is the liberal peace a manifestation of a hegemonic agenda? Donor – generally Western – states certainly want the free market in post-conflict societies but their commitment to justice or genuine democracy is less clear; similarly they are interested in an outcome (which often simply means stability) which fits their geostrategic interests. There is real concern that "post-conflict" peacebuilding programs sow the seeds of their own failure by exacerbating social tensions that resulted in violent conflict in the first place, and that different components of the liberal peace cannot be reconciled.

Democracy promotion

The clearest expression of the international community's embrace of the liberal peace is in the promotion of democracy. The ideal of democratic governance underpins much of the contemporary work of the UN. The founding of the organization, in addition to being an alliance against aggression, was premised upon the belief that stable, peaceful conditions within states underpin peaceful and stable relations between states. The range of democracy assistance activities is wide. It covers organizing, conducting and validating elections; developing civil society and political parties; bolstering the rule of law, judicial institutions and security architecture; strengthening accountability, oversight and transparency; enhancing legislative training and effectiveness; and civic education and protecting human rights. Bottom-up democracy assistance focuses on strengthening civil society, public awareness and the capacity for societal deliberation. It is often implemented through local and international non-governmental actors. In contrast, top-down assistance is implemented through governments and concentrates more on formal institutions and processes.

The UN is involved in all such approaches to the promotion of democracy. The normative basis for such activities includes the UN Charter, the Universal Declaration of Human Rights and other major human rights instruments. Until relatively recently these legal instruments did not imply an international democratic entitlement or a mandate for democracy promotion. However, the end of the Cold War opened up political space and an increased opportunity to address democracy and human rights issues at the international level, and a growing acceptance of a wider conception of peace and security which includes issues of governance inside states. Since the end of the Cold War almost half of the UN's members have requested the organization's assistance in conducting elections.

No form of intervention is value free. Different actors involved in democracy promotion – global and regional multilateral organizations, non-governmental organizations, individual governments – approach their work with different ideological and normative premises. Democracy is "rule for and by the people," but there are different emphases in its application, and these differences are reflected in the doctrine and practice of actors involved in democracy promotion. US democracy promotion has a clear agenda, for example.[56] Ideologically, it reflects a commitment to liberal democracy, free market economics and formal democratic procedures, rather than welfare outcomes. It also clearly reflects a commitment to US economic and strategic interests. Countries outside the US sphere of interest are less likely to receive assistance than those within, and the decision on which political actors receive assistance reflects the nature of their relationship with the US and their ideological credentials. This is not the promotion of a "level playing field"; it intentionally privileges certain political ideas and actors above others for both pragmatic and ideological reasons. Other national democracy promotion programs – such as those of West European states – also have their own agenda.

112   Civil war, state failure & peacebuilding

In theory, the UN is free from such an overtly ideological approach. The UN's Agenda for Democratization stated that the UN should not promote a specific model of democracy: "to do so could be counterproductive to the process of democratization that, in order to take root and to flourish, must derive from the society itself. Each society must be able to choose the form, pace and character of its democratization process."[57] The UN's approach is supposedly sensitive to cultural difference as well as, generally, politically impartial. The UN pursues its work with a view to building the capacity of communities to develop their own forms of participation and collective decision-making, in the context of indigenous social conditions.[58]

Nevertheless, all substantial forms of intervention have an impact upon the future of a political community – if not, there would be no point in undertaking them. The concepts of national representation, equality, individual rights of citizenship, and secular and accountable forms of civil authority – all represented in the UN's approach to democracy – are premised upon the liberal vein of democracy. In some settings, this is a departure from traditional structures, including family, clan and religious authority. Parakh has argued that: "the liberal principle of individuation and other liberal ideas are culturally and historically specific. As such a political system based on them cannot claim universal validity."[59] Building liberal democracy may therefore require deep changes in societies and disruptions in the status quo, a process that can attract resistance.

The impact of external actors upon local politics is one of the most difficult questions relating to democracy promotion and assistance. In engaging the local political situation inside a target state, UN actors and the international community in general are faced with the conundrum of influencing local politics to allow the people to have a proper choice. Most people recognize that it is not simply the process that matters, but also the results. Ideally, the design of the process will marginalize militants and encourage pluralism and inclusive politics. The UN can be in a difficult position as it deals with local political actors, some of which may have dubious democratic credentials but have influence and thus cannot be ignored.

In democracy assistance and promotion the UN can find itself in the position of supporting various activities which may not all be perfectly complementary, especially in conflict-prone societies. For example, the democracy that Burundi experienced – including the elections of 1993 – had a questionable impact at that time. Indeed, elections may well have played a role in the ensuing instability and violence because they exacerbated an atmosphere of divisive political competition in a tense social environment. Ahmedou Ould-Abdallah served as the UN Secretary-General's special representative for Burundi between 1993 and 1995. He reflected that "majority rule simply could not be sustained given the realities of Burundi's political and security situation," and "in many African countries the introduction of democracy should be allied with a ten- to twenty-year transitional period of constitutional power sharing. Democratic habits and traditions are not formed overnight."[60] While this may be unduly pessimistic, the challenges of building meaningful democracy in societies such as Iraq and Afghanistan in the short term are demonstrable. To ignore these challenges and insist upon democracy prematurely brings enormous risks. Yet democracy is integral to the UN's peacebuilding agenda.

There is often pressure from the international community for countries in which the UN is involved to move towards democracy as a matter of priority, as if this is an end in itself. However, there is evidence that this can be in tension with other public needs – such as peacebuilding, reconciliation, efficient provision of public services, perhaps even economic reconstruction – especially in conflict-prone situations. Ill-timed or poorly designed elections in delicate political situations can be hazardous – as the experience of Angola and Burundi demonstrates. They can exacerbate existing tensions, result in support for extremists or encourage patterns of voting that reflect wartime allegiances, as in Bosnia. As Chesterman notes, "Bosnians elected to power the same nationalist parties that had torn their country apart in the first place."[61]

An election does not necessarily resolve deep-seated problems, particularly when some of the situations in which the UN finds itself facilitating or promoting democracy – such as East Timor, Iraq, Kosovo and Afghanistan – are societies deeply traumatized by conflict. In Iraq, for example, elections were divisive in 2005: they highlighted political, religious and ethnic divisions. They also exacerbated the insurgency, because the insurgents resisted any public initiative organized under what they claimed was an illegitimate interim government; because they feared that a successful election would further marginalize them; and because they judged that the inherent volatility of an election campaign in such circumstances would be a conducive environment for one of their goals: to foment civil war. Perhaps most sensitively, though, elections threatened the minority Sunni community – in a dominant position under Saddam Hussein before his fall – with marginalization as a result of majority Shiite mobilization.

But there are significant benefits to holding elections even when the circumstances are not ideal. They are a step towards democracy and form a milestone in the post-conflict transition. They strengthen the sense of "ownership" amongst the public concerning the country's political destiny, something which is desperately needed. Elections can also marginalize the extremists as many political actors – including some radical groups – participate in the political process and turn their backs upon violence.

Nevertheless, the limitations of the liberal peace model in rebuilding war-torn societies are illustrated in a number of cases. If we consider the cases where the UN has had a major electoral or democracy-assistance role – Cambodia, Bosnia, West Sahara, Angola, El Salvador, Eritrea, Haiti, Mozambique, Nicaragua, South Africa, Liberia, Kosovo, East Timor – the record is not wholly positive. The extent to which durable institutions have been created in some of these cases is doubtful. The quality of democracy – of accountability, transparency in political decision-making, an ethos of participation and inclusion, and a constructive civil society – is also questionable. In some cases these elements are completely absent, in the context of violence, nationalist/ethnic extremism, and corruption. Yet one could argue that the problems in these high-profile cases do not necessarily undermine the liberal premise, because the volatility of many of these cases hardly allowed the liberal approach to take root. Looking at all countries in which the UN had a role, the record is somewhat better (for example, considering Freedom House's assessments of these countries).[62]

Huntington's study of "third wave" democracies found that by the late 1980s external observers had become a "familiar and indispensable presence" in almost all transitional elections.[63] Yet beyond the observation of elections, the major democracy-assistance operations demonstrate the limitations of outside parties attempting to install democracy. UN assistance is most effective when applied to situations where a tradition of democracy is already ingrained, even if latent, where a certain level of social stability exists, and where facilitation and confidence building are necessary to ensure trust and validation. In major operations in divided or post-conflict societies UN involvement seems fruitful only when a convergence of forces – both within the society and internationally – coalesce around a democratic future and when the new rules of the game are accepted. Such a convergence was not present for Angola in 1992, but was for Namibia in 1989.

It is important to be realistic about what any international actor can achieve in terms of democracy promotion. It is reasonable to suggest that people everywhere have an inherent desire to have at least some control over their lives. Having a say in the organization of their communities would therefore seem to be a universal human desire. If the UN is facilitating this process, then it is quite possible for the organization to have a significant impact in helping a society move forward to democracy. But the conditions under which the UN works are of critical importance. The modest progress towards consolidated democracy in many of the countries in which the UN has been involved seems to support this cautious conclusion. The social and economic context, the security situation and the policies and attitudes of powerful political actors are decisive factors. Yet even when democratic "convergence" occurs, democracy does not necessarily take root because of inadequate capacity and institutions, lack of trust, and lack of resources. This is where the UN and other external actors can have a real impact, by facilitating local will for democracy.

Conclusion: peacebuiding as a holistic concept

Many cease-fires and peace agreements in civil wars are initially unsuccessful and give way to renewed violence. In other cases, peace processes have become interminably protracted: lengthy and circular negotiations in which concessions are rare, and even if agreements are reached, they falter at the implementation phase. State building and peacebuilding processes are also often subject to outbreaks of violence, as recent experience in Haiti, Afghanistan, Iraq, Kosovo and East Timor illustrates. Given the huge material and human costs of a failed peace process, the consolidation of conflict settlement and dealing with threats to peacebuilding are critical challenges for the international community. After a history of painful experience in cases such as Angola and Bosnia the importance of this was finally recognized with the creation of the UN Peacebuilding Commission in 2006.[64] This new organ was established to improve effectiveness and coordination amongst all agencies involved in peacebuilding, peacekeeping, disarmament and demobilization.

The UN Security Council Resolution of December 2005, which laid the groundwork for the new UN Peacebuilding Commission, represents a milestone in UN institutional mechanisms for supporting peace and security. It observed the need for a "coordinated, coherent and integrated approach to post-conflict peacebuilding and reconciliation" and prepared the way for an organ that will bring together relevant actors to marshal resources and to advise on integrated strategies for peacebuilding.[65] The remit of the Commission is progressive, based upon the idea that development, peace and security and human rights are interlinked and mutually reinforcing, and stressing the importance of women and civil society in peacebuilding.

However, the limited remit given to the Peacebuilding Commission indicates that caution is called for and that a radical change in thinking amongst states towards civil war is unlikely. The background to the establishment of the Commission gives an illustration of this. The Report of the High Level Panel, endorsed by the UN Secretary-General, suggested that the core functions of the Peacebuilding Commission should include identifying "countries which are under stress and risk sliding towards State collapse" and organizing, in partnership with the national Government, "proactive assistance in preventing that process from developing further." However, the 2005 World Summit Outcome Final Document prescribed more modest – and less proactive – ambitions for the new Peacebuilding Commission. The main purposes of the new Commission will be "to bring together all the relevant actors to marshal resources and to advise on and propose integrated strategies for post-conflict peacebuilding and recovery." The question remains: what responsibility does the international community – through the United Nations and regional organizations – have in intervening in societies which are sliding into conflict and state failure?

7 Terrorism

Formalized multilateralism has a mixed record as a framework through which states coordinate their efforts to address terrorism. From an institutionalist theoretical perspective, terrorism presents peculiar challenges to collective action, for a number of reasons. Political and legal differences on what constitutes terrorism have hindered agreement on a definition of terrorism. This, in turn, has hindered agreement on how to address terrorism. Many states have also been reluctant to address terrorism in public international forums; terrorist challenges have often related to sensitive "domestic" issues that states have generally not wished to subject to international scrutiny. Some states themselves have been directly or indirectly involved in the perpetration of terrorism, making the sharing of information on terrorism difficult in a multilateral context, and commitments amongst states of questionable credibility. States have disagreed on how much emphasis or priority should be given to collective efforts to tackle terrorism, in contrast to other pressing problems such as poverty and disease. And there has been difficulty reaching agreement on how states can respond to terrorism both unilaterally and in cooperation with other states. The historical record of the UN's response to terrorism, as Edward Luck has observed, has been "tentative, halting, even ambivalent."[1]

The terrorist attacks of 11 September 2001 and the ensuing "war on terror" made terrorism unavoidable for the UN, and also most regional organizations. In the wake of those attacks most international organizations – and particularly those with any political, economic or security role – have taken significant steps, with varying effect, towards developing counterterrorism strategies. As the UN Secretary-General stated:

> Terrorism is a global threat with global effects; its consequences affect every aspect of the United Nations agenda from development

to peace to human rights and the rule of law ... By its very nature, terrorism is an assault on the fundamental principles of law, order, human rights, and the peaceful settlement of disputes upon which the United Nations is established ... The United Nations has an indispensable role to play in providing the legal and organizational framework within which the international campaign against terrorism can unfold.[2]

The UN Security Council has become a key focal point for collective action. Under the leadership of the US, it acted with speed and unity in promoting a norm of condemnation against terrorism and coordinating member state policy, passing landmark resolutions and creating a significant new counterterrorist apparatus. The activity of the Security Council has involved targeting state support for terrorism and the growing threat of non-state, "privatized" terrorism. The UN in general has made great strides towards a coordination, capacity building and in particular a normative role in addressing terrorism.

Boulden and Weiss have argued that: "As the organization with the primary responsibility for the maintenance of international peace and security, the UN should be at the forefront of the international response to terrorism."[3] However, a number of questions remain about the long-term prospects of the UN in this area. Does the UN have a strategy and a doctrine for addressing terrorism? Is it successful? Is there institutional coherence in the UN for addressing terrorism? Is there a "structural challenge": does the structure of the UN or international law limit the effectiveness of the UN in addressing terrorism, as an unconventional security challenge driven by non-state actors? Is the UN a part of (and thus problematized by) the "war on terror," a controversial approach dominated by the US? Is terrorism dominating the multilateral agenda and resulting in the alienation of developing countries? Is there really a "new security dilemma" as a result of changing strategic demands?[4] Is the UN taking a balanced approach to tackling terrorism, including addressing "root causes," and also upholding its commitment to human rights? Many assessments of the UN's role in addressing terrorism are broadly positive.[5] However, according to one judgment on the organization's role in this area, "the response of the UN has not been sufficiently effective in countering continuing attacks by terrorist cells that have proven adaptable and capable of exploiting gaps in law enforcement, border security, and domestic intelligence."[6] What explains such differences of opinion?

Terrorism and the UN

There have been three phases in the UN's involvement in terrorism: during the Cold War the organization was characterized by ambivalence; after the Cold War, in the 1990s, consensus emerged in the Security Council especially in addressing state-sponsored terrorism; after 9/11, the UN took a particularly active – although not completely unproblematic – leadership role in strengthening norms against terrorism and coordinating national counterterrorism policy.

Terrorism is not a new challenge for international organizations. The League of Nations produced a draft Convention for the Prevention and Punishment of Terrorism and a Convention for the Creation of an International Criminal Court to cover terrorism. Neither convention went into effect. In the UN, states have sought to coordinate their policies since the early 1960s through conventions and resolutions. However, the UN has not, until recently, embraced a broad based strategy for addressing terrorism. The reasons for this are basically political; the constraints are not an inevitable result of the structure or legal framework of the UN. First, debate and decision-making at the UN regarding terrorism has been characterized by political and legal disagreements on what constitutes terrorism. Subsequently, it has been difficult to reach consensus on a workable definition of terrorism and thus agreement on how to address it. Disagreement has focused on whether terrorism includes actions by states, in addition to non-state actors, and whether the use of violence can be permissible in certain circumstances.

Defining terrorism is an analytical as well as a political challenge. From an analytical perspective Laqueur has stated that generalizations with regard to terrorism "are almost always misleading."[7] This has led to the academic study of terrorism being described as "descriptively rich but analytically barren."[8] Indeed, to use one term – "terrorism" – to describe a very wide array of phenomena is very problematic from a methodological perspective. The broadest definition of terrorism encapsulates a range of factors: the deliberate and illegal use of violence with no regard for – or deliberately targeting – civilians; a political objective; and the intention to exert influence and change upon third parties. From a political perspective a particular point of contention has been whether the definition of terrorism should exclude the inherent right of resistance of people living under occupation or colonial oppression. That is, should people living under oppression – who have no recourse to democratic or peaceful political action – have a right to use violence, even against civilians, in order to make their voice heard and seek freedom? A significant proportion of countries in the developing world and in the Middle East have certainly had sympathy and solidarity with people in territories under colonial control or occupation. Therefore, "national liberation" organizations such as the South West African People's Organization (SWAPO) in Namibia, the Front for the Liberation of Mozambique (FRELIMO), the African National Congress (ANC) in South Africa, and the Palestine Liberation Organization (PLO) which may have been associated with violent activities were never censored by the majority in the UN during their struggle for independence. The UN majority has notably endorsed the "inherent" right of the people of Palestine to struggle against the "illegal" occupation by Israel, even when this has involved violence.

As a result, the UN – and especially the General Assembly – has historically tended to focus more on condemning the causes of terrorism rather than developing a strategy of tackling terrorism itself. A typical Assembly resolution in 1985

> urges all States unilaterally and in co-operation with other States, as well as relevant United Nations organs, to contribute to the progressive elimination of causes underlying international terrorism and to pay special attention to all situations, including colonialism, racism and situations involving mass and flagrant violations of human rights and fundamental freedoms and those involving alien occupation, that may give rise to international terrorism and may endanger international peace and security.[9]

The moral ambivalence of the UN majority towards certain types of terrorism and the obvious sympathies harbored by many member states towards resistance – including violence – in colonial territories and occupied Palestine has alienated many Western states. Indeed, conservative commentators have accused the UN of not only turning a blind eye to terrorism but actively supporting terrorists.[10] Of course, the Western members of the UN have also indulged in double standards when considering which "terrorists" to condemn and which "liberation movements" to support. The result of this has been that discussions on terrorism have been extremely politicized and divisive, especially until the end of the Cold War (and perhaps until 9/11).

A second, and related, historical problem which has undermined the UN's effectiveness and legitimacy in addressing terrorism concerns the fact that some states themselves have been directly or indirectly involved in the perpetration of terrorism. This has made it difficult to produce significant, binding norms for combating terrorism or to coordinate state policy to this end (apart from the narrow remit of the international conventions). It is reasonable to suggest that an organization which represents, on the basis of "sovereign equality," states which have supported terrorism would not enjoy the confidence of all members in addressing the challenge. International agreements forged in this context lack legitimacy. John Bolton argued that "experience has shown that treaties and agreements are an insufficient check against state sponsors of terrorism."[11] This reality has also made the sharing of information and intelligence on terrorism difficult, or even impossible, in a multilateral context.

A third reason for the mixed record of the UN and many other international and regional organizations in addressing terrorism results from the reluctance that many states have to address terrorism in public international forums when it may relate to sensitive "domestic" issues. Addressing terrorist issues in a multilateral context might introduce unwelcome opinions to the agenda – or even sympathy towards the "terrorist" group in question. It might constrain the action of governments in dealing with the terrorist challenge; and it might have the unintended and equally unwelcome effect of gaining international recognition – or even support – for the terrorist organization in question. The United Kingdom, for example, was reluctant to accept any UN involvement in the terrorism connected with the separatist struggle in Northern Ireland. India, similarly, has been reluctant to put the question of terrorism in Kashmir on the international agenda for fear of giving Kashmiri separatists an international platform from which they could promote their cause. Indeed, India – and other states facing similar separatist challenges which have generated terrorism – regards the efforts of adversaries in the Kashmir dispute to put the issue onto the UN agenda as a ploy aimed at internationalizing the dispute and strengthening the position of separatists.

Fourth, multilateral approaches to terrorism have been limited for the simple reason that there has been difficulty reaching agreement, from a legal perspective, on how states can respond to terrorism both unilaterally and in cooperation with other states. Under international law and according to the UN Charter, states may use military force in self-defense, collective self-defense, and when authorized to do so by the UN Security Council in response to a threat to international peace and security. Customary international law and the UN Charter are based upon a traditional model of international security: preventing and if necessary addressing military aggression by one state against another. The legal framework governing the response of states to terrorism committed against their interests or in their territory is ambiguous, especially when it involves international terrorism. Obviously, states have a right to respond to terrorism within their borders. However, responses which involve action in the territory of other states or in international territory or airspace are more complicated. A number of states have taken direct military action against terrorist organizations in international territory or in the territory of other states on an *ad hoc* basis. Since 9/11, a number of states have argued that they have a right, as an extension of self-defense, and in the interests of international security, to take coercive action within the territory of other states against terrorist organizations. The argument increasingly aired is that if states are unwilling or unable to prevent their territory being used as a base for terrorist activity, they forfeit their claim to territorial inviolability, at least temporarily.

State sponsorship of terrorism and harboring terrorist organizations are much less tolerated since 9/11 than during the Cold War, when states could hide behind the veil of sovereignty quite effectively. Nevertheless, states differ in their opinion of how they may respond to international terrorism in principle and as a matter of pragmatism. In principle, some states – most notably the US, Australia, Israel and Russia – have declared a right to unilaterally pursue terrorists operating from within the sovereignty of other states, including the right to use military force without the consent of the target state. Most other countries, however, continue to respect the sovereignty of states and would prefer to address the foreign terrorist challenge in cooperation with the target state. And where the state in question is recalcitrant, most states would still prefer to address the issue within the framework of international law. But the issue of pragmatism is probably the biggest challenge in gaining multilateral agreement on how states can respond to terrorism. While the norm of condemnation of terrorism is growing, states still view terrorism through the prism of their perceived national interest. Allies which might be associated with terrorism – such as Saudi Arabia and Pakistan, in the case of the US – are much less likely to receive the opprobrium of the US than "rogue" states such as Cuba, Iran, North Korea, Sudan, Syria and until recently Libya.

Major powers therefore are reluctant to support powerful and binding multilateral norms which coordinate action on terrorism because they are wary of committing themselves to unforeseen circumstances. *Ad hoc* responses, in line with national interests, have characterized the positions of leading states. There is evidence that this is finally giving way to a strong general norm against terrorism, but differences amongst states in principle and according to their pragmatic calculations remain a major challenge in the multilateral coordination of states.

For much of the Cold War formal multilateral coordination regarding terrorism was stilted, even when international terrorism increased in the 1960s and 1970s. The approach of the General Assembly was politicized by broader disputes and bloc maneuvering, and the Security Council was "slow and hesitant."[12] Much of the most high-profile terrorism – including hijackings of planes and ships, assaults upon airports, kidnappings and assassinations – was associated with the Israel-Palestine conflict. Security Council Resolution 286 called upon states to "take all possible legal steps to prevent further hijackings or any other interference with international civil air travel."

However the infamous 1972 Munich Olympic atrocity – along with other terrorist outrages in the same year – did not galvanize the membership of the UN into a united front against terrorism. Indeed, it had the effect of illuminating the divisions which existed. A draft resolution submitted by the non-aligned states – and vetoed by the US – did not mention terrorism or the Munich deaths, and further drafts failed to bridge the differences which existed between states which wished to focus upon terrorism and those which insisted upon addressing the sources of terrorism as a part of a broader political solution.[13] The General Assembly, perhaps inevitably, provided no solution to this standoff. At that time a form of wording emerged which was reiterated in many subsequent resolutions and declarations of the General Assembly and which typified the ambivalence of the UN majority – or the belief that terrorism is a manifestation of injustice and oppression. It focused upon "the underlying causes of those forms of terrorism and acts of violence which lie in misery, frustration, grievance and despair and which cause some people to sacrifice human lives, including their own, in an attempt to effect radical changes."[14] This wording first appeared in 1972, and can be seen – more or less identically – in General Assembly Resolutions adopted regularly until 1990. The divisions and politicization engendered by the issue thus persisted for two decades until the end of the Cold War.

Multilateral approaches did produce some results during the Cold War, in terms of declaratory conventions. These conventions – 13 in total between 1963 and 2005 – have generally dealt with fairly narrow terrorist activity rather than tackling the broad phenomenon of terrorism. They have defined a particular type of terrorist violence as an offence under the convention, such as the violent seizure of an aircraft in flight; required state parties to penalize that activity in their domestic law; and created an obligation on states in which a suspect is found in terms of extradition.[15]

Four of the conventions deal with aviation and the rest address internationally protected persons, hostage taking, nuclear material and nuclear terrorism, maritime issues, plastic explosives, bombings, and the suppression of financing of terrorism. The word "terrorism" is not even featured in seven of the conventions; the word is first used in the 1979 convention, on one occasion in the preamble and without definition. Only in 1988 did the convention related to maritime navigation allude to acts of terrorism "which endanger or take innocent human lives, jeopardize fundamental freedoms and seriously impair the dignity of human beings."

International Conventions Relating to Terrorism

- Convention on Offences and Certain Other Acts Committed Onboard Aircraft ("Tokyo Convention," 1963).
- Convention for the Suppression of Unlawful Seizure of Aircraft ("Hague Convention," 1970).
- Convention for the Suppression of Unlawful Acts Against the Safety of Civil Aviation ("Montreal Convention," 1971).
- Convention on the Prevention and Punishment of Crimes Against Internationally Protected Persons (1973).
- International Convention Against the Taking of Hostages ("Hostages Convention," 1979).
- Convention on the Physical Protection of Nuclear Material ("Nuclear Materials Convention," 1980).
- Protocol for the Suppression of Unlawful Acts of Violence at Airports Serving International Civil Aviation, supplementary to the Convention for the Suppression of Unlawful Acts against the Safety of Civil Aviation (Extends and supplements the Montreal Convention on Air Safety) (1988).
- Convention for the Suppression of Unlawful Acts Against the Safety of Maritime Navigation (1988).
- Protocol for the Suppression of Unlawful Acts Against the Safety of Fixed Platforms Located on the Continental Shelf (1988).
- Convention on the Marking of Plastic Explosives for the Purpose of Detection (1991).
- International Convention for the Suppression of Terrorist Bombing (UN General Assembly Resolution, 1997).
- International Convention for the Suppression of the Financing of Terrorism (1999).
- The International Convention for the Suppression of Acts of Nuclear terrorism (adopted by the General Assembly and open for signature since September 14, 2005. Not in effect as of April 2007).

The 1990s: the Security Council takes the lead

The end of the Cold War was characterized by a number of trends in the UN's role in addressing terrorism: there was a move to enforcement in the decisions of the Security Council, including the use of Chapter VII powers; the politicization of the issue was toned down – but not eliminated – in debates and statements; and Security Council action against state sponsorship of terrorism, albeit selective, was achieved. The activism of the Security Council can be explained by the fact that all permanent members felt threatened by the most prominent form of terrorism – jihadi militancy – and none felt they could benefit from an ambivalent stance towards this. Moreover, many developing countries – who might earlier have sympathized with certain types of terrorism in the context of the struggle against Israel – themselves felt threatened by the emerging forms of Islamist terrorism. Governments of Muslim countries – especially secular ones – are a primary target of Islamist terrorism, and while their solidarity with the struggle against Israeli "oppression" continues, they have become increasingly cautious in sympathizing with terrorism. According to a cost-benefit analysis, the incentives for state involvement in terrorism declined, and the potential costs of complicity increased.

As a result of this the number of states willing to block Security Council action on terrorism declined; and the number of states actively involved in terrorism became fewer in number and increasingly isolated. In 1989 Security Council Resolutions 635 and 638 represented a significant step forward. Resolution 635, in an unequivocal condemnation of the misuse of explosives and interference in civil aviation, noted the "implications of acts of terrorism for international security." A number of other Security Council resolutions were passed in response to terrorist activities in the 1990s, although the states which were targeted – and those which were ignored – suggest that it was an uneven and selective process.[16] Resolution 731 (1992) related to the destruction of Pan American flight 103 and UTA flight 772. Resolution 1189 (1998) concerned the terrorist bomb attacks of August 1998 in Kenya and Tanzania. Other resolutions targeted specific states. In 1992 Council Resolution 748 imposed sanctions against Libya in response to its involvement in international terrorism, specifically the bombing of the Pan Am and UTA flights. That resolution noted that "the suppression of acts of international terrorism, including those in which States are directly or indirectly involved, is essential for the maintenance of international peace and security." It was passed under Chapter VII of the Charter, and therefore had mandatory authority. Resolution 1044 (1996) called upon Sudan to extradite the three suspects wanted in connection with the assassination attempt against President Mubarak of Egypt. In turn, Resolution 1054 (1996) imposed sanctions upon Sudan for failing to comply with the extradition demand.

Four resolutions specifically targeted Afghanistan and the Taliban regime: 1214 (1998), 1267 (1999), 1333 (2000) and 1363 (2001). They denounced the Taliban's support of international terrorism, demanded that the Taliban regime extradite Osama Bin Laden and cease all support for terrorism, imposed arms and diplomatic sanctions, and created a committee to administer these mandatory Chapter VII measures. Resolution 1269 (1999) formed the most significant general statement on international terrorism prior to 9/11. It condemned "all acts of terrorism irrespective of motive, wherever and by whomever committed." It emphasized the necessity of intensifying the fight against terrorism and specified a number of concrete measures that states should undertake, including the suppression of terrorist financing, denying safe haven to terrorists and extraditing those involved in terrorism, and strengthening coordination and information sharing among states, international and regional organizations.

General Assembly resolutions also reflected an evolution in the 1990s, although the Assembly could not fully move beyond the divisions and politicization of the past. Compared to the Cold War years, Assembly resolutions reflected less emphasis upon terrorism as a response to injustice, occupation and oppression, and more on seeking to build consensus on responding to terrorism. For example, Resolution 51 of 1991 stated that members were "Deeply disturbed by the world-wide persistence of acts of international terrorism in all its forms, including those in which States are directly or indirectly involved, which endanger or take innocent lives, have a deleterious effect on international relations and may jeopardize the territorial integrity and security of States." It unequivocally condemned, "as criminal and unjustifiable, all acts, methods and practices of terrorism wherever and by whomever committed." The references to the legitimate struggle of "peoples under colonial and racist regimes or other forms of alien domination" had less prominence. Other Assembly resolutions in the 1990s, such as the resolution on human rights and terrorism (A/RES/48/122) and measures to eliminate international terrorism (A/49/743) unequivocally condemn all forms of terrorism without reference to the "root causes." The latter resolution was an elaborate document which included a range of practical steps which member states should follow in this regard.

The impact of 9/11

In the 1990s the Security Council agreed upon meaningful (although selective and inconsistent) collective action to address terrorism on a number of occasions, targeting a number of specific states and strengthening norms proscribing terrorism. To a lesser extent, Council resolutions also established operational guidelines amongst states for addressing terrorism. With the attacks of 9/11, the activities of the UN went into new territory in terms of the intrusive and binding obligations imposed upon states to combat terrorism, the capacity-building functions designed to assist states to meet their obligations to combat terrorism, and the willingness to deal with the increasing "privatization" of terrorism. A number of landmark decisions were reached which had real practical effect.

Edward C. Luck – a supporter of the UN, but in no way an uncritical one – wrote that "the rapidity, unanimity, and decisiveness with which the Security Council responded to the September 11, 2001, terrorist assault on the United States were without precedent."[17] Resolution 1368, passed on the 12 September 2001, unequivocally condemned in the strongest terms the attacks the previous day as a threat to international peace and security. Both the promptness and the substance of this resolution were very significant. By recognizing the inherent right of self-defense, and the threat posed by terrorism to international peace and security, the resolution implied that a state could respond to such an attack as if it was a victim of aggression, without further Security Council authorization. Resolution 1368 is therefore seen as giving authorization to the US for the military action it eventually took against the Taliban regime in Afghanistan which had harbored al-Qaeda terrorists. Some analysts have expressed concern about this resolution, apparently legitimizing as it does the unilateral use of force in response to terrorist attacks.[18]

More substantively still, Resolution 1373, passed on 28 September, under Chapter VII of the Charter – and thus mandatory for all UN member states – imposed a range of obligations relating to domestic policy. These include: preventing and suppressing the financing of terrorism; refraining from providing any form of support, active or passive, to entities or individuals involved in terrorism; providing early warning of terrorist acts to other states; denying safe haven to those who finance, plan, support, or commit terrorism; ensuring that any person so involved in terrorism is brought to justice in the context of laws which constitute terrorism as a serious criminal offence; providing assistance to other states in the course of criminal investigations or proceedings relating to terrorism; preventing the movement of terrorists by effective border controls and the prevention of forged travel documentation; and ensuring that asylum-seekers have not in any way been involved in terrorism.

The resolution established a committee of the Security Council to monitor member states' compliance with these mandatory obligations, thus establishing the Counter Terrorism Committee (CTC). The deadline for the first submission of reports from member states to indicate progress in implementing obligatory measures was 90 days after the adoption of the resolution, and the compliance rate – in terms of submission – was an impressive 100 percent. Resolution 1535 (March 2004) established a Counter-Terrorism Committee Executive Directorate to collate the progress of member states in complying with Resolution 1373 and to facilitate the capacity building work. It is worth noting that in the post-9/11 period state ratification of the counterterrorism conventions has also increased.

Other key Council resolutions have been intended to convey UN condemnation in response to specific terrorist attacks (Bali in 2002, Moscow in 2002, Kenya in 2002, Colombia in 2003, Istanbul in 2003, Madrid in 2004, London in 2005, and Iraq in a 2005 resolution) and have had the effect of strengthening the norm of condemnation of terrorism in two ways. First, such resolutions have explicitly condemned the egregious abuse of human rights that these terrorist attacks have entailed, often resulting in the deaths of – or even targeting – children and women. Second, the Security Council has explicitly emphasized that terrorism is a threat to international peace and security and the Council is thus willing and able to respond under the powers of Chapter VII, with mandatory effect upon member states. Indeed, Resolution 1566 (adopted 8 October 2004) even condemned terrorism "as one of the most serious threats to peace and security."

These resolutions are also intrusive, requiring member states to fulfill certain requirements in their domestic legal apparatus. The mandatory obligations they impose upon member states have implications for domestic legal policy. In addition to the far-reaching requirements of resolution 1373, for example, resolution 1624 (September 2005) calls upon states to prohibit by law the incitement of terrorism, which clearly has implications for free speech, traditionally considered to be a "domestic" matter.

However, the UN still lacked a doctrine for addressing terrorism, and this finally emerged in 2005. The High-level Panel on Threats, Challenges and Change asked the Secretary-General to develop a comprehensive global strategy that "incorporates but is broader than coercive measures" and that "addresses root causes and strengthens responsible States and the rule of law and fundamental human rights."[19] In 2005 the Secretary-General presented a five-part strategy – the "5 Ds" – to the International Summit on Democracy, Terrorism and Security in Madrid. His five pillars were: 1) dissuading disaffected groups from choosing terrorism as a tactic to achieve their goals; 2) denying terrorists the means to carry out their attacks; 3) deterring states from supporting terrorists; 4) developing state capacity to prevent terrorism; and 5) defending human rights in the struggle against terrorism.[20]

The September 2005 World Summit also produced a clear statement against terrorism, including 11 paragraphs dealing with this subject and 18 direct references to "terrorism."[21] Reflecting the political interest and consensus on this topic, this was in conspicuous contrast to the issue of weapons of mass destruction, which was not dealt with at all in the world summit statement, partly because of the standoff over the NPT regime. (Nuclear weapons feature only once in the statement, and that is in connection with nuclear terrorism.) In the UN Summit Outcome Document, member states declared that:

- Paragraph 81: We strongly condemn terrorism in all its forms and manifestations, committed by whomever, wherever, and for whatever purposes, as it constitutes one of the most serious threats to international peace and security.
- Paragraph 82: We welcome the Secretary-General's identification of the elements of a counter-terrorism strategy. These elements should be developed by the General Assembly without delay ...
- Paragraph 83: We stress the need to make every effort to reach an agreement on and conclude a comprehensive convention on international terrorism during the Sixtieth session of the General Assembly (September 2006).
- Paragraph 85: We recognize that international cooperation to fight terrorism must be conducted in conformity with international law, including the Charter and relevant international conventions and protocols. States must ensure that any measures taken to combat terrorism comply with their obligations under international law, in particular human rights law, refugee law and international humanitarian law.
- Paragraph 86: We reiterate our call upon States to refrain from organizing, financing, encouraging, providing training for or otherwise supporting terrorist activities and to take appropriate measures to ensure that their territories are not used for such activities.

- Paragraph 88: We urge the international community, including the United Nations, to assist States in building national and regional capacity to combat terrorism. We invite the Secretary-General to submit proposals to the General Assembly and the Security Council, within their respective mandates, to strengthen the capacity of the United Nations system to assist States in combating terrorism and to enhance the coordination of the United Nations activities in this regard.
- Paragraph 90: We encourage the Security Council to consider ways to strengthen its monitoring and enforcement role in counter-terrorism, including by consolidating State reporting requirements...

While the Security Council has attempted to develop a comprehensive strategy for addressing terrorism, it also continues to respond to specific terrorist outrages, such as the assassination of former Lebanese President Rafik Hariri in Beirut in 2004. Responding to the assassination, the Council established a Commission under Resolution 1595 to assist the Lebanese authorities to investigate the case.

The principal organs of the UN are not alone in adjusting their work to the increased salience of terrorism. The International Atomic Energy Agency (IAEA) has reviewed its ability to assess the security of nuclear facilities in member states, with the aim of preventing nuclear material falling into the hands of non-state groups. In 2002, the IAEA Board of Governors approved an action plan designed to upgrade worldwide protection against acts of terrorism involving nuclear and other radioactive materials. The International Civil Aviation Organization spearheaded efforts to gain agreement on air safety. The International Maritime Organization has reviewed international arrangements and treaties regarding terrorism at sea. The UN's work has also proceeded in parallel with regional efforts.

The effectiveness of and debates over the UN's role in addressing terrorism

The UN – and especially the Security Council – has taken an active and important role in addressing terrorism since the end of the Cold War, first in targeting state sponsorship in the 1990s and then in broadening its attention to non-state actors after 9/11. Most observers agree that the role of the UN in coordinating action against terrorism is significant, although some conservatives remain deeply skeptical.[22] A number of challenges and questions do remain regarding the UN's ability to play a significant role. There has been considerable attention devoted to the question of whether the structure, decision-making processes and legal bases of the UN allow it to take an effective role in addressing terrorism. Some analysts have argued that the UN is inherently flawed with regard to such a role, as a result of its state-centric structure and mostly voluntary decision-making. Terrorism is complex and multifaceted, requiring a response which goes far beyond the diplomatic approach of the UN. As O'Neill has observed, "New allies in the struggle include financial analysts, bankers, arms control experts, educators, communications specialists, development planners and religious leaders."[23]

Others have suggested that the Charter concepts covering the use of force, armed attack, self-defense, and threats to peace, "are not geared to situations of serious attacks against a state by a group of foreign-based and often loosely organized international terrorists."[24] In terms of performance, according to a scoping study prepared for the UN Foundation, "the response of the UN has not been sufficiently effective in countering attacks by terrorist cells that have proven adaptable and capable of exploiting gaps in law enforcement, border security, and domestic intelligence."[25] In contrast, others, such as Edward Luck, have argued that nothing in the structure or rules of procedure of the UN preclude it from playing a significant and effective role in addressing terrorism: "Political and strategic factors, much more than constitutional constraints, have shaped how and whether the world body has taken on the challenge of terrorism."[26]

The purposes and principles of the UN, enshrined in the Charter, are to maintain international peace and security, which calls for collective measures to address threats to the peace. While the primary focus is on acts of aggression and international disputes – implying a traditional inter-state conception of international security – Article 1 also broadly refers to "situations which might lead to a breach of the peace." The tone of Chapter VII – which deals with action with respect to threats to the peace and aggression – is, again, somewhat state centric. However, Article 39 gives the Security Council the authority to determine the existence of "any threat" to the peace, without qualification. In determining such a threat, the Council has "considerable discretion."[27] Moreover, any response, including coercion, that may be authorized by the Security Council is not explicitly confined to states as the culprit. And while Article 2 (7) states that "nothing contained in the present Charter shall authorize the United Nations to intervene in matters which are essentially within the domestic jurisdiction of any state," it also observes that "this principle shall not prejudice the application of enforcement measures under Chapter VII." Moreover, Article 99 states that the Secretary-General "may bring to the attention of the Security Council *any matter* which in his opinion may threaten the maintenance of international peace and security" (italics added).

The Charter can and has been interpreted to allow a broad definition of security. At the same time, terrorism has been interpreted as relevant to traditional notions of international peace and security. It is interesting, for example, that Council Resolution 748 in 1992, dealing with sanctions against Libya, stated that states must refrain from supporting terrorist acts in accordance with Article 2 (4). Moreover, an Assembly resolution on measures to eliminate international terrorism (A/49/743) was drafted with clear reference to landmark treaties and conventions related to peaceful relations between states, human rights, and the UN Charter. Both of these resolutions tie terrorism to "conventional" peace and security challenges and thus allow the UN and states to respond as they would do to threats to international peace and security. In addition, Council resolutions on terrorism have clearly been able to address "behind the border" issues – such as legal issues, border policies, financial and banking regulations relating to terrorist funding – without being in violation of Charter norms. Finally, the performance and decision-making record of the Council since the end of the Cold War has amply demonstrated that the UN is capable of adapting to a broadening peace and security mandate, if the political will exists. Indeed, if the Council can approach AIDS as a threat to international peace and security, as it did in 2000, then it is surely able to approach terrorism in such terms.

An additional concern is that, notwithstanding the assertive stance taken by the Council in relation to specific states – such as Libya, Sudan and Afghanistan – the general mechanisms established by the UN "lack teeth." The reporting requirements of the CTC are essentially voluntary. There are no plans to "name and shame" states which do not meet their Resolution 1373 obligations. Moreover, the committee itself cannot impose sanctions. In theory, as the resolution was passed under Chapter VII of the UN Charter, if a state was found to be in violation of its obligations, a further Council decision could interpret this as a threat to international peace and security and agree upon coercive measures, including sanctions. However, there is little or no expectation that this will happen (unless a state is found to be directly supporting terrorism), and so most of the general requirements of the Security Council relating to terrorism are non-enforceable. The emphasis of the CTC has clearly been upon creating positive incentives for compliance, rather than negative threats, and this is the approach that member states prefer. State compliance has been impressive – at least in terms of the submission of reports on national performance – but it remains to be seen if this voluntary approach is sustainable and will continue to enjoy the confidence of leading states, such as the US.

The feeling amongst the UN community has – characteristically – been that a non-confrontational approach which emphasizes capacity building is the most fruitful. As a corollary, the threat of sanctions or "naming and shaming" is considered less likely to result in state compliance. This practice relates to theories of state compliance which contrast different strategies – the so-called "enforcement" and "management" schools of thought.[28] According to these theories of state compliance, a confidence-building/incentive-based approach cannot be combined with an approach which poses possible sanctions. Positive incentives can indeed be more efficient as a mechanism to gain state compliance in the UN system, but there are limitations to this which may weaken the credibility of the organization in this field.

Other concerns about the UN's bureaucratic culture in its approach to terrorism – and thus a lack of coherence – have also been raised.[29] A number of different UN units and agencies now have a responsibility in this field, including the CTC (and its executive directorate) and the Terrorism Prevention Branch of the Vienna-based Office on Drugs and Crime. One study has observed the duplication and potentially conflicting mandates in the UN system, and a lack of coordination in the UN system regarding the response to terrorism.[30] It also observes the complications which can arise from the UN counterterrorism apparatus being embroiled in Security Council politics.

A further concern is the politicization of the terrorism debate globally. The US has been the driving force behind the UN's work on terrorism since 9/11. However, the US "war on terror" is highly controversial. It emphasizes a military approach and it also, according to many observers, is not even-handed, and perhaps even hypocritical. The states named by the US as sponsors of terrorism in 2006 (Cuba, Iran, North Korea, Sudan and Syria) are conspicuous as states which are estranged from the US, whereas other states which are allies of the US and might have been associated with terrorism (such as Pakistan) are absent from the list. The apparently unconditional US support for Israel in its use of force – especially its attacks against Hezbollah militants in Lebanon in the summer of 2006, resulting in a high number of civilian casualties – has made the double standard all the more pointed. The US war on terror is thus regarded as an extension – or even a legitimation – of its broader foreign policy campaign, part of which targets certain states.

US prominence in forging the UN approach to terrorism has therefore generated tensions and alienated some states. States generally conform to new multilateral initiatives regarding terrorism, but in some cases increasingly half-heartedly, and there are signs of antagonism regarding the focus of the war on terror. The "war on terror" has clearly influenced the UN attempts to address terrorism, for example in the stress upon interdicting terrorist financing and the danger of terrorist groups acquiring nuclear weapons, rather than on root causes and safeguarding human rights. In addition, many analysts have observed that Resolution 1368, which confirmed the right of self-defense under the UN Charter, leaves discretion for powerful states to act militarily, and unilaterally, to perceived terrorism threats; some have suggested that this gave the US a "blank check" to respond. As the military – and if necessary, unilateral – response to terrorism has been a constant refrain of the US government since 9/11 it has given the impression of the US bending the UN to its will.

A further, related, concern regarding the UN's approach to terrorism, in the context of the "war on terror," is the place of human rights, and the concern that since 9/11 "the framework of international human rights standards has been attacked and undermined by both governments and armed groups."[31] The UN Secretary-General, in his report *In Larger Freedom*, stated that an effective strategy against terrorism must include, as one of its pillars, the defense of human rights: "In our struggle against terrorism, we must never compromise human rights. When we do so we facilitate achievement of one of the terrorist's objectives."[32] The Secretary-General recommended the creation of a special rapporteur who would report to the Commission on Human Rights on the compatibility of counterterrorism measures with international human rights laws. However, the balance between human rights and upholding security is a challenge for many societies. There have been claims that human rights are being disregarded in the fight against terrorism, or even that this fight is being used as a pretext for curtailing human rights. The use of extraordinary rendition and allegations of torture, and the introduction of national legislation which limits individual rights in the interests of enhancing public security, have caused great controversy internationally and within states.[33] While the UN has certainly not been silent on this issue, the widely held impression has been that human rights have been put in second place in terms of priorities, after combating terrorism.

A further source of antagonism concerns the different attitudes which are emerging regarding the prioritization of terrorism. After 9/11, almost every state rallied in support of the US, accepting that the US had a right to respond according to the norms of self-defense. There was consensus that terrorism represented a clear and present danger. However, in the years following 9/11, and despite constant reminders of the dangers of terrorism, many UN member states have expressed reservations about the diplomatic and material attention given to terrorism, when other challenges – such as underdevelopment, malnutrition and preventable diseases – have a far greater negative impact upon human life. There is the distinct feeling that terrorism is dominating the agenda and resulting in alienation, in particular, in developing countries. It is worth quoting Kofi Annan at length:

> The fight against terrorism cannot be used as an excuse for slackening efforts to put an end to conflicts and defeat poverty and disease. Nor can it be an excuse for undermining the bases of the rule of law – good governance, respect for human rights and fundamental freedoms. The long-term war on terrorism requires us to fight on all these fronts. Indeed, the best defense against these despicable acts is the establishment of a global society based on common values of solidarity, social justice and respect for human rights.[34]

A related theme concerns root causes. There is a widely held view that "Despite these calls for a broad counter-terrorism campaign that includes both preventive and protective measures, the global fight against terrorism has focused largely on denial and deterrence strategies."[35] The idea of "root causes" of terrorism suggests that there is some form of causal relationship between underlying social, economic, political and demographic conditions and terrorist activity. According to this proposition, certain underlying conditions and grievances help to explain how, where and why terrorism occurs. Therefore, certain conditions provide a social environment and widespread grievances which, when combined with certain precipitant factors, result in the emergence of terrorist organizations and terrorist acts. These conditions – such as poverty, demographic factors, social inequality and exclusion, dispossession and political grievances – can be either permissive or direct. The idea suggests, for example, that: "human insecurity, broadly understood, provides the enabling conditions for terrorism to flourish."[36] As a corollary, a failure to understand the linkages between these underlying conditions and terrorism may result in inadequate counterterrorist policies. Moreover, according to this argument, an approach to counterterrorism which ignores this relationship may even exacerbate the underlying conditions which give rise to terrorism and in turn intensify the terrorist threat.

"Root causes" can be broken down into permissive structural factors and direct underlying grievances. Structural factors create an enabling environment which, alone, is of no explanatory value, but when in conjunction with other factors, may have explanatory value. Underlying grievances are more than merely structural: they represent tangible political issues. Structural factors include poverty; demographic factors including rapid population growth and especially a burgeoning of young males, and uneven population shifts across different ethnic groups; and urbanization, especially in conjunction with unemployment and poverty. Direct root causes include exclusion and social inequality; dispossession, human rights abuse, alienation, and humiliation; and a clash of values, especially associated with ideological or "religious" terrorism. These ideas are not without controversy. Some people are clearly uncomfortable with the idea of root causes because it disturbs the "moral clarity" that they believe is necessary to confront terrorism.[37] They wish to deny that any form of terrorism could be associated with a legitimate political cause, because they wish to deny that terrorist groups have any legitimacy whatsoever. From another angle, a political scientist has claimed that root causes are "misleading as an explanation for terrorism or a prescription for dealing with it."[38]

The author's work elsewhere has suggested a number of propositions regarding the relationship between social conditions and terrorism.[39] Neither permissive nor direct root causes are alone effective in explaining or predicting terrorism. However, focusing on terrorist organizations (their nature and aims, their leadership, the background of key supporters and operatives, and their social base) suggests that root cause analysis may be helpful in explaining certain *types* of terrorism. In particular, a tentative correlation can be identified in terms of the social and political conditions of the societies from which the most deadly terrorist organizations emerge and are based, and this particular focus deserves further analysis. Qualitative case analyses which present a detailed picture of specific conflicts offer the most effective methodology for understanding the role of root causes in relation to other explanatory variables. Root causes are necessary, although not sufficient, factors in explaining and understanding certain types of terrorism, and only in conjunction with precipitant factors. Root causes tend to be most relevant in helping to understand terrorism associated with ideological, ethno-nationalist and Islamist groups in developing countries; of limited value in explaining nationalist groups in developed societies; and least relevant with regard to ideological groups in developed countries.

Even when it is not feasible to alter social and economic conditions in the short-term, a focus on root causes can form a part of an integrated counterterrorism program. In turn, projections of social and economic trends, urbanization and demography may hold implications for future patterns of terrorism. It is therefore prudent to include, in a long-term counterterrorist agenda, policies such as development aid, support for local democracy processes, human rights, the promotion and protection of minority rights, and the amelioration of the negative effects of globalization. However, in terms of the politics of dealing with terrorism through formal multilateral institutions, the impression is that root causes are being neglected.

The selective focus of the UN is reflected in the apparatus it established to address terrorism. The CTC, for example, does not focus on root causes or human rights, and it appears firmly controlled by the US and the UK.[40] This is causing antagonism which threatens to weaken the commitment of certain states to the UN approach. In particular, there are misgivings amongst states which are alienated by the perceived domineering approach of the US, which feel potentially threatened by the combative nature of the "war on terror," and those states which have concerns about human rights issues – such as the practice of extraordinary rendition, the detention facilities at Guantanamo Bay, and curtailment of civil liberties. A weakening of commitment can have negative repercussions for state compliance with international agreements. The evidence suggests a declining support amongst states for UN counterterrorism indicated by, for example, declining rates of report submission to the CTC.[41]

Conclusion

The principles of institutionalism are strained, but not undermined, by multilateral responses to terrorism. Most states, however powerful, see incentives in some level of coordination in addressing this challenge. Agreeing upon norms which condemn terrorism, and state support for terrorism, provides a framework through which to tackle terrorism, either unilaterally or multilaterally. Coordinating state action – in areas such as border control and travel, financial transfers, and fund-raising and in the prohibition of the training and incitement of terrorism – makes counterterrorism more effective. Establishing credible agreements to prohibit certain activities – such as the transfer of knowledge regarding weapons of mass destruction to non-state actors – is in the interests of almost all states. Sharing information about the activities of terrorist groups makes it easier to prevent attacks and interdict the movement of terrorists. Military action – the most sensitive issue – can be more effective and politically more legitimate when pursued multilaterally, in concert with other states. The incentives for states to hold out or renege are declining, even for the more recalcitrant states, in an era of jihad and when state sponsorship of terrorism can have serious consequences.

The principles of institutionalism – reciprocity, reducing transaction costs, creating credible expectations about the behavior of states – can certainly work in these functional areas, if political will exists. However, political will rests upon consensus regarding the threat of terrorism and how it should be addressed, and how to balance this with safeguards regarding human rights, and how it should be prioritized in relation to other challenges. Achieving agreement upon these issues is difficult. Moreover, more sensitive political issues continue to hinder the smooth functioning of a multilateral approach to terrorism: while consensus is building on the definition of terrorism – any violence which deliberately targets civilians for political ends – states are still selective about the types of terrorism that they target for opprobrium. Many states remain reluctant to address terrorism in public international settings when it is associated with their own sensitive "domestic" issues. While state sponsorship for terrorism has significantly declined some states remain directly or indirectly involved in the perpetration of terrorism. And there remains difficulty reaching agreement on how states can respond to terrorism both unilaterally and in cooperation with other states, as Israel's punitive response to Hezbollah's attacks in 2006 demonstrated.

The UN has not been hobbled by the "unconventional" nature of terrorism as a security threat. The UN can tackle "new" and unconventional security challenges, if the political will exists. Of course there are operational limitations upon multilateral organizations and a reliance upon alliances or powerful states for tackling terrorism militarily. But the organization is promoting norms and coordinating policy.

There is the sense that the West – and particularly the US and the UK – is driving this process. This is not necessarily a bad thing for multilateralism in a functional sense, in terms of terrorism or any other policy area. However, because counterterrorism strategy is dominated by Western – and particularly US – interests, it is characterized by its emphasis upon countering rather than preventing terrorism. Within the framework of the Council, the work is also politicized by the broader controversies which pervade the UN, and possibly hampered by consensus-based decision-making procedures.

In terms of the various agencies and programs relevant to tackling terrorism – even just within the UN – there is a lack of coherence and a need to consolidate. Efforts towards developing a coherent strategy for addressing terrorism have continued,[42] and there have been calls for a global counterterrorism organization.[43] However, the fundamental challenge to achieving effective multilateral approaches to terrorism – especially in the UN, which is the most difficult – is not coordination but political will.

Conclusion
Revisiting institutionalism in a post-Westphalian world

The preceding chapters suggest why some of the values and institutions of multilateralism may have to be re-envisioned in line with twenty-first century norms, the evolving security agenda, and the distribution and nature of power in international relations. Despite the constraints that multilateralism inevitably experiences in the security arena, there are ways to improve performance and in turn enhance legitimacy. If they are to be viable and legitimate, multilateral values and institutions must be constituted according to contemporary principles of governance and legitimacy, and capable of addressing contemporary challenges effectively. This involves moving beyond the Westphalian roots of multilateral institutions based upon sovereign equality, reassessing the values upon which multilateralism is based and which it is promoting, and recognizing that contemporary challenges demand greater flexibility and proactivity. Some policy areas can be used as examples to illustrate, in an ideal world, how the institutions and values of multilateralism might be re-envisioned.

A number of – mainly liberal internationalist – ideas for reforming the UN have emerged in recent years. The Secretary-General of the UN has argued that the world needs a broad and comprehensive framework of collective security appropriate for the new millennium, one which recognizes that contemporary security threats are interconnected and complex.[1] He argued that "we will not enjoy development without security, we will not enjoy security without development, and we will not enjoy either without respect for human rights. Unless all these causes are advanced, none will succeed."[2] According to this argument, the world would be better served by a system of collective security which responded to all critical threats, irrespective of source. The High Level Panel on Threats, Challenges and Change argued that: "Any event or process that leads to large-scale death or lessening of life chances and undermines States as the basic unit of the international system is a threat to international security."³ It identified, as priorities, economic and social threats, including poverty, infectious disease and environmental degradation; inter-state conflict; internal conflict, including civil war; nuclear, radiological, chemical and biological weapons; terrorism; and transnational organized crime.

This new collective security should be based upon the evolution of the institution of sovereignty and international norms. In terms of critical issues of human survival, states should recognize that sovereignty is conditional upon meeting certain standards of human welfare and human rights. There is a responsibility to protect human life; if states are unable or unwilling to meet this responsibility, the international community, through multilateral organizations, should be mandated and enabled to take over this responsibility.

In terms of international peace and security, and especially weapons of mass destruction (WMD) and terrorism, certain principles related to the presumption of sovereignty, non-interference and the use of force should also be reexamined. The established rules governing the use of military force (only in self-defense, collective self-defense or with reference to Chapter VII of the UN Charter) have been questioned in some circumstances, especially when states are faced with the hypothetical combination of terrorism and WMD. Clearly the idea of preventive force in response to latent or non-imminent threats is something that has appealed to some policy analysts. When this idea has arisen, the presumption has been that such preventive force would necessarily be outside the UN framework because of the UN Charter's emphasis upon the non-use of force except in self-defense or in response to cases of aggression.

The Secretary-General offered a rebuttal to this presumption in his report *In Larger Freedom* by observing that the Charter does give authority to the Council to use force, even preventively, to preserve international peace and security.⁴ Few observers – whether UN supporters or detractors – accept that the organization is sufficiently constituted to authorize preventive force in response to latent threats. It will therefore not have the full confidence of some key countries on critical issues related to international security, unless it undergoes a radical transformation in its rules of procedure and its definition of "threats to international peace and security." The first step should be the promotion of a threat-based system of international peace and security, in the broadest sense: including a comprehensive convention on terrorism in all its aspects, and a declaration on the responsibility to protect human life. Once members have signed up to these core conventions, they must be enforced and the Security Council must be prepared to make decisions, including authorizing the use of coercion in response to violations.

Multilateral institutions should recognize and involve non-state actors on the basis of criteria which ensure their legitimacy and effectiveness. In particular, in the areas of social and economic welfare and humanitarianism, non-state actors are an essential component of multilateralism and must be embraced centrally. In this sense, the multilateralism of the twenty-first century should not be confined to relationships amongst states; it must reflect the plurality of international relations and the key role of non-state actors.

Revisiting institutionalism

However, the reality appears to be different from the liberal internationalist vision. The preceding chapters illustrate that the incentives which exist for states to commit to formal multilateral arrangements, according to the dominant institutionalist theory of multilateralism, falter in important policy areas related to security. The principles of non-discrimination, indivisibility and diffuse reciprocity – which have functioned well in many areas of policy since 1945 – appear less viable in more sensitive and less predictable areas such as the use of military force and intervention, WMD, terrorism and civil war.

According to the principle of non-discrimination, states should fulfill the obligations of membership in a multilateral regime or organization without reservations or conditions based upon the circumstances of a particular issue, or their perception of their particular national interests. Thus, members of a multilateral arrangement must not take a "case-by-case" approach to issues depending upon individual preferences. Related to this is the principle of *indivisibility*, which suggests that the members should behave according to fixed rules on the given policy matter in relation to all members of the multilateral arrangement, sharing the benefits and costs of cooperation. According to *diffuse reciprocity*, states conform to expectations in terms of their behavior because they can expect to receive roughly equivalent benefits over time, if not necessarily every time.

The theoretical principles of multilateralism are upheld quite reliably in the area of international trade, despite the collapse of the Doha round of trade liberalization in 2006 (indeed, these principles emerged from the study of this policy area). In the area of international trade, multilateral commitments to liberalize trade and dispute settlement have become increasingly regularized and robust over time:

"Multilateralism has been crucial to an enhanced international flow of goods and services over the past century."[5] In other areas of cooperation, state practice upholds these principles even more faithfully. The Universal Postal Union, for example, has 190 member countries. It was established in 1874 and basically facilitates cooperation between national postal services to ensure that international mail posted in one member country is delivered in other member countries. The acceptance of the regulations of the UPU makes the member countries an interconnected single postal territory. The technical standards of the UPU are fairly uncontroversial, and there is little incentive for a member state to withdraw from the union and seek to achieve the objectives of international postal delivery unilaterally or in cooperation with like-minded states. No viable alternative exists because there is no need for an alternative and the costs of a unilateral, or even multilateral, alternative would be prohibitive. Similar principles exist with an even older international organization – the International Telecommunication Union – where governments and the private sector coordinate global telecommunication networks and services.

There *are* incentives to committing to formal multilateral arrangements in international security issues and such arrangements do exist, as the preceding chapters demonstrate. All states have an interest in following rules which regulate the use of military force, because this strengthens confidence and reduces the costs – and risks – of being on a permanent war-footing. It is in the general interest that military force is only used in self-defense or collective self-defense and the decline of inter-state war since the Second World War supports this consensus. Similarly, states have an interest in supporting binding agreements which clarify the circumstances in which military intervention might be used – to prevent or stop genocide, state failure or civil war, for example. The incentives for this are clear. These phenomena are disruptive to the international system, they are contrary to human rights standards which reflect wide consensus, and they are associated with a range of security problems which can threaten other countries, including insurgency, the trafficking of narcotics and weapons, and terrorism. Unilateral intervention can arouse suspicion and hostility, and so there are incentives to agree on when and how intervention might legitimately be undertaken.[6] Such an agreement can also make intervention more effective and cost-efficient.

The multilateral rationale for binding agreements in terms of WMD is also obvious, at least in theory. States find incentives in agreeing to limit the destructiveness and quantity of weapons, and agreeing when they might be used. In recent years it has also become clear that almost all states have an incentive to agree to binding obligations which prevent non-state groups – and particularly terrorists – acquiring WMD technology and materials. Moreover, states have incentives to agree to binding obligations which prevent other states from assisting non-state groups to acquire WMD. The means of achieving this are more effective when they embrace as many states as possible, and when they are obligatory – they represent binding obligations amongst states, irrespective of the power of states or their particular interests. Such agreements would be more robust – and hence enjoy greater credibility and thus legitimacy – if they are non-discriminatory. That is, a regime is stronger if the parties have confidence that no other party would breach the rules under any circumstances.

The norm of diffuse reciprocity can function also. States forgo the temptation of assisting an ally or a favored non-state actor to develop WMD (even if such a thing would be possible without being discovered) because states have an interest, in the longer term, in other states similarly restraining themselves. If they undermine the system by defecting due to short-term preferences, they endanger themselves in the longer term because a weakened system may permit security threats against themselves in different circumstances. In addition, of course, there are other disincentives to violating such a norm: in particular, the high risk of being the target of international opprobrium or coercion.

A similar logic applies to terrorism, in theory. Most – but not all – states have a clear interest in accepting binding agreements which seek to limit the activities of terrorist organizations. States may not be equally threatened by terrorism in general or by specific terrorist organizations. Indeed, sometimes their perceived interests might be served by the objectives and activities of certain terrorist groups, or they may have sympathies for certain terrorist causes. However, the institutionalist logic is gaining ground: in the long-term, states have an interest in supporting norms and regulations which proscribe terrorism, even if they forego short-term advantages, because of the incentives of reciprocal expectations which benefit them over time. Thus, a credible system which limits the actions of terrorist groups is in the interests of most states. Even if they might have sympathies for or share tactical interests with certain terrorist groups, states need to consider that different terrorist groups – or unforeseen terrorist groups which may emerge in the future – may be hostile to their interests. According to the logic of institutionalism, therefore, states should support generalized, non-discriminatory and binding agreements which prevent

Conclusion: revisiting institutionalism 145

terrorist organizations from fund raising, operating, and recruiting on their territory.

However, the limitations of institutionalism are equally obvious. Non-discrimination does not function reliably in certain areas of international security because the dangers of defection by another party – for example, in breaking out of the nuclear Non-Proliferation Treaty (NPT) and developing WMD – are intolerable, especially to states which have the power to act unilaterally in a given area.

The normal theoretical constructions for explaining the emergence of cooperation – for example, game theory – have limitations when seeking to explain the most sensitive security issues. Game theory – such as the Prisoner's Dilemma – sees the emergence of cooperation in iterated (and not sole) encounters. However, while this provides an interesting model for the study of a policy area such as trade, where mistakes are tolerable – and adjustments possible over time – most states view critical security challenges as non-negotiable. A single mistake – or defection by an adversary – can be fatal. Therefore, while cooperation can and does occur in these areas, states will generally "hedge": that is, they will hold out on making absolute or irreversible commitments and reserve the capacity to defect themselves in light of unforeseen or "special" circumstances.

A number of examples will illustrate this further. The potential advantages of developing WMD for some states – or the costs of an adversary developing such weapons – are breaking down the multi-lateral rules of the game enshrined in the non-proliferation regime. There is a danger that increasing numbers of states will be unwilling to forego the advantage of the nuclear option for two reasons. First, the legitimacy of the NPT is in serious doubt due to the failure of the established nuclear powers to fulfill their disarmament obligations. Second, the NPT regime has a major weakness: it does not contain sufficient safeguards against violation, or sufficient means to ensure transparency or verifiability. The NPT allows civilian nuclear activities – such as enriching nuclear materials for peaceful energy purposes – which could be diverted to military purposes. Nuclear-capable states have the capacity and have in many cases undertaken the preparations for the development of nuclear weapons and could promptly move to weaponization as soon as the incentives outweigh the costs. This weakness, if not addressed, will grow as more countries develop civilian nuclear programs which might have military potential. For non-nuclear states, especially those in volatile regions, this leaves a worrying erosion of credibility. The risks of an adversary defecting from the regime – as long as the regime is not strengthened – and gaining the

146 Conclusion: revisiting institutionalism

advantage of nuclear weapons are immense. One response is, if it is within a state's capacity, to plan for the contingency of developing some form of WMD.

For existing nuclear states, the credibility of the NPT is also on the decline. The US does not accept the assurances of certain states, even within the context of the NPT, that they are not pursuing nuclear weapons programs. This means that the US, and other countries, will not seriously consider disarmament. Britain's official position is quite telling in this regard: that as long as a potential enemy has a nuclear weapon the UK should retain the capacity.

The challenge of terrorism provides another example which is particularly difficult for multilateralism, although multilateral consensus is gaining ground. There are incentives for supporting global norms which proscribe terrorism and state support for terrorism, and agreements which require coordination amongst states to combat terrorism. There are also, of course, disincentives to be seen to be outside the "new consensus"; state supporters of terrorism are increasingly likely to be isolated or even targeted. At least superficially, then, states have incentives in appearing to comply with regional and UN requirements relating to terrorism.

Yet the sensitivity of terrorist challenges has meant that reservations continue to exist in terms of the commitment of states to multilateral action. States continue to have reservations about placing their domestic terrorist challenges on the international agenda because of the risks of them becoming complicated by international scrutiny or constraining their response. There is also the possible unwelcome effect of gaining international recognition for the terrorist organization in question. Similarly, there may be times when, for broader geostrategic reasons, it may be convenient to focus less on certain types of terrorism than others. Therefore, the multilateral principles of non-discrimination and indivisibility do not entirely hold up. While a wide-ranging body of international law and regulations exists to address terrorism, states will continue to apply "case-by-case" analysis in deciding how thoroughly they apply multilateral norms and agreements relating to terrorism. The Report of the Secretary-General's High-level Panel on Threats, Challenges and Change complained, quite correctly, that "Too often, the United Nations and its Member States have discriminated in responding to threats to international security."[7] There is little reason to hope for a radical transformation of this situation.

This contingency-based approach – which defies true multilateral principles – is equally demonstrated in the area of the use of force for human protection purposes ("humanitarian intervention"). Most people,

Conclusion: revisiting institutionalism 147

including government leaders, share a humanitarian impulse to help people who are suffering genocide, war crimes, or crimes against humanity. The "responsibility to protect" human life, especially in times of violent conflict or persecution, has established itself in the terminology of diplomacy and international politics. However, it is not a norm; it is not supported by consistent state behavior. Therefore, it is unlikely that a robust multilateral framework will ever emerge in this area. The reasons are clear enough; the difficulties and sensitivities of humanitarian intervention defy the principles of non-discrimination, indivisibility and reciprocity. Given the sensitivities of using military force – the material costs, the risk to personnel, the legal complications, and geostrategic factors – states will not commit themselves to act in a non-discriminatory manner through a responsibility to protect human life. They are more likely to judge every case on its individual merits, considering a range of interests and issues, including humanitarianism. The principle of diffuse reciprocity is similarly unlikely to take root in this issue area; it is highly unlikely that powerful states would become involved in a multilateral military intervention to protect human lives where no other interest exists on the basis that they might require support from other states for a similar intervention in the future. For smaller, weaker countries – especially in the developing world – the subject is moot, because they are fundamentally against the concept of humanitarian intervention.

Similar dynamics have obstructed a formal multilateral framework for approaching civil war, although consensus is slowly growing that such a framework must be developed. As indicated elsewhere in this book, there are incentives for states to support some form of international arrangement to prevent, contain or resolve civil war because such conflicts present a range of international security problems. It is clearly in the interest of all states to suppress these problems. Moreover, it is in the interests of states to support a *system* which addresses these problems; even though not all civil wars would appear to represent a direct security challenge, a future civil war may do so. Therefore it makes sense to support a system which may be necessary to respond to a future, sometimes unforeseen, contingency. However, the costs involved in actively participating in such an operation – in terms of financial costs and the risks to personnel – defy the multilateral logic. States would prefer to respond to unforeseen circumstances on an *ad hoc* – discriminatory – basis. They are prepared to forego the potential benefits of reciprocity in this issue area (for example, participating in a military intervention into a conflicted society in support of other states, in the hope that other states will return the favor in the future).

148 Conclusion: revisiting institutionalism

This does sometimes happen, but the principle of reciprocity is not strong enough to constitute a multilateral system to address civil wars.

The UN Secretary-General argued that "there is an urgent need for the nations of the world to come together and reach a new consensus – both on the future of collective security and on the changes needed if the United Nations is to play its part."[8] UN Member States did indeed reaffirm their commitment "to work towards a security consensus" based upon an "efficient collective security system pursuant to the purposes and principles of the Charter."[9] Yet it would appear that the structure of international politics is not currently constituted in a way which is conducive to such a transformation. The *Responsibility to Protect* and the High Level Panel Report sought to introduce rational policy options for challenges such as the use of force for human protection purposes and for maintaining international peace and security, but this normative progress has not resulted in a policy transformation. Moreover, this situation reflects the inherent dynamics of international politics. As such, it may not be helpful to think in terms of the UN facing a "moment of truth."[10] The challenges that the UN faces are perennial.

Multilateral alternatives and alternatives to multilateralism

The inherent limitations of multilateralism in the area of international security are unlikely to be overcome at the global level. Changes in the structure of international politics – such as the growing salience of non-state actors – do not at present alter this conclusion because the international system is still essentially state-centric. In many ways, this is at the heart of much of the multilateral malaise. US preeminence coupled with an ideologically conservative government, frustrated with the perceived limitations of traditional forms of international organizations, has facilitated a pattern of US behavior which has had important implications for global multilateralism. On occasions, the US has withdrawn from or operated outside established multilateral arrangements – sometimes in cooperation with a coalition of allies. In other instances the US has sought to create new, alternative forms of multilateralism, such as the Security Proliferation Initiative. And in other instances the US has sought to mould existing multilateral arrangements in line with its interests, such as in the area of terrorism. None of this is new. Nevertheless, as this book illustrates, most observers believe that it has reached new levels.

In the regional context, and amongst more exclusive multilateral arrangements – for example based upon shared values amongst allies –

Conclusion: revisiting institutionalism 149

there is greater promise for addressing some of these evolving security challenges. One theory holds that regional blocs embrace a more limited range of interests, and so therefore regularized cooperation can be easier to attain. The primary example of this is Western Europe, where integration has resulted in the pooling of sovereignty in a number of issue areas based upon shared functional needs and also shared values. Proximity does not automatically result in affinity, of course. East Asia embraces a range of diverse – and often conflicting – interests which have hindered the emergence of regional institutions.

An alternative theory advocates increasing cooperation based not upon elusive global interests, or regionalism, but upon exclusive shared values. Emanuel Adler, for example, has written of communitarian multilateralism in constructions such as the European Union and NATO. Adler claims that: "Communitarian multilateralism, which transcends liberal transaction-based relations and relies instead on communitarian practices of collective-identity formation that depend, not only on material power, but also on collective epistemic understandings, is thriving."[11] The implication of this, however, is that communitarian multilateralism is unlikely to contribute to global governance because its practices are inherently exclusive.

Conservative analysts – who challenge the legitimacy of the UN because it seeks to bring together states which have incompatible values and interests – also suggest alternative forms of multilateral cooperation. Cooperation amongst democracies – even a League of Democracies – is one such idea. This rests upon the democratic peace theory that liberal democracies never go to war against other democracies. It also embraces a range of liberal assumptions which are worth reporting at length:

> Countries that govern themselves in a truly democratic fashion do not go to war with one another. They do not aggress against their neighbors to aggrandize themselves or glorify their leaders. Democratic governments do not ethnically "cleanse" their own populations, and they are much less likely to face ethnic insurgency. Democracies do not sponsor terrorism against one another. They do not build weapons of mass destruction to use on or to threaten one another. Democratic countries form more reliable, open, and enduring trading partnerships. In the long run they offer better and more stable climates for investment. They are more environmentally responsible because they must answer to their own citizens, who organize to protest the destruction of their environments. They are better bets to honor international treaties

since they value legal obligations and because their openness makes it much more difficult to breach agreements in secret. Precisely because, within their own borders, they respect competition, civil liberties, property rights, and the rule of law, democracies are the only reliable foundation on which a new world order of international security and prosperity can be built.[12]

The implications of this reasoning are two-fold. It has led to an emphasis upon democracy promotion in the foreign policy of many countries, and it has led to calls for collaboration amongst democracies – as a community of shared values – as the effectiveness and legitimacy of more inclusive multilateral arrangements, such as the UN, have come into question.[13] In theory, the benefits of such collaboration will have a demonstration effect and encourage other states to become democratic. Such a process is under way in Western Europe, where the prospect of joining the liberal security community has had the effect of contributing to incentives for democracy and liberalization in central and Eastern Europe.

The idea, is, however, controversial and divisive. It represents a challenge to the legalist principle of sovereign equality amongst states upon which the UN, for example, is based. According to the legalist tradition, as long as states conform to established international norms and laws, they are legitimate members of the community of states. Imposing a conditionality based upon the nature of domestic governance raises suspicions of cultural imperialism or ethnocentrism. The idea that an exclusive league of democracies has superior moral legitimacy to non-democratic societies is highly adversarial, especially if it implies that new forms of "liberal" multilateralism can transcend "old" Westphalian forms of multilateralism when they collide. However, perhaps the main concern with the idea of new forms of multilateralism on the basis of shared values is that it is inconsistent. Indeed, it often appears to be a part of the repertoire of US-led *ad hoc* alliances, bilateralism and unilateralism.

A specific example of an alternative form of exclusive multilateralism amongst allies is the Proliferation Security Initiative (PSI). Launched by the US in 2003, the PSI aims to stop trafficking of WMD, their delivery systems, and related materials to and from states and non-state actors of concern. The emphasis is upon aggressive interdiction, particularly of maritime activity, including boarding and searching ships. The leading states emphasize the "global" and "multilateral" nature of PSI and the endorsement that it has received from the UN High-level Panel on Threats, Challenges and Change and

UN Secretary-General Kofi Annan who applauded the efforts of the PSI to "fill a gap in our defenses."[14] The US State Department observes that more than 60 countries around the world have indicated their support for PSI. The idea that the PSI is an activity, not an organization, and that it is based upon flexibility conforms with the new emphasis in the US and amongst its allies for multilateral forms which respond to needs – following the "coalition of the willing" model – rather than existing arrangements. It is notable that the PSI originated as a flexible working arrangement, not as a convention or treaty.

The arrangement has certainly shown its effectiveness. In October 2003, the US, UK, Germany and Italy, acting under the auspices of the PSI, stopped an illegal cargo of centrifuge parts for uranium enrichment destined for Libya. Some have claimed that this was instrumental in Libya's decision to recant its desire to pursue nuclear weapons.

However, even though few states would object to the intentions of PSI, there are concerns about what it represents. As it does not give member states any powers which did not already exist under international law, it appears as an alternative initiative under US leadership. The core participants – Australia, Canada, France, Germany, Italy, Japan, the Netherlands, Norway, Poland, Portugal, Russia, Singapore, Spain, the UK and the US – are within the Western camp, with the exception of perhaps Russia. The PSI has become associated with US dominance in non-proliferation efforts. Even if this impression can be eradicated, the fact remains that the initiative was begun as an *ad hoc* and proactive arrangement outside of established multilateral arrangements, as a flexible US-led coalition. It is exactly the type of response that the neoconservatives had advocated, seeking UN endorsement after the fact rather than working through the UN at the outset. Some have called for the PSI to be more closely aligned with the UN, but the point is that the US and its allies sought to avoid the perceived structural limitations of the UN in creating it.[15] While some countries – such as China – are in principle wary of such an approach, there are also some specific reasons why some states have reservations. In East Asia the PSI is seen as primarily targeting North Korea – especially after that country's nuclear test in October 2006 – and is certainly exerting pressure upon the country. China and South Korea – which both have ties to North Korea and also have certain views about how North Korea should be engaged – have not been convinced that pressure is the best way to achieve results. As the PSI is construed as a form of pressure, these countries are wary of it.[16]

152 Conclusion: revisiting institutionalism

Another form of alternative multilateralism is found in the Shanghai Cooperation Organization (SCO). Founded in 2001 by Russia, China, and the Central Asian republics of Kazakhstan, Kyrgyzstan, Tajikistan, and Uzbekistan, the SCO calls for "closer political and economic cooperation and coordinated action among the member states to fight terrorism, extremism and separatism." Mongolia became the first country to receive observer status at the 2004 Tashkent Summit. Pakistan, India and Iran received observer status in 2005. The declaration on the establishment of the SCO stated that: "The Shanghai Cooperation Organization is not an alliance directed against other States and regions and it adheres to the principle of openness." However, most analysts believe that one of the original purposes of the SCO was to serve as a counterbalance to the US and to resist the influence – or interference – of the US in areas near Russia and China. Iranian President Mahmoud Ahmadinejad, in arguing that the SCO should be enlarged, stated in June 2006 that: "We want this organization to develop into a powerful body influential in regional and international politics, economics and trade, serving to block threats and unlawful strong-arm interference from various countries."[17]

The SCO is certainly not a military alliance between Russia and China – which would represent a significant challenge. However, it is significant as an alternative form of multilateralism interpreted by many as a response to a hegemonic US approach to pursuing its interests. Multilateralism, in this sense, is a vehicle for counterbalancing US influence.

Given the inherent strains of maintaining viable multilateral arrangements – which are most acute in sensitive peace and security areas – it is very unsurprising that there are problems. The fundamental *principle* of multilateralism, with all its limitations, is not in crisis. Indeed, this principle is validated and vindicated by the demands of the contemporary world. Multilateralism involves collective, cooperative action by states – when necessary, in cooperation with non-state actors – to deal with common challenges and problems when these are best managed collectively at the international level. Areas such as maintaining and promoting international peace and security, economic development and international trade, human rights, functional and technical cooperation, and the protection of the environment – amongst others – require joint action to reduce costs, and to bring order and regularity to international relations. Powerful states can act unilaterally, but such common problems cannot be addressed unilaterally to optimum effectiveness. Some policy areas find agreement on collective action easier than others. Nevertheless, the multilateral rationale

Conclusion: revisiting institutionalism 153

persists because all states – which remain the key although not the sole actors in international relations – face mutual vulnerabilities and share interdependence. Even the most powerful states cannot achieve security, environmental safety, and economic prosperity as effectively (if at all) in isolation or unilaterally. We have seen this demonstrated many times, and so the international system rests upon a network of regimes, treaties, international organizations and shared practices that embody common expectations, reciprocity and equivalence of benefits.

In an interdependent, globalizing world, multilateralism will continue to be a key aspect of international relations. Limitations do and always will exist, and the utility and effectiveness of formal multilateral institutions are inevitably conditioned and constrained by the exigencies of power and leadership. Powerful states may work through formal institutions at their pleasure and selectively. Some issues may defy multilateral approaches. Moreover, changing normative expectations may cast doubt upon the constitutive values of specific international institutions. But the theoretical rationale of multilateralism is broadly intact.

However, the values and institutions of multilateralism as *currently constituted* – and with them, the conceptual tools and presumptions with which multilateralism has been approached hitherto – are arguably under serious challenge. Thus, the distinction between the principle of multilateralism, and the specific forms of institutionalized multilateralism, is fundamentally important. This challenge involves the unit of analysis of multilateralism – presumed to be viable states – as well as the norms which govern multilateral behavior. The problem, in essence, is that states are not all viable, they do not all embrace the rules and changing norms of "international society," and that non-state actors, while an important part of the equation, are not sufficiently integrated into multilateralism.

The US – the most important actor in international relations – clearly does continue to recognize the value of multilateralism in promoting its interests. However, it is able to withhold support or operate outside existing multilateral arrangements when it perceives it to be necessary. It can create new or alternative multilateral arrangements which better suit its values and needs, or use coercion or persuasion to mould multilateralism to its interests. Because of its preeminence, the US can bend the rules of the "institutional bargain" without undermining international organizations and regimes. An extension of this bargain – or a new bargain, in light of US power and its ideological disposition towards unilateralism – is that other states will tolerate and accommodate US autonomy out of necessity. But there are limits

Conclusion: revisiting institutionalism

to this. On the one hand, while the US continues to work multilaterally where it can, its patience is short in the face of ineffectiveness. This brings with it the possibility of a genuine estrangement between the US and the UN, for example. On the other hand, we cannot rule out a serious rift between the US and its traditional allies – especially in Europe – who are more tied to a multilateral international community and to the defense of a rule-based order. But it is certainly not a question of multilateralism versus unilateralism for the US. Rather, it is a choice between different types of multilateralism: established, formalized multilateralism versus new, *ad hoc* forms of multilateralism. A pattern of *ad hoc* coalitions of the willing based upon shared values – especially amongst liberal democracies – is therefore likely to continue.

In some areas of security, the institutionalist tenets of multilateralism (indivisibility, generalized principles of conduct, and diffuse reciprocity) are not functional. But this has always been the case; it is absolutely not new. We cannot apply the same institutionalist theories to both trade policy and to the defense of territory against critical security threats. Different policy areas illustrate different limits to cooperation amongst states. Powerful states have the capacity to disregard the long-term costs of "defection" from multilateral commitments; the trade off between long-term and short-term costs and benefits will be different in the area of security. In this sense institutionalist theory needs to be revisited in light of the evolving security environment. Caporaso observes that multilateralism "requires its participants to renounce temporary advantages and the temptation to define their interests narrowly in terms of national interests, and it also requires them to forgo ad hoc coalitions and to avoid policies based on situational exigencies and momentary constellations of interests."[18] In the area of international security, this principle is no longer sacred – if it ever was – and certainly not for the most powerful states in the international system.

A further institutionalist tenet of multilateralism which requires serious reconsideration is the assumption that multilateral processes, by their very nature, have greater legitimacy than unilateral or *ad hoc* coalition approaches to foreign policy. Ruggie wrote that "multilateral diplomacy has come to embody a procedural norm *in its own right* – though often a hotly contested one – in some instances carrying with it an international legitimacy not enjoyed by other means."[19] The actions and statements of the US – and a number of other powerful countries – would suggest that this principle is eroding.

The traditional – Westphalian – model of multilateralism emphasized equality of state sovereignty and privileged consensus in decision-making.

Conclusion: revisiting institutionalism 155

It coordinated relationships amongst states which were presumed to be rational and stable. Non-state actors were of secondary importance and the distinction between "domestic" and "international" politics was clear. In academic theories of international relations, this conformed to a material approach to "high politics" amongst self-centered actors, free from the complications of changing norms. Ineffectiveness and status quo were tolerated, often according to the lowest common denominator. This resulted in perverse outcomes: international organizations failed to respond to genocide, and this was legally sound according to the rules of procedure of international organizations. Moreover, established multilateral approaches to maintaining international security appeared to be severely tested by changing threats. The Westphalian model therefore cannot remain the constitutive principle of multilateralism in the twenty-first century; the rules of procedure of multilateral arrangements must be questioned when they result in decisions and performance according to the lowest common denominator. There is a responsibility to act in response to – and in anticipation of – pressing global problems, and this should be the starting point for multilateralism.

Notes

Foreword

1 Chris Patten, "Jaw-Jaw, Not War-War," *Financial Times*, 15 February 2002.
2 See United Nations, Report of the High-level Panel on Threats, Challenges and Change, *A More Secure World: Our Shared Responsibility* (New York: UN, 2004); and *2005 World Summit Outcome*, General Assembly resolution A/60/1, 24 October 2006.
3 "Last of the Big Time Spenders: US Military Budget Still the World's Largest, and Growing," Center for Defense Information, Table on "Fiscal Year 2004 Budget," based on data provided by the US Department of Defense and International Institute for Strategic Studies, Washington, DC, available at www.cdi.org/budget/2004/world-military-spending.cfm, 1 March 2004.
4 Donald J. Puchala, "World Hegemony and the United Nations," *International Studies Review* 7, no. 4 (2005): 571–84.
5 Edward C. Luck, *Mixed Messages: American Politics and International Organization, 1919–1999* (Washington, DC: Brookings, 1999). He also has a book in this series, *UN Security Council: Practice and Promise* (London: Routledge, 2006).
6 Edward Newman, *The UN Secretary-General from the Cold War to the New Era: A Global Peace and Security Mandate?* (New York: Palgrave Macmillan, 1998).
7 These include: Edward Newman and Oliver Richmond, eds., *Challenges to Peacebuilding: Managing Spoilers During Conflict Resolution* (Tokyo: UNU Press, 2004); Edward Newman and Roland Rich, eds., *The UN Role in Promoting Democracy: Between Ideals and Reality* (Tokyo: UNU Press, 2004); and Edward Newman and Joanne Van Selm, eds., *Refugees and Forced Displacement: International Security, Human Vulnerability, and the State* (Tokyo: UNU Press, 2003).

Introduction

1 John Gerard Ruggie, "Multilateralism: The Anatomy of an Institution," in *Multilateralism Matters. The Theory and Praxis of an Institutional Form*, ed. John Gerard Ruggie (New York: Columbia University Press, 1993), 10–12.

Notes 157

2 The peace of Westphalia of 1648 – which ended the Thirty Years War – is often said to have signaled the beginning of an interstate system (at least in Europe). A Westphalian system is therefore said to rest upon the concept of sovereignty of political units, territoriality, and non-intervention. In the following centuries, "international" norms, diplomatic practices, international law, and rules of interaction developed. This European state system then spread through the world. International "orders" underscored the concept of state co-existence.
3 Ruggie, "Multilateralism: The Anatomy of an Institution," 7–8.
4 John Gerard Ruggie, "This Crisis of Multilateralism is Different," paper presented at the United Nations Association National Forum on the United Nations, Capital Hilton Hotel, Washington DC, 26–28 June 2003.

1 Multilateral malaise – sources and manifestations

1 Edward D. Mansfield, "The Organization of International Relations," in *International Organization: A Reader*, ed. Friedrich Kratochwil and Edward D. Mansfield (New York: Harper Collins, 1994), 3.
2 Stephen D. Krasner, "Structural Causes and Regime Consequences," in *International Organization: A Reader*, ed. Friedrich Kratochwil and Edward D. Mansfield, 97.
3 Robert O. Keohane, "International Institutions: Two Approaches," in *International Organization: A Reader*, ed. Friedrich Kratochwil and Edward D. Mansfield, 48–9.
4 John Gerard Ruggie, "Multilateralism: The Anatomy of an Institution," in *Multilateralism Matters: The Theory and Praxis of an Institutional Form*, ed. John Gerard Ruggie (New York: Columbia University Press, 1993), 11.
5 Ruggie, "Multilateralism: The Anatomy of an Institution," 10–11.
6 Robert O. Keohane, "Reciprocity in International Relations," *International Organization* 40, no. 1 (1985): 1–27.
7 Robert O. Keohane, *Power and Governance in a Partially Globalized World* (London: Routledge, 2002).
8 Ruggie, "Multilateralism: The Anatomy of an Institution," 8.
9 Stephen Krasner, ed., *International Regimes* (Ithaca, NY: Cornell University Press, 1983).
10 Ruggie, "Multilateralism: The Anatomy of an Institution," 33.
11 *American Interests and UN Reform*, Report of the Task Force on the United Nations (Washington DC: United States Institute of Peace, 2005), 3.
12 *A More Secure World: Our Shared Responsibility*, Report of the Secretary-General's High-level Panel on Threats, Challenges and Change, Report of the Secretary-General to the General Assembly, A/59/565 (2 December 2004): 14.
13 Michael J. Glennon, "Idealism at the UN," *Policy Review* no. 129 (February/March 2005), 15.
14 Paul Heinbecker, "Washington's Exceptionalism and the United Nations," *Global Governance* 10, no. 3 (2004): 273.
15 Anne-Marie Slaughter, "Security, Solidarity, and Sovereignty: The Grand Themes of UN Reform," *The American Journal of International Law* 99, no. 3 (2005): 620.
16 Jeremy Rabkin, *Law Without Nations? Why Constitutional Government Requires Sovereign States* (Princeton, NJ: Princeton University Press, 2005).

Notes

17 President Bush Addresses UN General Assembly, 23 September 2003.
18 Keith Krause and W. Andy Knight, eds., *State, Society, and the United Nations System: Changing Perspectives on Multilateralism* (Tokyo: UNU Press, 1995).
19 Remarks as prepared for Secretary of Defense Donald Rumsfeld, the National Defense University in Washington, DC, Thursday, 31 January 2002, available at http://www.oft.osd.mil/library/library_files/speech_136_rumsfeld_speech_31_jan_2002.doc
20 G. John Ikenberry, "America's Imperial Ambition," *Foreign Affairs* 81, no. 5 (2002): 45.
21 Ikenberry, "America's Imperial Ambition," 54.
22 *American Interests and UN Reform, Report of the Task Force on the United Nations*, 7.
23 Speech of John R. Bolton, Under-Secretary for Arms Control and International Security, on "Beyond the Axis of Evil: Additional Threats From Weapons of Mass Destruction," to the Heritage Foundation, Washington DC, 6 May 2002.
24 Joseph S. Nye, "Seven Tests. Between Concert and Unilateralism," *National Interest*, no. 66 (Winter 2001/2002): 5–13.
25 John G. Ruggie, "This Crisis of Multilateralism is Different."
26 Robert O. Keohane, "The Contingent Legitimacy of Multilateralism," in *Multilateralism Under Challenge? Power, International Order, and Structural Change*, ed. Edward Newman, Ramesh Thakur and John Tirman (Tokyo: United Nations University Press, 2006), 56–76.
27 Yoshikazu Sakamoto, *Global Transformations: Challenges to the State System* (Tokyo: UNU Press, 1994); Keith Krause and W. Andy Knight, *State, Society, and the United Nations System: Changing Perspectives on Multilateralism* (Tokyo: UNU Press, 1995); Stephen Gill, ed. *Globalization, Democratization and Multilateralism* (New York: St. Martin's Press, 1997); Michael G. Schechter, ed., *Innovation in Multilateralism* (London: Macmillan for UNU Press, 1999); Michael G. Schechter, ed., *Future Multilateralism: The Political and Social Framework* (London: Macmillan for UNU Press, 1999).
28 Robert W. Cox ed., *The New Realism: Perspectives on Multilateralism and World Order* (London: Macmillan for UNU Press, 2000).
29 J. Pérez de Cuéllar, "Report of the Secretary-General on the Work of the Organization" (New York: United Nations, 1982).
30 Kurt Waldheim, *In the Eye of the Storm* (London: Weidenfield and Nicolson, 1980), 121.
31 Michael J. Glennon, "Why the Security Council Failed," *Foreign Affairs* (May/June 2003): 25.
32 Hans J. Morgenthau, *Politics Among Nations* (New York: Alfred A. Knopf, 1948).
33 Kenneth Waltz, *Theory of International Politics* (Reading, MA: Addison-Wesley, 1979).
34 *A More Secure World: Our Shared Responsibility*, 62.
35 Waheguru Pal Singh Sidhu and Ramesh Thakur, "Iraq's Challenge to World Order," in *The Iraq Crisis and World Order: Structural, Institutional and Normative Challenges*, ed. Ramesh Thakur and Waheguru Pal Singh Sidhu (Tokyo: UNU Press, 2006), 3–15.

36 Ernest W. Lefever, "Reining in the UN: Mistaking the instrument for the actor," *Foreign Affairs* 72, no. 3 (1993): 17.
37 F.S. Northedge, *The International Political System* (London: Faber, 1976), 181.
38 Georg Schwarzenberger, *Power Politics*, 2nd ed. (New York: Praeger, 1951), 712.
39 Kenneth N. Waltz, "Structural Realism After the Cold War," *International Security* 25, no. 1 (2000): 10.
40 John Gerard Ruggie, "What Makes the World Hang Together? Neoutilitarianism and the Social Constructivist Challenge," *International Organization* 52, no. 4 (1998): 879.
41 Alexander Wendt, "Anarchy is What States Make of It: The Social Construction of Power Politics," *International Organization* 46, no. 2 (1992): 399.
42 Kofi Annan, "Secretary-General Address to the General Assembly," New York, 23 September 2003. Also Joachim Krause, "Multilateralism: Behind European Views," *The Washington Quarterly* 27, no. 2 (Spring 2004): 43–59; Gwyn Prins, "Lord Castlereagh's Return: The Significance of Kofi Annan's High Level Panel on Threats, Challenges and Change," *International Affairs* 81, no. 2 (2005): 373–91; Lord Hannay of Chiswick GCMG, "Reforming the United Nations," *Conflict, Security and Development* 5, no. 1 (2005): 109–17.
43 Ruggie, "This Crisis of Multilateralism is Different."
44 Thomas G. Weiss, "An Unchanged Security Council: The Sky Ain't Falling," *Security Dialogue* 36, no. 3 (2005): 367. Edward C. Luck agrees, calling the "fork in the road" idea a "gross overstatement," in "How Not to Reform the United Nations," *Global Governance* 11, no. 4 (2005): 407.

2 The United States, power, and multilateralism

1 David M. Malone and Yuen Foong Khong, "Introduction," in *Unilateralism and US Foreign Policy: International Perspectives*, ed. David M. Malone and Yuen Foong Khong (Boulder, Colorado: Lynne Rienner Publishers, 2003), 4.
2 Charles Krauthammer, "The Unipolar Moment," *Foreign Affairs* (Winter 1990/1991): 23–33.
3 The SIPRI Yearbook Summary (Stockholm: SIPRI, 2006), 11; and the SIPRI Military Expenditure Database, at http://www.sipri.org.
4 Joseph S. Nye, *Soft Power: The Means to Success in World Politics* (New York: Public Affairs, 2004).
5 George W. Bush, foreword, *The National Security Strategy of the United States of America* (Washington DC: The White House, March 2006).
6 See Stefano Guzzini, "From (Alleged) Unipolarity to the Decline of Multilateralism? A Power-Theoretical Critique," in *Multilateralism Under Challenge? Power, International Order, and Structural Change*, ed. Edward Newman, Ramesh Thakur and John Tirman (Tokyo: UNU Press, 2006): 119–38.
7 Nico Krisch, "Weak as Constraint, Strong as Tool: The Place of International Law in US Foreign Policy," in *Unilateralism and US Foreign Policy: International Perspectives*, ed. David M. Malone and Yuen Foong Khong, 41–70.

8 See, for example, Peter Brookes, *A Devil's Triangle: Terrorism, Weapons of Mass Destruction, and Rogue States* (New York: Rowman and Littlefield, 2005).
9 Remarks of Secretary of Defense Donald Rumsfeld on the "21st Century Transformation of the US Armed Forces," National Defense University, Washington DC, 31 January 2002.
10 The President's State of the Union Address, The United States Capitol, Washington, DC, 29 January 2002.
11 *American Interests and UN Reform: Report of the Task Force on the United Nations* (Washington DC: United States Institute of Peace, 2005), 12.
12 Richard Perle, "Coalitions of the Willing Are Our Best Hope," American Enterprise Institute for Public Policy Research, Short Publications, 21 March 2003, at http://www.aei.org/publications/filter.all,pubID.16666/pub_detail.asp.
13 Bruce W. Jentleson, "Tough Love Multilateralism," *The Washington Quarterly* 27, no. 1 (2004): 8. See also Steven Holloway, "US Unilateralism at the UN: Why Great Powers Do Not Make Great Multilateralists," *Global Governance* 6, no. 3 (2000): 361–81.
14 John R. Bolton, "Kofi Annan's UN Power Grab," American Enterprise Institute for Public Policy Research, Short Publications, 1 January 2000, at http://www.aei.org/publications/pubID.14912/pub_detail.asp
15 Paul Heinbecker, "Washington's Exceptionalism and the United Nations," *Global Governance* 10, no. 3 (2004): 274.
16 G. John Ikenberry, "America's Imperial Ambition," *Foreign Affairs* 81 (September 2002): 53.
17 Edward C. Luck, *Mixed Messages: American Politics and International Organization 1919–1999* (Washington DC: Brookings Institution Press, 1999), 2. See also Barbara Crossette, "Killing One's Progeny: America and the United Nations," *World Policy Journal* 19, no. 3 (2002): 54–9.
18 John R. Bolton, "The Creation, Fall, Rise, and Fall of the United Nations," in *Delusions of Grandeur: The United Nations and Global Intervention*, ed. Ted Galen Carpenter (Washington DC: Cato Institute, 1997), 46.
19 Miles Kahler, "Multilateralism with Small and Large Numbers," in *Multilateralism Matters: The Theory and Praxis of an Institutional Form*, ed. John Gerard Ruggie (New York: Columbia University Press, 1993), 681–708.
20 Robert O. Keohane and Joseph S. Nye Jr., "The Club Model of Multilateral Cooperation and Problems of Democratic Legitimacy," in *Power and Governance in a Partially Globalized World*, ed. Robert O. Keohane (London: Routledge, 2002), 219–44.
21 Kurt Waldheim, *In the Eye of the Storm* (London: Weidenfield and Nicolson, 1980), 111.
22 Daniel Patrick Moynihan, *A Dangerous Place* (Boston: Little, Brown & Co., 1978).
23 Seymour Maxwell Finger and Arnold A. Saltzman, *Bending with the Winds: Kurt Waldheim and the United Nations* (New York: Praeger Publishers, 1990), 33.
24 Henry Kissinger, *Years of Upheaval* (London: Weidenfeld and Nicolson, 1982), 471–4 and 480, 486, 502.

25 Paul Taylor and A. J. R. Groom, *The United Nations and the Gulf War, 1990–91: Back to the Future?* (London: The Royal Institute of International Affairs Discussion Paper 38, 1992), 2.
26 Anthony Parsons, "The UN and the National Interest of States," in *United Nations, Divided World. The UN's Roles in International Relations*, ed. Adam Roberts and Benedict Kingsbury (Oxford: Clarendon Press, 1993), 111.
27 Robert O. Keohane and Jospeh S. Nye Jr., "Two Cheers for Multilateralism," *Foreign Policy*, no. 60 (Fall 1985): 148.
28 Thomas M. Franck, "Soviet Initiatives: US Responses – New Opportunities for Reviving the United Nations System," *The American Journal of International Law* 83, no. 3 (1989): 532–3; see also Brian Urquhart, *A Life in Peace and War* (New York, Harper and Row, 1987), 326.
29 Stephen Krasner, *Structural Conflict: The Third World Against Global Liberalism* (California: University of California Press, 1985), 300.
30 E. B. Haas, "Regime Decay: Conflict Management and International Organizations, 1945–1981," *International Organization* 37, no. 2 (1983): 189–256.
31 See Yves Beigbeder, *Threats to the International Civil Service* (London: Pinter Publishers, 1988), 56–7.
32 Bolton, "The Creation, Fall, Rise, and Fall of the United Nations," 47.
33 Charles Krauthammer, *Democratic Realism: An American Foreign Policy for a Unipolar World* (Washington, DC: The AEI Press, 2004), 6.
34 Bolton, "The Creation, Fall, Rise, and Fall of the United Nations," 45. See also Eric Shawn, *The U.N. Exposed: How the United Nations Sabotages America's Security and Fails the World* (New York: Sentinel HC, 2006); Thomas P. Kilgannon, *Diplomatic Divorce: Why America Should End Its Love Affair with the United Nations* (Macon, GA: Stroud & Hall Publishers, 2006).
35 John G. Ruggie, "This Crisis of Multilateralism is Different," paper presented at the United Nations Association National Forum on the United Nations, Capital Hilton Hotel, Washington DC, 26–28 June 2003, 7.
36 Jed Babbin, *Inside the Asylum: Why the UN and Old Europe are Worse Than You Think* (Washington DC: Regnery Publishing Inc., 2004), 4, 60.
37 Dore Gold, *Tower of Babble: How the United Nations has Fueled Global Chaos* (New York: Crown Forum, 2004), 223; Bolton, "The Creation, Fall, Rise, and Fall of the United Nations."
38 Newt Gingrich, "A Limited UN is Best for America," *The Boston Globe*, 12 September 2005.
39 Jed Babbin, *Inside the Asylum: Why the UN and Old Europe Are Worse Than You Think*, 2.
40 "President Bush Addresses the United Nations General Assembly," United Nations, New York, 23 September 2003.
41 Secretary Condoleezza Rice, Remarks at the 60th United Nations General Assembly, New York, 17 September 2005.
42 *A More Secure World: Our Shared Responsibility*, Report of the Secretary-General's High-level Panel on Threats, Challenges and Change, Report of the Secretary-General to the General Assembly, A/59/565 (2 December 2004): 78.
43 Jesse Helms, "Saving the UN," *Foreign Affairs* 75, no. 5 (1996): 2–7.

162 Notes

44 Bolton, "The Creation, Fall, Rise, and Fall of the United Nations," 52. See also Charles Krauthammer, *Democratic Realism: An American Foreign Policy for a Unipolar World.*
45 Paul A. Volcker, Richard J. Goldstone and Mark Pieth constituted the Independent Inquiry Committee into the United Nations Oil-for-Food Program whose five-volume report is available at www.iic-offp.org.
46 Joachim Krause, "Multilateralism: Behind European Views," *The Washington Quarterly* 27, no. 2 (Spring 2004): 43–59.
47 Robert Kagan, *Of Paradise and Power: America and Europe in the New World Order* (New York: Alfred A. Knopf, 2003), 3.
48 Mohammed Ayoob and Matthew Zierler, "The Unipolar Concert: Unipolarity and Multilateralism in the Age of Globalization," in *The Iraq Crisis and World Order: Structural, Institutional and Normative Challenges,* ed. Ramesh Thakur and Waheguru Pal Singh Sidhu (Tokyo: UNU Press, 2006), 37–56.
49 Ruggie, "This Crisis of Multilateralism is Different."
50 James Dobbins, "Bush's Second Term: We're all Multilateralists Now," *International Herald Tribune*, 13 November 2004.
51 President Bush Delivers Graduation Speech at West Point, United States Military Academy, 1 June 2002. This was reiterated in The National Security Strategy of the United States of America, March 2006.
52 Ikenberry, "America's Imperial Ambition," 53.
53 UN Secretary-General Kofi Annan's Address to the UN General Assembly, New York, United Nations, 12 September 2002.
54 Speech of President Chirac to the General Assembly, 23 September 2003.
55 President George W. Bush Graduation Speech at West Point, United States Military Academy, 1 June 2002.
56 Andrew Kydd, "In America We (Used to) Trust: US Hegemony and Global Cooperation," *Political Science Quarterly* 120, no. 4 (2005–6): 619–36.
57 Ruggie, "Multilateralism: The Anatomy of an Institution," 23.
58 Secretary Condoleezza Rice, "Remarks at the Institut d'Etudes Politiques de Paris – Sciences Po" (8 February 2005).
59 Speech of President Chirac to the General Assembly, 23 September 2003.
60 Bolton, "The Creation, Fall, Rise, and Fall of the United Nations," 58.
61 *American Interests and UN Reform. Report of the Task Force on the United Nations* (Washington DC: United States Institute of Peace, 2005), 5.
62 President Bush Addresses the United Nations General Assembly, United Nations, New York, 23 September 2003.
63 Krauthammer, "The Unipolar Moment," 25.

3 Collective security and the use of force

1 Speech of President Chirac to the General Assembly, 23 September 2003.
2 *American Interests and UN Reform, Report of the Task Force on the United Nations* (Washington DC: United States Institute of Peace, 2005), vii.
3 Michael J. Glennon, "Why the Security Council Failed," *Foreign Affairs* 82, no. 3 (2003): 23. Robert Howse similarly derides the "internationalist fantasy of an effective UN-based collective security system" in "The Road to Baghdad is Paved with Good Intentions," *European Journal of International Law* 13, no. 1 (2002): 89. See also Charles Krauthammer, "The

Unipolar Moment," *Foreign Affairs* (Winter 1990/1991): 23–33; and John C. Yoo and Will Trachman, "Less than Bargained for: The Use of Force and the Declining Relevance of the United Nations," *Chicago Journal of International Law* 5, no. 2 (2005): 379–94. For a response to the Glennon article see Edward C. Luck, Anne-Marie Slaughter and Ian Hurd, "Stayin' Alive," *Foreign Affairs* 82, no. 4 (2003): 201–5.
4 Richard Perle, "United They Fall," *The Spectator* (22 March 2003): 22.
5 John G. Ruggie, "This Crisis of Multilateralism is Different," paper presented at the United Nations Association National Forum on the United Nations, Capital Hilton Hotel, Washington DC, 26–28 June 2003.
6 Thomas M. Franck, "What Happens Now? The United Nations After Iraq," *The American Journal of International Law* 97, no. 3 (2003): 608.
7 Edwin M. Smith, "Collective Security: Changing Conceptions and Institutional Adaptation," in *Adapting the United Nations to a Postmodern Era: Lessons Learned*, ed. W. Andy Knight (New York: Palgrave, 2005), 43.
8 Ramesh Thakur, *The United Nations, Peace and Security* (Cambridge: Cambridge University Press, 2006), 10.
9 Robert W. Tucker and David C. Hendrickson, "The Sources of American Legitimacy," *Foreign Affairs* 83, no. 6 (2004).
10 Thakur, *The United Nations, Peace and Security*, 222.
11 Joachim Krause, "Multilateralism: Behind European Views," *The Washington Quarterly* 27, no. 2 (Spring 2004): 43.
12 Sally Marks, *The Illusion of Peace. International Relations in Europe 1918–1933* (London: Macmillan Press, 1976).
13 Alexandru Grigorescu, "Mapping the UN-League of Nations Analogy: Are There Still Lessons to Be Learned from the League?" *Global Governance* 11, no. 1 (2005): 25–42; Glennon, "Why the Security Council Failed."
14 E. H. Carr, *The Twenty Years Crisis, An Introduction to the Study of International Relations*, 2nd ed. (New York: Palgrave, 2001).
15 Glennon, "Why the Security Council Failed," 21.
16 Adam Roberts, "The Use of Force," in *The UN Security Council. From the Cold War to the 21st Century*, ed. David Malone (Boulder CO: Lynne Rienner Publishers, 2004), 150.
17 *Human Security Report 2005 – War and Peace in the 21st Century* (New York: Oxford University Press, 2005); Monty G. Marshall and Ted Robert Gurr, *Peace and Conflict 2005: A Global Survey of Armed Conflicts, Self-Determination Movements, and Democracy* (Maryland, Center for International Development and Conflict Management, University of Maryland, 2005) at http://www.cidcm.umd.edu/peace_and_conflict.asp; War archive data trends of Hamburg University (Kriege-Archiv: Kriege und bewaffnete Konflikte seit 1945) at http://www.sozialwiss.uni-hamburg.de/publish/Ipw/Akuf/kriege_archiv.htm; *Conflictbarometer 2005*, Heidelberg University Institute on International Conflict Research (Heidelberg University: Department of Political Science, 2005) at http://hiik.de/en/barometer2005/ConflictBarometer2005.pdf; *Uppsala Conflict Database*, Uppsala University Department of Peace and Conflict Research, at http://www.pcr.uu.sc/database/index.php.
18 Lotta Harbom and Peter Wallensteen, "Armed Conflict and Its International Dimensions, 1946–2004," *Journal of Peace Research* 42, no. 5 (2005): 623.

19 Monty G. Marshall and Ted Robert Gurr, *Peace and Conflict 2005*; Lotta Harbom and Peter Wallensteen, "Armed Conflict and Its International Dimensions, 1946–2004."
20 Michael J. Glennon, *Policy Review*, no. 129 (February-March 2005): 3.
21 *A More Secure World: Our Shared Responsibility*, Report of the Secretary-General's High Level Panel on Threats, Challenges and Change (New York: United Nations, 2004), 54.
22 *The National Security Strategy of the United States of America* (Washington: DC: The White House, 2002). Thomas M. Franck wrote that this strategy "aims at ending all collective control over the US resort to force. This is not system transformation by system abrogation. Instead of the law of the Charter, we find an unabashed return to the Melian principle." "What Happens Now? The United Nations After Iraq," 620.
23 *The National Security Strategy of the United States of America* (Washington: DC: The White House, 2006).
24 *The National Security Strategy of the United States of America* (2002), 15.
25 Franck, "What Happens Now? The United Nations After Iraq," 619.
26 *In Larger Freedom: Towards Development, Security and Human Rights for All*, Report of the Secretary-General (New York: United Nations, 21 March 2005), para. 125.
27 Lawrence Ziring, Robert E. Riggs and Jack C. Plano, *The United Nations. International Organization and World Politics*, 4th ed. (Belmont CA: Thomas Wadsworth, 2005), 173.
28 Franck, "What Happens Now? The United Nations after Iraq."
29 *A More Secure World: Our Shared Responsibility*, 62. Brian Frederking also argues that, contrary to popular opinion, "the dominant post-cold war global security trend is the gradual construction of collective security rules." See "Constructing Post-Cold War Collective Security," *American Political Science Review* 97, no. 3 (2003): 363.
30 *A More Secure World: Our Shared Responsibility*, 33.
31 Shashi Tharoor, "Saving Humanity From Hell," in *Multilateralism Under Challenge? Power, International Order, and Structural Change*, ed. Edward Newman, Ramesh Thakur and John Tirman (Tokyo: UN University Press, 2006), 21–33.
32 *A More Secure World: Our Shared Responsibility*, 61.

4 Humanitarian intervention

1 *A More Secure World: Our Shared Responsibility*, Report of the Secretary-General's High Level Panel on Threats, Challenges and Change (New York: United Nations, 2004), 66.
2 Roméo Dallaire, *Shake Hands with the Devil. The Failure of Humanity in Rwanda* (New York, Carroll and Graf Publishers, 2004), 6–7.
3 Dallaire, *Shake Hands with the Devil*, 89–90.
4 See for example Nicholas J. Wheeler, *Saving Strangers: Humanitarian Intervention in International Society* (Oxford: Oxford University Press, 2000); Stanley Hoffman, ed., *The Ethics and Politics of Humanitarian Intervention* (Notre Dame: University of Notre Dame Press, 1996); Thomas G. Weiss and Don Hubert, *et al.*, *The Responsibility to Protect*,

Supplementary Volume to the Report of the International Commission on Intervention and States Sovereignty (Ottawa: International Development Research Centre, 2001).

5 For example General Assembly Resolution 2131(20) 1965; *The Declaration on Principles of International Law Concerning Friendly Relations and Cooperation Among States in Accordance with the Charter of the United Nations*, Annex to Resolution 2625(25) 1970; and Resolution 103(36) 1981 on the "inadmissibility of intervention and interference in the internal affairs of States," stressing "the duty of a State to refrain from the exploitation and deformation of human rights issues as a means of interference in the internal affairs of States."

6 For example Charles R. Beitz, *Political Theory and International Relations* (Princeton: Princeton University Press, 1979); David R. Mapel, "Military Intervention and Rights," *Millennium* 20, no. 1 (1991): 41–55; Terry Nardin, "The Moral Basis of Humanitarian Intervention," *Ethics and International Affairs* 16, no. 1 (2002): 57–70.

7 Albrecht Schnabel, "Playing with Fire: Humanitarian Intervention Post-Kosovo," in *The United Nations and Human Security*, ed. Edward Newman and Oliver P. Richmond (Basingstoke: Palgrave, 2001), 137–50.

8 See "Forum: Humanitarian Intervention and International Society," *The International Journal of Human Rights* 6, no. 1 (2002): 81–102; and "Special Issue: The Kosovo Tragedy: The Human Rights Dimensions," *The International Journal of Human Rights* 4, no. 3 (2000).

9 Kofi Annan, "The legitimacy to intervene: International action to uphold human rights requires a new understanding of state and individual sovereignty," *Financial Times*, 31 December 1999.

10 Kofi Annan, "We the Peoples: The Role of the United Nations in the 21st Century" (New York: United Nations, 2000), para. 217.

11 Dallaire, *Shake Hands with the Devil*, 1, 7.

12 *The Responsibility to Protect* – Report of the International Commission on Intervention and State Sovereignty (Ottawa: International Development Research Centre, December 2001).

13 *The Responsibility to Protect*, 69.

14 *The Responsibility to Protect*, 3 and 6.

15 *The Responsibility to Protect*, 8.

16 The following three paragraphs draw directly from the synopsis of the report.

17 See Edward Newman and Albrecht Schnabel, eds., *Recovering from Civil Conflict: Reconciliation, Peace and Development* (London: Frank Cass, 2002).

18 *Srebrenica – Reconstruction, background, consequences and analyses of the fall of a Safe Area* – Report of the Netherlands Institute for War Documentation (Amsterdam: Boom Publishers, 2002).

19 Report prepared by the Netherlands Advisory Committee on Issues of Public International Law and the Advisory Council on International Affairs, 2000.

20 Report prepared by the Netherlands Advisory Committee, 3

21 Report prepared by the Netherlands Advisory Committee, 3 and 5.

22 Report prepared by the Netherlands Advisory Committee, 7.

23 Report prepared by the Netherlands Advisory Committee, 9.

24 Report prepared by the Netherlands Advisory Committee, 13.
25 Report prepared by the Netherlands Advisory Committee, 24.
26 Report prepared by the Netherlands Advisory Committee, 25.
27 Report prepared by the Netherlands Advisory Committee, 26.
28 Report prepared by the Netherlands Advisory Committee, 30–1.
29 Report prepared by the Netherlands Advisory Committee, 36.
30 Report prepared by the Netherlands Advisory Committee, 34.
31 Report prepared by the Netherlands Advisory Committee, 36.
32 *The Responsibility to Protect*, xii.
33 *Humanitarian Intervention: Legal and political aspects*, Danish Institute of International Affairs, 1999, 128.
34 *Humanitarian Intervention: Legal and political aspects*, Danish Institute of International Affairs, 1999, 24.
35 *Humanitarian Intervention: Legal and political aspects*, Danish Institute of International Affairs, 1999, 26.
36 *Humanitarian Intervention: Legal and political aspects*, Danish Institute of International Affairs, 1999, 15.
37 *Humanitarian Intervention: Legal and political aspects*, Danish Institute of International Affairs, 1999, 30.
38 *Humanitarian Intervention: Legal and political aspects*, Danish Institute of International Affairs, 1999, 61.
39 *Humanitarian Intervention: Legal and political aspects*, Danish Institute of International Affairs, 1999, 62.
40 *Humanitarian Intervention: Legal and political aspects*, Danish Institute of International Affairs, 1999, 93.
41 *Humanitarian Intervention: Legal and political aspects*, Danish Institute of International Affairs, 1999, 69.
42 *Humanitarian Intervention: Legal and political aspects*, Danish Institute of International Affairs, 1999, 74.
43 *Humanitarian Intervention: Legal and political aspects*, Danish Institute of International Affairs, 1999, 106–9.
44 *Humanitarian Intervention: Legal and political aspects*, Danish Institute of International Affairs, 1999, 124.
45 *The Report of the Independent International Commission on Kosovo* (Oxford: Oxford University Press, 2000), 4.
46 *The Report of the Independent International Commission on Kosovo*, 10.
47 *The Report of the Independent International Commission on Kosovo*, 187.
48 *The Report of the Independent International Commission on Kosovo*, 187.
49 *The Report of the Independent International Commission on Kosovo*, 193.
50 *The Report of the Independent International Commission on Kosovo*, 194.
51 *The Report of the Independent International Commission on Kosovo*, 195.
52 *The Report of the Independent International Commission on Kosovo*, 196.
53 *The Report of the Independent International Commission on Kosovo*, 196.
54 *A More Secure World: Our Shared Responsibility*, 17.
55 *A More Secure World: Our Shared Responsibility*, vii.
56 *In Larger Freedom: Towards Development, Security and Human Rights for All*, Report of the United Nations Secretary-General, New York, 21 March 2005, para. 132.
57 *In Larger Freedom*, para. 135.
58 2005 World Summit Outcome, A/60/150, 20 September 2005, para. 139.

Notes 167

59 Thomas G. Weiss, "Using Military Force For Human Protection: What Next?" in *Multilateralism Under Challenge? Power, International Order, and Structural Change*, ed. Edward Newman, Ramesh Thakur and John Tirman (Tokyo: United Nations University Press, 2006), 376–94.
60 *A More Secure World: Our Shared Responsibility*, 66.
61 David P. Forsythe, "International Humanitarianism in the Contemporary World: Forms and Issues," in *Multilateralism Under Challenge? Power, International Order, and Structural Change*, 253.

5 Weapons of mass destruction

1 Michael A. Levi and Michael E. O'Hanlon, "Arms Control and American Security," *Current History* 104, issue 681 (2005): 163.
2 Wade Boese, "Nuclear Nonproliferation Treaty Meeting Sputters," *Arms Control Today* 35, no. 6 (2005): 22.
3 Trevor Findlay, "Weapons of Mass Destruction," in *Multilateralism Under Challenge? Power, International Order, and Structural Change*, ed. Edward Newman, Ramesh Thakur and John Tirman (Tokyo: UNU Press, 2006), 224.
4 *National Strategy to Combat Weapons of Mass Destruction* (Washington DC: The White House, December 2002), 1. See also Jon B. Wolfsthal, "The Next Nuclear Wave; the Future of Arms Control," *Foreign Affairs* 84, no. 1 (2005): 156–61; Graham Allison, *Nuclear Terrorism: The Ultimate Preventable Catastrophe* (New York: Times Books, 2004).
5 National Strategy to Combat Weapons of Mass Destruction, 1 and 4.
6 Levi and O'Hanlon, "Arms Control and American Security." See also Derek D. Smith, "Deterrence and Counterproliferation in an Age of Weapons of Mass Destruction," *Security Studies* 12, no. 4 (2003): 152–97.
7 For example the EU Strategy against proliferation of weapons of mass destruction, endorsed by the European Council on 9 December 2003, 15708/03. However, there are clearly divisions regarding arms control within Western Europe and it would be wrong to present a simple contrast between the US and the EU; see Oliver Meier and Gerrard Quille, "Testing Time for Europe's Nonproliferation Strategy," *Arms Control Today* 35, no. 4 (2005): 6–12.
8 Findlay, "Weapons of Mass Destruction," 207.
9 Hans M. Kristensen, "The Role of US Nuclear Weapons: New Doctrine Falls Short of Bush Pledge," *Arms Control Today* 35, no. 7 (2005): 13–19; National Strategy to Combat Weapons of Mass Destruction, 3.
10 Keir A. Lieber and Daryl G. Press, "The Rise of US Nuclear Primacy," *Foreign Affairs* 85, no. 2 (2006): 42–54.
11 Levi and O'Hanlon, "Arms Control and American Security," 169.
12 Ramesh Thakur, "North Korea Test as Spur to Nuclear Disarmament," *Economic and Political Weekly*, 21 October 2006, 4403.
13 See the opinion of C. G. Weeramantry in the collection of opinions in Miles A. Pomper, "Is there a Role for Nuclear Weapons Today?" *Arms Control Today* 35, no. 6 (2005): 5.
14 Madeleine Albright and Robin Cook, "We Must Cut Our Nuclear Arsenals: Unless the US and Europe Act Now, Non-Nuclear States Will Rebel," *The Guardian*, 9 June 2004.

168 Notes

15 Leonard Weiss, "Nuclear-Weapon States and the Grand Bargain," *Arms Control Today* 33, no. 10 (2003): 6–7.
16 *A More Secure World: Our Shared Responsibility*, Report of the Secretary-General's High Level Panel on Threats, Challenges and Change (New York: United Nations, 2004), 39.
17 IAEA Board of Governors, "Implementation of the NPT Safeguards Agreement in the Islamic Republic of Iran Resolution," (GOV/2006/13), 4 February 2006, preamble.
18 Statement by the President of the Security Council, S/PRST/2006/15, 29 March 2006.
19 *A More Secure World: Our Shared Responsibility*, 39.
20 US Withdrawal From the ABM Treaty: President Bush's Remarks and US Diplomatic Notes, *Arms Control Today*, Arms Control Association, January/February 2002, http://www.armscontrol.org/act/2002_01-02/docjanfeb02.asp.
21 "Entry Into Force of Nuclear-Test-Ban Treaty Would Strengthen Security of States, Peoples Everywhere, Secretary-General Says at Launch of Ministerial Statement," UN Press Release SG/SM/9499 DC/2935, 23 September 2004.
22 The Missile Technology Control Regime at a Glance, September 2004, Arms Control Today Factsheets, http://www.armscontrol.org/factsheets/mtcr.asp
23 The Chemical Weapons Convention at a Glance, September 2004, Arms Control Association, http://www.armscontrol.org/factsheets/cwcglance.asp
24 Ere Haru, "Conclusion: Seize the Moment," in *The Chemical Weapons Convention: Implementation, Challenges and Opportunities*, ed. Ramesh Thakur and Ere Haru (Tokyo: UN University Press, 2006).
25 Ralf Trapp, "The Chemical Weapons Convention – Multilateral Instrument With a Future," in *The Chemical Weapons Convention: Implementation, Challenges and Opportunities*, 15–43.
26 *A More Secure World: Our Shared Responsibility*, 39.
27 Kurt M. Campbell, Robert J. Einhorn, Mitchell B. Reiss, eds., *The Nuclear Tipping Point: Why States Reconsider Their Nuclear Choices* (Washington DC: Brookings Institution Press), 2004.
28 Charles Krauthammer, *Democratic Realism. An American Foreign Policy for a Unipolar World* (Washington, DC: The AEI Press, 2004), 10.

6 Civil war, state failure and peacebuilding

1 See, for example, Peter J. Hoffman and Thomas G. Weiss, *Sword and Salve. Confronting New Wars and Humanitarian Crises* (Oxford: Rowman and Littlefield Publishers, 2006) and Cynthia J. Arnson and I. William Zartman, *Rethinking the Economics of War: The Intersection of Need, Creed, and Greed* (Washington DC: The Johns Hopkins University Press, 2005).
2 Stephen M. Walt, "The Renaissance of Security Studies," *International Studies Quarterly* 35 (1991): 212.
3 Donald M. Snow, *Uncivil Wars: International Security and the New Internal Conflicts* (Boulder, Colorado: Lynne Rienner Publishers, 1996), 1.
4 Mary Kaldor, *New and Old Wars: Organized Violence in a Global Era* (Cambridge: Polity Press, 2001), 6.
5 Mary Kaldor, "Wanted: Global Politics," *The Nation* (5 November 2001): 16.

6 ICISS – International Commission on Intervention and State Sovereignty, *The Responsibility to Protect*: Report of the International Commission on Intervention and State Sovereignty (Ottawa: International Development Research Centre, 2001), 4.
7 Dietrich Jung, "A Political Economy Of Intra-State War: Confronting a Paradox," in *Shadow Globalization, Ethnic Conflicts and New Wars: A Political Economy of Intra-State War*, ed. Dietrich Jung (London: Routledge, 2003), 12.
8 Dietrich Jung, "Introduction: Towards Global Civil War?," in *Shadow Globalization, Ethnic Conflicts and New Wars*, ed. Dietrich Jung, 2.
9 Kaldor, *New and Old Wars*, 70.
10 Kaldor, *New and Old Wars*, 92.
11 Kaldor, *New and Old Wars*, 5.
12 Kaldor, *New and Old Wars*, 9.
13 Duffield, *Global Governance and the New Wars*, 14.
14 David Keen, "The Economic Functions of Violence in Civil Wars," *Adelphi Paper* 320 (Oxford: Oxford University Press for the International Institute for Strategic Studies, 1998), 11–12.
15 Mats Berdal and David M. Malone, "Introduction," in *Greed and Grievance. Economic Agendas in Civil Wars*, ed. Mats Berdal and David M. Malone (Boulder, Colorado: Lynne Rienner, 2000), 3.
16 William Reno, "Shadow States and the Political Economy of Civil Wars," in *Greed and Grievance: Economic Agendas in Civil Wars*, ed. Mats Berdal and David M. Malone; and Donald M. Snow, *Uncivil Wars: International Security and the New Internal Conflicts*.
17 Paul Collier, "Doing Well out of War: An Economic Perspective," in *Greed and Grievance: Economic Agendas in Civil Wars*, ed. Mats Berdal and David M. Malone, 91
18 Indra de Soysa, "The Resource Curse: Are Civil Wars Driven by Rapacity or Paucity?," in *Greed and Grievance: Economic Agendas in Civil Wars*, ed. Mats Berdal and David M. Malone; Michael L. Ross, "The Political Economy of the Resource Curse," *World Politics* 51, no. 2 (1999): 297–322.
19 Donald Snow, *Uncivil Wars: International Security and the New Internal Conflicts*, 57.
20 Kaldor, *New and Old Wars*, 6.
21 ICISS – International Commission on Intervention and State Sovereignty, 2001, *The Responsibility to Protect*, 4.
22 Kaldor, *New and Old Wars*, 99.
23 Donald M. Snow, *Uncivil Wars: International Security and the New Internal Conflicts*, ix.
24 *Carnegie Commission on Preventing Deadly Conflict*, Final Report, (Washington DC: Carnegie Commission on Preventing Deadly Conflict, 1997), xvii and 11.
25 Kaldor, *New and Old Wars*, 100; Simon Chesterman, "Introduction," in *Civilians in War*, ed. Simon Chesterman (Boulder, Colorado: Lynne Rienner Publishers, 2001), 2.
26 Kaldor, *New and Old Wars*, 8.
27 United Nations High Commissioner for Refugees, "The State of the World's Refugees: Fifty Years of Humanitarian Action" (Oxford: Oxford University Press, 2000), 276–80.

28 United Nations High Commissioner for Refugees, "The State of the World's Refugees," 277, italics added.
29 United Nations High Commissioner for Refugees, "The State of the World's Refugees," 282.
30 Albrecht Schnabel, "Preventing the Plight of Refugees," *Peace Review* 13, no. 1 (2001): 109.
31 United Nations High Commissioner for Refugees, "The State of the World's Refugees," 306–10.
32 Kaldor, *New and Old Wars*, 5.
33 Edward Newman, "The 'New Wars' Debate: A Historical Perspective is Needed," *Security Dialogue* 35, no. 2 (2004): 173–89.
34 *Human Security Report 2005 – War and Peace in the 21st Century* (New York: Oxford University Press, 2005); Monty G. Marshall and Ted Robert Gurr, *Peace and Conflict 2005: A Global Survey of Armed Conflicts, Self-Determination Movements, and Democracy* (Maryland, Center for International Development and Conflict Management, University of Maryland, 2005) at http://www.cidcm.umd.edu/peace_and_conflict.asp
35 Nils Petter Gleditsch, Peter Wallensteen, Mikael Eriksson, Margareta Sollenberg and Håvard Strand, "Armed Conflict 1946–2001: A New Dataset," *Journal of Peace Research* 39, no. 5 (2002): 621.
36 Paul Heinbecker, "Washington's Exceptionalism and the United Nations," *Global Governance* 10, no. 3 (2004): 277.
37 For example, *A More Secure World: Our Shared Responsibility*, Report of the Secretary-General's High-level Panel on Threats, Challenges and Change, Report of the Secretary-General to the General Assembly, A/59/565 (2 December 2004).
38 Kofi Annan, *In Larger Freedom: Towards Development, Security and Human Rights for All* (New York: United Nations, 21 March 2005), para. 114.
39 Boutros Boutros-Ghali, "Report on the Work of the Organization" (New York: United Nations, September 1993), para. 6. The UN Security Council also integrated human rights dimensions within peace operations: See Julie A. Mertus, *The United Nations and Human Rights: A Guide For a New Era* (New York: Routledge, 2005), chapter 5.
40 For example Bruce D. Berkowitz, "Rules of Engagement for UN Peacekeeping Forces in Bosnia," *Orbis* 38, no. 4 (1994): 635–46.
41 For domestic peace-keeping and its hazards, see Alan James, "Internal Peace-keeping: A Dead End for the UN?" *Security Dialogue* 24, no. 4 (1993); Thomas G. Weiss, "The United Nations and Civil Wars," *The Washington Quarterly* 17, no. 4 (1994): 175–84; David Rieff, "The Illusions of Peacekeeping," *World Policy Journal* xi, no. 3 (1994): 1–8.
42 Boutros Boutros-Ghali, *Building Peace and Development*, para. 705.
43 Michael N. Barnett, "The United Nations and Global Security: The Norm is Mightier than the Sword," *Ethics and International Affairs* 9 (1995): 37–54; Richard K. Betts, "The Delusion of Impartial Intervention," *Foreign Affairs* 73, no. 6 (1994): 20–33.
44 Rosalyn Higgins, "The New United Nations and Former Yugoslavia," *International Affairs* 69, no. 3 (1993): 468.
45 Panel on United Nations Peace Operations (the "Brahimi report") (New York: United Nations, A/55/305 - S/2000/809, 21 August 2000), viii.

46 *A More Secure World: Our Shared Responsibility*, 34. A similar conclusion can be found in *Human Security Report 2005 – War and Peace in the 21st Century*. A RAND study also came to a generally positive conclusion about the UN's peacebuilding work: James Dobbins, Seth G. Jones, Keith Crane, Andrew Rathmell, Brett Steele, Richard Teltschik and Anga Timilsina, *The UN's Role in Nation-Building: From the Congo to Iraq* (Santa Monica, CA: RAND Corporation, 2005).
47 *A More Secure World: Our Shared Responsibility*, 34–5.
48 Thomas G. Weiss, "UN Responses in the Former Yugoslavia: Moral and Operational Choices," *Ethics and International Affairs* 8 (1994): 20.
49 Roméo Dallaire, *Shake Hands with the Devil: The Failure of Humanity in Rwanda* (New York: Carroll and Graf Publishers, 2004), 6–7.
50 *Report of the Independent Inquiry into the Actions of the United Nations During the 1994 Genocide in Rwanda*, submitted to the UN as S/1999/1257, 4.
51 The Secretary-General, *Statement on Receiving the Report of the Independent Inquiry into the Actions of the United Nations During the 1994 Genocide in Rwanda*, 16 December 1999.
52 Panel on United Nations Peace Operations (the "Brahimi report"), ix.
53 See, for example, Roland Paris, *At War's End: Building Peace After Civil Conflict* (Cambridge: Cambridge University Press, 2004); Edward Newman and Oliver Richmond, eds., *Challenges to Peacebuilding: Managing Spoilers During Conflict* (Tokyo: UN University Press, 2006).
54 Paris, *At War's End*, ix.
55 John Tirman, "Civil Wars, Globalization, and the 'Washington Consensus'," in *Multilateralism Under Challenge? Power, International Order, and Structural Change*, ed. Edward Newman, Ramesh Thakur and John Tirman (Tokyo: UNU Press, 2006), 356–75.
56 Thomas Carothers, *Aiding Democracy Abroad: The Learning Curve* (Washington DC:, Carnegie Endowment for International Peace, 1999); Michael Cox, John Ikenberry, Takashi Inoguchi, eds., *American Democracy Promotion: Impulses, Strategies, and Impacts* (Oxford: Oxford University Press, 2000).
57 Boutros Boutros-Ghali, *An Agenda for Democratization* (New York: United Nations, 20 December 1996 - A/51/761), 4.
58 See Edward Newman and Roland Rich, eds., *The UN Role in Promoting Democracy: Between Ideals and Reality* (Tokyo: UNU Press, 2004).
59 Bhikhu Parakh, "The Cultural Particularity of Liberal Democracy," in *Prospects for Democracy: North, South, East, West*, ed. David Held (Cambridge: Polity Press, 1996), 169.
60 Ahmedou Ould-Abdallah, *Burundi on the Brink 1993–1995. A UN Special Envoy Reflects on Preventive Diplomacy* (Washington DC: USIP Press, 2000), 71.
61 Simon Chesterman, "Building Democracy Through Benevolent Autocracy: Consultation and Accountability in UN Transitional Administrations," in *The UN Role in Promoting Democracy: Between Ideals and Reality*, ed. Edward Newman and Roland Rich, 90.
62 Edward Newman, "(Re)building Political Society: the UN and Democratization," in *The United Nations and Human Security*, ed. Edward Newman and Oliver P. Richmond (London: Palgrave, 2001), 47–64.
63 Samuel P. Huntington, *The Third Wave: Democratization in the Late Twentieth Century* (Norman: University of Oklahoma Press, 1991), 184.

172 Notes

64 United Nations Security Council Resolution 1645, 20 December 2005.
65 United Nations Security Council Resolution 1645, preamble.

7 Terrorism

1 Edward C. Luck, "The Uninvited Challenge: Terrorism Targets the United Nations," in *Multilateralism Under Challenge? Power, International Order, and Structural Change*, ed. Edward Newman, Ramesh Thakur and John Tirman (Tokyo: UNU Press, 2006), 336.
2 Kofi Annan, Press Release SG/SM/8417-SC/7523, 4 October 2002.
3 Jane Boulden and Thomas G. Weiss, "Whither Terrorism and the United Nations?," in *Terrorism and the UN: Before and after September 11*, ed. Jane Boulden and Thomas G. Weiss (Bloomington and Indianapolis: Indiana University Press, 2004), 8.
4 Philip G. Cerny, "Terrorism and the New Security Dilemma," *Naval War College Review* 58, no. 1 (2005): 10–34.
5 Edward C. Luck, "Tackling Terrorism," in *The UN Security Council. From the Cold War to the 21st Century*, ed. David M. Malone (Boulder: Lynne Rienner Publishers, 2004), 85–100; Chantal de Jonge Oudraat, "The Role of the Security Council" and Jane Boulden and Thomas G. Weiss, "Whither Terrorism and the United Nations?," in *Terrorism and the UN: Before and after September 11*, ed. Jane Boulden and Thomas G. Weiss.
6 Alistair Millar and Daniel Benjamin, *The Future of Multilateral Counter-Terrorism Policy Coordination, Monitoring, and Implementation* (Center for Strategic and International Studies: University of Notre Dame, 2005), 3.
7 Walter Laqueur, *The New Terrorism. Fanaticism and the Arms of Mass Destruction* (New York: Oxford University Press, 1999), 21.
8 Jeffrey Ian Ross, "Structural Causes of Oppositional Political Terrorism: Towards a Causal Model," *Journal of Peace Research* 30, no. 3 (1993): 326.
9 Resolution 40/61 of the General Assembly of the United Nations of 9 December 1985.
10 Jed Babbin, *Inside the Asylum: Why the UN and Old Europe are Worse Than You Think* (Washington DC: Regnery Publishing Inc., 2004), 3, 18–20, 85.
11 Speech of John R. Bolton, Under-Secretary for Arms Control and International Security, on "Beyond the Axis of Evil: Additional Threats from Weapons of Mass Destruction," to the Heritage Foundation, Washington DC, 6 May 2002.
12 Luck, "Tackling Terrorism," 93.
13 Luck, "Tackling Terrorism," 87–8.
14 General Assembly Resolution 3034 (XXVII), 18 December 1972.
15 UN Office on Drugs and Crime, Implementing international action against terrorism.
16 Monika Heupel, "Adapting to the 'Privatization' of Terrorism: The UN Security Council's Approach to Terrorism in Change," unpublished paper, UN University.
17 Luck, "Tackling Terrorism," 85.
18 For example, Chantal de Jonge Oudraat, "The Role of the Security Council," in *Terrorism and the UN*, ed. Jane Boulden and Thomas G. Weiss, 164.

19 *A More Secure World: Our Shared Responsibility*, Report of the Secretary-General's High-level Panel on Threats, Challenges and Change, Report of the Secretary-General to the General Assembly, A/59/565 (2 December 2004), 148.
20 SG/SM/9757, 10 March 2005.
21 2005 World Summit Outcome, A/RES/60/1, 15 September 2005, 22, paras. 81–3.
22 Joshua Muravchik, "Terrorism's Silent Partner at the United Nations," *On the Issues*, American Enterprise Institute for Public Policy Research, October 2004, www.aei.org
23 William G. O'Neill, "Conference Report," in International Peace Academy, *Responding to Terrorism: What Role for the United Nations* (New York: International Peace Academy, 2003), 5.
24 Nico Schrijver, "September 11 and Challenges to International Law," in *Terrorism and the UN: Before and After September 11*, ed. Jane Boulden and Thomas G. Weiss, 62.
25 Alistair Miller and Daniel Benjamin, *The Future of Multilateral Counter-Terrorism Policy: Coordination, Monitoring, and Implementation*, 3.
26 Luck, "The Uninvited Challenge: Terrorism Targets the United Nations," 338. See also Jane Boulden and Thomas G. Weiss, "Whither Terrorism and the United Nations?"
27 Nico Krisch and Jochen Abr. Frowein, "Article 39," in *The Charter of the United Nations: A Commentary*, ed. Bruno Simma (Oxford: Oxford University Press, 2002), 719.
28 Jonas Tallberg, "Paths to Compliance: Enforcement, Management, and the European Union," *International Organization* 56, no. 3 (2002): 609–43.
29 Edward C. Luck, "Another Reluctant Belligerent: The United Nations and the War on Terrorism," in *The United Nations and Global Security*, ed. Richard M. Price and Mark W. Zacher (London: Palgrave, 2004): 95–108.
30 Alistair Miller and Daniel Benjamin, *The Future of Multilateral Counter-Terrorism Policy: Coordination, Monitoring, and Implementation*.
31 *Amnesty International Annual Report* (London: Amnesty International, 2005), 12. See also Neil Hicks, "The Impact of Counter Terror on the Promotion and Protection of Human Rights: A Global Perspective," in *Human Rights in the 'War on Terror'*, ed. Richard Ashby Wilson (Cambridge: Cambridge University Press, 2005), 209–24.
32 Kofi Annan, *In Larger Freedom: Towards Development, Security and Human Rights for All* (New York: United Nations, 21 March 2005), para. 94.
33 Charles H. Brower II, Nigel Rodley and Oren Gross, "Torture, Violence, and the Global War on Terror," *American Society of International Law*, Proceedings of the Annual Meeting (Washington: ASIL, 2005): 401–10.
34 UN Press Release, SG/SM/7999 AFR/344, 22 October 2001.
35 David Cortright, "A Critical Evaluation of the UN Counter-Terrorism Program: Accomplishments and Challenges," paper presented at: Global Enforcement Regimes – Transnational Organized Crime, International Terrorism and Money Laundering, Transnational Institute, Amsterdam (28–29 April 2005), 2.
36 William O'Neill, "Conference Report," in "Responding to Terrorism: What Role for the United Nations?," report of a conference organized by the International Peace Academy, New York, 25–26 October 2002, published by International Peace Academy, 20.

37 William J. Bennett, *Why We Fight: Moral Clarity and the War on Terrorism* (Washington DC: Regnery Publishing Inc., 2002), 67–9.
38 Robert Jervis, "An Interim Assessment of September 11: What Has Changed and What Has Not?" *Political Science Quarterly* 117, no. 1 (2002): 1.
39 Edward Newman, "Exploring the 'Root Causes' of Terrorism," *Studies in Conflict and Terrorism* 29, no. 8 (2006): 749–72.
40 David Cortright, "A Critical Evaluation of the UN Counter-Terrorism Program: Accomplishments and Challenges."
41 191 member states responded in the first round, 164 to the second, 124 to the third, and 88 to the fourth.
42 *United Against Terrorism: Recommendations for a Global Counter-Terrorism Strategy*, A/60/825, 27 April 2006.
43 Alistair Miller and Daniel Benjamin, *The Future of Multilateral Counter-Terrorism Policy: Coordination, Monitoring, and Implementation*, 18–33.

8 Conclusion: revisiting institutionalism in a post-Westphalian world

1 "Foreword by the United Nations Secretary-General," in *A More Secure World: Our Shared Responsibility, Report of the Secretary-General's High-level Panel on Threats, Challenges and Change, Report of the Secretary-General to the General Assembly*, A/59/565 (2 December 2004).
2 *In Larger Freedom: Towards Development, Security and Human Rights for All, Report of the Secretary-General* (New York: United Nations, 21 March 2005), para. 17.
3 *A More Secure World: Our Shared Responsibility*, 23.
4 *In Larger Freedom*, para. 125.
5 Beth A. Simmons, "From Unilateralism to Bilateralism: Challenges for the Multilateral Trade System," in *Multilateralism Under Challenge? Power, International Order, and Structural Change*, ed. Edward Newman, Ramesh Thakur and John Tirman (Tokyo: UN University Press, 2006), 457.
6 This is something attempted in *The Responsibility to Protect* – Report of the International Commission on Intervention and State Sovereignty, Ottawa, International Development Research Centre, December 2001.
7 *A More Secure World: Our Shared Responsibility*, 19.
8 "Foreword by the United Nations Secretary-General," in *A More Secure World: Our Shared Responsibility*, ix.
9 2005 World Summit Outcome, A/60/150, 20 September 2005, para. 72.
10 Kofi Annan, "Moment of Truth for UN – Reform for Benefit of Peoples," *The Daily Yomiuri*, 17 June 2006, 13.
11 See Emanuel Adler, "Communitarian Multilateralism," in *Multilateralism Under Challenge?* ed. Edward Newman, Ramesh Thakur and John Tirman, 34–55.
12 Larry Diamond, *Promoting Democracy in the 1990s: Actors and Instruments, Issues and Imperatives*, A Report to the Carnegie Commission on Preventing Deadly Conflict (New York: Carnegie Corporation of New York, December 1995).
13 For example, Allen Buchanan and Robert O. Keohane, "The Preventive Use of Force: A Cosmopolitan Institutional Proposal," *Ethics & International Affairs* 18, no. 1 (2004): 1–22.

14 Secretary-General's keynote speech to the International Summit on Democracy, Terrorism and Security in Madrid SG/SM/9757, 10 March 2005.
15 Mark J. Valencia, "Bring the Proliferation Security Initiative into the UN," *Policy Forum Online,* 05–101A: 20 December 2005. http://www.nautilus.org/fora/security.
16 Mark J. Valencia, *The Proliferation Security Initiative: Making Waves in Asia,* Adelphi Paper, no. 376 (2006).
17 "Iran urges Central Asian bloc to counter West," CBC News, 15 June 2006, at www.cbc.ca/world/story/2006/06/15/iran-thurs.html.
18 James A. Caporaso, "International Relations Theory and Multilateralism: The Search for Foundations," in *Multilateralism Matters: The Theory and Praxis of an Institutional Form,* ed. John Gerard Ruggie (New York: Columbia University Press, 1993), 56.
19 John Gerard Ruggie, "Multilateralism: The Anatomy of an Institution," in *Multilateralism Matters: The Theory and Praxis of an Institutional Form,* ed. John Gerard Ruggie, 23.

Select bibliography

United Nations

Kofi Annan, *In Larger Freedom: Towards Development, Security and Human Rights for All* (New York: United Nations, 2005). This report focuses on three themes: freedom from fear, freedom to live in dignity and strengthening the United Nations. The report contains a comprehensive package of reforms to revitalize the General Assembly and make the Security Council more broadly representative of the international community. It is praiseworthy for its eloquence, arguing that "we will not enjoy development without security, we will not enjoy security without development, and we will not enjoy either without respect for human rights." However, it was based on the unhelpful idea that the UN faces a defining "moment of truth" and many of its arguments and proposals were lost within the clamor surrounding the proposals for Security Council reform which are found in the report.

Leon Gordenker, *The UN Secretary-General and Secretariat* (Oxford: Routledge – Global Institutions Series, 2005). This book, written by an eminent authority on the subject, describes the evolution of the office of Secretary-General in international politics. It illustrates how the Secretary-General can play a significant role, but generally within the confines of the power politics of the major states.

High-level Panel on Threats, Challenges and Change, *A More Secure World: Our Shared Responsibility*, General Assembly, A/59/565, 2 December 2004. The panel was created by Secretary-General Kofi Annan in November 2003 in order to propose ways of strengthening international security in response to new and evolving threats. Implicit in this was the task of making the UN more relevant after historic challenges such as the rise of catastrophic terrorism and the US-led war against Iraq. A key message is that contemporary threats to security are interconnected and must be addressed in an integrated manner. Proposals included the creation of a new UN Peacebuilding Commission and a new Human Rights Council. In terms of UN-sponsored reports, it is genuinely interesting and creative.

Keith Krause and W. Andy Knight, *State, Society, and the United Nations System: Changing Perspectives on Multilateralism* (Tokyo: UNU Press, 1995).

Select bibliography   177

An interesting attempt at a critical approach to multilateralism, focusing upon the UN.

Edward C. Luck, *The UN Security Council: A Primer* (London: Routledge – Global Institutions Series, 2006). This book provides a contemporary analysis of the politics and process of the Security Council by an author with great insights. It focuses on historical perspectives; the founding vision; procedures and practices; economic enforcement; peace operations and military enforcement; human security; proliferation and WMD; terrorism; and reform, adaptation and change.

Edward Newman and Roland Rich, eds., *The UN Role in Promoting Democracy: Between Ideals and Reality* (Tokyo: UNU Press, 2004). A collection of essays which explores the modalities, effectiveness and controversies of the UN's work in promoting and assisting democracy. It considers whether the UN can help to build the foundations of democracy and whether, as an "external" actor, it can have a substantive positive impact upon the development of democratic governance inside societies. The conclusion is mixed.

M. J. Peterson, *The UN General Assembly* (London: Routledge – Global Institutions Series, 2005). A book on an organ which has been neglected by scholars in recent years – because of its own ebbing fortunes – but one which remains important to multilateralism.

Ramesh Thakur, *The United Nations, Peace and Security: From Collective Security to the Responsibility to Protect* (Cambridge: Cambridge University Press, 2006). This book examines the transformation of the UN in the area of international peace and security. It examines a range of themes – such as human security and UN reform – and issue areas, such as international criminal justice, collective security, and the use of force for human protection purposes. The book has an emphasis upon the normative and political debates and controversies which underlie these challenges.

US foreign policy

American Interests and UN Reform, Report of the Task Force on the United Nations (Washington DC: United States Institute of Peace, 2005). The report of the bipartisan task force co-chaired by Newt Gingrich and George Mitchell argues that supporting the UN is in America's interests – for helping to maintain international peace and security and to promote liberal values – but that reform of the organization is essential if it is to retain the confidence of the US.

Robert Kagan, *Of Paradise and Power: America and Europe in the New World Order* (New York: Alfred A. Knopf, 2003). Written by a leading conservative, this book suggests that a new phase has begun in the relationship between the US and Europe based upon fundamentally different and incompatible values. It argues that the US must acknowledge a growing transatlantic split which will have implications for international order.

Charles Krauthammer, *Democratic Realism: An American Foreign Policy for a Unipolar World* (Washington, DC: The AEI Press, 2004). A conservative commentary on US foreign policy which examines four schools of foreign policy: isolationism, liberal internationalism, realism and democratic globalism. He proposes an alternative – democratic realism – aimed at democracy promotion in key regions of the world which are of relevance to the US national interest.

Edward C. Luck, *Mixed Messages: American Politics and International Organization 1919–1999* (Washington DC: Brookings Institution Press, 1999). This book explores how and why the US has been both a leader and detractor in its relationship with international organizations. Luck identifies a number of recurring themes which characterize this ambivalence: exceptionalism, sovereignty, nativism and racism, unilateralism, security, commitments, reform and burden-sharing.

David M. Malone and Yuen Foong Khong, eds., *Unilateralism and US Foreign Policy: International Perspectives* (Boulder, CO: Lynne Rienner Publishers, 2003). A solid collection of essays examining the sources and impact of US unilateralism.

Stewart Patrick and Shepard Forman, eds., *Multilateralism and US Foreign Policy: Ambivalent Engagement* (Boulder, CO: Lynne Rienner Publishers, 2001). This volume, although written before 9/11, remains an excellent analysis of the sources of US skepticism towards international organizations.

The National Security Strategy of the United States of America (Washington, DC: The White House, 2002). A keynote document which outlines the preventive use of force doctrine of the US and the intention of the US to remain a military power beyond peer. A similar message can be found in the 2006 edition.

Terrorism and weapons of mass destruction

Jane Boulden and Thomas G. Weiss, eds., *Terrorism and the UN: Before and After September 11* (Bloomington: Indiana University Press, 2004). This provides an excellent account of the role and history of the UN in addressing terrorism and its prospects in this area. It demonstrates the limitations and political obstacles which exist but shows that if the political will exists the UN can play an important role.

Michael A. Levi and Michael E. O'Hanlon, *The Future of Arms Control* (Washington DC: Brookings Institution Press, 2005). This volume argues that the traditional tenets of arms control – to regulate and manage WMD between rational stable states – is not suitable for the evolving strategic environment of the twenty-first century which includes weak and failed states, "rogue states," and the possibility of terrorist groups acquiring WMD.

Conflict and humanitarianism

Roméo Dallaire, *Shake Hands with the Devil. The Failure of Humanity in Rwanda* (New York: Carroll and Graf Publishers, 2004). General Dallaire was the commander of the UN peacekeeping force in Rwanda which was forced to stand by and witness the genocide unfold. This is a harrowing personal indictment of the callousness of international politics and the lack of humanity which allowed the genocide to happen. It also makes the argument that the early use of military force could have halted the descent into mass murder and chaos.

Peter J. Hoffman and Thomas G. Weiss, *Sword and Salve: Confronting New Wars and Humanitarian Crises* (Oxford: Rowman and Littlefield Publishers, 2006). This book examines the evolution of the international humanitarian system since the nineteenth century and focuses on the challenges which are inherent in contemporary "new wars" which are characterized by state weakness, atrocities and war economies. The volume illustrates how the classical principles of humanitarianism have been severely strained.

ICISS – International Commission on Intervention and State Sovereignty, *The Responsibility to Protect* (Ottawa: International Development Research Centre, 2001). A landmark report which changed the vocabulary of the "humanitarian intervention" debate, focusing upon the needs of victims rather than the right to intervene. It argued that states have the primary responsibility to protect the fundamental needs and rights of their citizens; if they are unable or unwilling to do this, the responsibility may fall to the international community. The responsibility to protect principle was endorsed by UN member states in the 2005 World Summit.

Mary Kaldor, *New and Old Wars: Organized Violence in a Global Era* (Cambridge: Polity Press, 2001). This book made a major impact upon conflict studies, arguing that violent conflict – and especially civil war – since the end of the Cold War displays social, economic and military characteristics that suggest a pattern of "new wars."

Thomas G. Weiss and Don Hubert, *et al.*, *The Responsibility to Protect: Supplementary Volume to the Report of the International Commission on Intervention and States Sovereignty* (Ottawa: International Development Research Centre, 2001). This substantial collection includes chapters on the core issues relating to the humanitarian intervention debate – such as state sovereignty and legitimacy – and a number of cases. It also includes a very extensive bibliography.

Nicholas J. Wheeler, *Saving Strangers: Humanitarian Intervention in International Society* (Oxford: Oxford University Press, 2000). An authoritative monograph on the use of force for human protection. A particular contribution of this book is that it examines the subject in the context of theories of international relations.

International order and theories of international relations

E. H. Carr, *The Twenty Years Crisis, An Introduction to the Study of International Relations*, 2nd ed. (New York: Palgrave, 2001). A classical realist text, first published in 1939, which argued that international norms, institutions and organizations cannot bring stability if they do not reflect prevailing power politics.

Select bibliography

Thomas M. Franck, "What Happens Now? The United Nations after Iraq," *The American Journal of International Law* 97, no. 3 (2003): 607–20. In a good example of a liberal legalist response to the war against Iraq in 2003, Franck argues that this crisis has overturned the UN-based rules regulating the use of force.

Michael J. Glennon, "Why the Security Council Failed," *Foreign Affairs* (May/June 2003): 16–35. A realist article which argues that the war against Iraq in 2003 demonstrated that the UN and collective security are doomed to failure, as the League of Nations was in the 1930s.

G. John Ikenberry, *Liberal Order and Imperial Ambition: Essays on American Power and World Politics* (Cambridge: Polity, 2006). This collection examines the consequences and implications of America's preeminent power and questions how international institutions can work in this environment.

Robert O. Keohane, *Power and Governance in a Partially Globalized World* (London: Routledge, 2002). A compilation of articles by the leading figure of the institutionalist school of international relations. It seeks to demonstrate how international institutions can emerge in an anarchic environment, based upon the need for reciprocity and regularized interaction amongst states.

Edward Newman, Ramesh Thakur and John Tirman, eds., *Multilateralism Under Challenge? Power, International Order, and Structural Change* (Tokyo: UN University Press, 2006). This collection explores the performance and future of multilateral approaches and institutions with reference to major global challenges such as international security, terrorism, HIV/AIDS, environmental sustainability, economic justice, human rights and humanitarian assistance.

Panel on United Nations Peace Operations (the "Brahimi report") (New York: United Nations, A/55/305 - S/2000/809, 21 August 2000). A landmark UN report on peacekeeping which represented a defining moment for the organization in coming to terms with the post-Cold War world. The report argued that the principles of classical peacekeeping – impartiality, neutrality and the non-use of force except in self-defense – are not appropriate for many of the conflicts faced by the UN in the contemporary world. Peacekeeping operations must be robustly mandated and equipped.

John Gerard Ruggie, ed., *Multilateralism Matters: The Theory and Praxis of an Institutional Form* (New York: Columbia University Press, 1993). An important collection of theoretical essays on multilateralism edited by the leading scholar on the subject.

Ramesh Thakur and Waheguru Pal Singh Sidhu, eds., *The Iraq Crisis and World Order: Structural, Institutional and Normative Challenges* (Tokyo: UN University Press, 2006). A large collection which examines every angle of the war against Iraq and the impact this has had upon international order. On balance, the book tends to view the war as a key moment in recent history and a fundamental challenge to the UN.

Index

Adler, Emmanuel 149
Advisory Committee on Issues of Public International Law (Netherlands) 64–68
Afghanistan 101, 103, 109, 113, 115, 126, 132
African National Congress (ANC) 120
Agenda for Democratization 112
Aggression (international) 5, 22, 44–49, 52–55, 121, 127, 131, 141
Al-Qaeda 127
Anarchy (international) 23–25
Anarchy, international 10, 23–26
Angola 101, 103, 105, 114
Annan, Kofi 12, 21, 38, 89, 103, 108, 151
Anti-Ballistic Missile (Treaty) 13, 79–81
Argentina 103
Australia Group 92

Balance of power 46, 55
Biological weapons 32, 92–93
Bolton, John 17, 33, 36, 41, 121
Bosnia 74, 100, 101, 103, 104–7, 113
Brahimi Report (on peacekeeping) 106, 108
Bretton Woods institutions 17, 19, 50
Burundi 101, 103, 106, 109, 112, 113
Bush, President George W., 28, 31, 32, 33, 37, 40, 52, 80, 88

Cambodia 101, 103, 105
Carnegie Commission on Preventing Deadly conflict 100

Chechnya 76, 101
Chemical weapons 90–92
Chesterman, Simon 113
Chile 103
China 13, 59, 83, 152
Chirac, President Jacques 41, 43
Civil war: civilian casualties 100–101; impact of 95; and globalization 98; and identity 98; and UN 102–3
Cold War 23, 30, 32, 42, 52, 83, 89, 97, 120
Collective security, chapter 3
Collier, Paul 99
Colombia 103
Comprehensive Nuclear Test Bank (CTBT) 79, 89
Conference on Disarmament (UN) 79, 81
Congo, Democratic Republic of 76, 101, 108
Congressional study on the UN 43
Constructivism 25–26
Counter Terrorism Committee 128, 133, 137
Cuba 92, 122, 133

Dallaire, Roméo 58, 60
Danish Institute of International Affairs (report of) 60, 68–70
Darfur 76
Democracy promotion 111
Democracy 18, 109, 110–15; and Africa 113
Democratic peace 21
Duffield, Mark 99

182 Index

East Timor 59, 73, 103, 109, 113
Egypt 92, 104, 126
El Salvador 103, 104
Ethiopia 103
European Union 80

First World War 22, 47, 49
Forced displacement: of humans 15, 96, 100–102
Fourteen Points 48
Franck, Thomas 35, 5
Freedom House 114
Front for the Liberation of Mozambique (FRELIMO) 120

Game theory 145
General Assembly 28, 60; and terrorism 123
Germany 48
Glennon, Michael 43, 50
Great powers 46
Guatemala 103
Gulf War (1990) 44, 51

Haiti 59, 69, 73, 104, 106, 115
Heinbecker, Paul 103
Hezbollah 133, 138
Higgins, Rosalyn 106
Hobbes 24, 55
Humanitarian intervention: definition of 57; and solidarism 59
Huntington, Samuel 114
Idealism (Liberal internationalism) 22–23

Ikenberry, G. John 16, 17
ILO 36
"In Larger Freedom", Report of the Secretary-General 53, 74, 134, 141
Independent International Commission on Kosovo 70–72, 73
India 59, 90, 103
India 78, 84, 85, 89, 90, 121
"Institutionalist bargain" of U.S. 2
International Atomic Energy Agency (IAEA) 82, 86, 91, 130
International Civil Aviation Organization 130
International Commission on Intervention and State

Sovereignty 60, 97; see also Responsibility to Protect
International Conventions relating to terrorism 124
International Criminal Court 13
International Maritime Organization 130
International Monetary fund 110
International relations studies 21–27
Iran 86–88, 92, 94, 122, 133, 152
Iraq 12, 16, 44, 45, 50, 51, 54, 59, 73, 87, 92, 94, 113
Israel 91, 92, 104, 125, 133, 138
Italy 48, 49

Japan 48
Justice: and international relations theory 21; and peacebuilding 110; and political legitimacy 18

Kagan, Robert 39
Kaldor, Mary 98, 100
Kant, Immanuel 22–23, 39
Kashmir 121
Keen, David 99
Keohane, Robert, O., 11, 19
Kirkpatrick, Jeane 35
Kissinger, Henry 35
Kosovo 57, 59, 60, 70–72, 77, 113

Laqueur, Walter 119
Law of the Sea 36
League of Nations 22, 47–49, 119
Lebanon 133
Legitimacy: of UN 3, 13, 37,
Liberal institutionalism 11, 142–48
Liberal internationalism ("Idealism") 22–23
Liberal peace 1, 20, 108–10, 114
Liberia 100, 101, 103, 114
Libya 37, 78, 85, 92, 122, 132
Luck, Edward 33, 117, 127, 131

Middle East 35, 103, 120
"Moral relativism" of the UN 37
Moynihan, Patrick 34
Mozambique 103
Multilateralism: definition of 10–12; crisis of 21, 26
Multipolar world 38–39

Index

Munich Olympic terrorist attacks 123

National Security Strategy of the U.S., 52, 53
National Strategy to Combat Weapons of Mass Destruction (U.S.) 80
NATO 13, 70–72, 149
Neoconservatives 32, 41–42
New International Economic Order 34
"New wars" 96–102
NGOs 16, 19
Nicaragua 103, 104
Nigeria 101, 103
Non-Proliferation Treaty (NPT) 78, 79, 81, 82–90, 93, 145–46
Normative, challenges to multilateralism 17–20
North Korea 42, 78, 82, 85, 89, 90, 91, 92, 94, 122, 133, 151
NPT 6
Nuclear Suppliers Group 90
Nye, Joseph 17

Osama Bin Laden 126
Ould-Abdallah, Ahmedou 113

Pakistan 78, 82, 83, 85, 89, 90, 103, 122
Palestine Liberation Organization (PLO) 36, 120
Pan Am flight 103 terrorist attack 125
Paris, Roland 109
Peacebuilding Commission 7, 115–16
Peacekeeping 58, 104–5, 108
Pérez de Cuéllar, Javier 21
Permanent Members of the Security Council (P5) 48, 49
Political legitimacy 18–19
Precautionary principles (of humanitarian intervention) 63
Preventive use of military force 52–54
Public goods: international 2, 10, 12, 42, 98–100

Realism 23–24, 45, 50, 55
Reciprocity 11

Refugees 101; see forced displacement
Regimes 11
Responsibility to Protect 60–64, 67, 74, 147, 148
Rice, Condoleeza 38, 40
Roberts, Adam 50
"Rogue states" 80, 122
Ruggie, John, G., 3, 4, 11, 12, 19, 29, 36, 39, 40, 43, 154
Rumsfeld, Donald 16, 32
Russia 13, 59, 83, 152
Rwanda 57, 59, 60, 74, 76, 100, 103, 104, 106, 107–8, 109

Saddam Hussein 45, 113
"Safe havens": in Bosnia 64, 106, 107
Saudi Arabia 122
Second World War 17, 23, 55, 95, 143
Secretary-General's High Level Panel on Threats, Challenges and Change 24, 52, 54–55, 75–76, 85, 88, 93, 106, 128, 140, 145
Security Council: and collective security 44, 51; and humanitarian intervention 59, 61, 65, 70, 72; and terrorism 125–26; and use of force 43
Security Proliferation Initiative (SPI) 148, 151
September 11, 2001 terrorist attacks (9/11) 32, 39, 52, 53, 117, 122, 127
Shanghai Cooperation Organization (SCO) 152
Sierra Leone 101
Somalia 69, 73, 100, 101, 104, 105, 106
South Africa 78
South West African People's Organization (SWAPO) 120
Sovereignty: of states 13–15; and UN 13
Srebrenica 64, 107, 108
Sri Lanka 103
Sudan 37, 76, 103, 108, 122, 126, 132
South West African People's Organization (SWAPO) 36, 120
Syria 91, 122, 133

184 Index

Taliban 126
Terrorism 117–39; and human rights 134; international conventions 124; root causes of 126, 135–36; and Security Council 118; and UN 17, 19, 121–22, 131–32
Terrorism Prevention Branch, Office on Drugs and Crime 133
Thakur, Ramesh 45, 19 (note 26) 24, (note 35) 44 (note 8)
Tharoor, Shashi 55
Treaty of Chaument (1814) 47
Trusteeship Council 27

US: and International Criminal Court 13; Kyoto Protocol 13; power and unilateralism 13, 16–17, 30–42, 94
UK 84, 94, 104, 121
UN Conference on Trade and Development 34
UN Emergency Force (UNEF I) 104
UN High Commissioner for Refugees 101
UN Peacebuilding Commission 115–16
UN Protection force (UNPROFOR) 105–6
UNESCO 36

Unilateralism: of U.S., 1, 2,5, 13, 16, 31, 39, 150, 153, 154
United Nations: Charter of 28, 43, 44, 49, 52, 53, 55, 56, 58, 59, 97, 111
"Uniting for Peace" Resolution 63, 66, 69
Universal Declaration of Human Rights 111
Universal Postal Union 143
Uppsala University 51, 102

Versailles Treaty 48
Vietnam War 35, 103
Volcker, Paul 38

Waldheim, Kurt 21
Walt, Stephen 97
Waltz, Kenneth 25
"War on terror" 133–34
Weapons of mass destruction 78–94
Weiss, Thomas 29
Wendt, Alexander 25
Westphalian international system and post-Westphalianism 3, 14, 15, 18, 19, 46, 57, 61, 154, 155
Wilson, Woodrow 48
World Bank 110
World Summit (UN) 116, 129
Yugoslavia 59, 105